STUDY GUIDE

for use with

CANADIAN SIXTH EDITION

Management Accounting

Hansen Mowen Senkow Pollanen

PREPARED BY

Deborah Mortimer, University of Manitoba

THOMSON

NELSON

Australia   Canada   Mexico   Singapore   Spain   United Kingdom   United States

Contents

To the Student

This study guide, a supplement to *Management Accounting,* Canadian Sixth Edition, by Don R. Hansen, Maryanne M. Mowen, David Senkow, and Raili Pollanen is designed to assist you in reviewing important concepts and testing your understanding of the material. The study guide contains the following:

- **CHAPTER REVIEW.** A summary of the important points in each chapter.

- **KEY TERMS TEST.** A test of your understanding of the key terms in each chapter.

- **CHAPTER QUIZ.** Multiple-choice, true-false, and completion questions to test your comprehension of the chapter material.

- **PRACTICE TEST.** A test of your ability to apply the concepts.

- **ANSWERS.** Suggested solutions, which appear at the end of each chapter.

The following sequence is recommended to make the most effective use of your study time:
- Read the assigned chapter in the text.
- Read the Chapter Review in the study guide. Add your notes or questions to the Chapter Review.
- Complete the Key Terms Test, Chapter Quiz, and Practice Test in the study guide.
- Review any difficult topics, if necessary.
- Prepare text exercises and problems assigned by your instructor.

Additional suggestions to assist you in your course preparation are as follows:
- Try to understand the important concepts and how they are applied. Do not try to memorize formulas and plug in numbers without first understanding *why* the formulas work.

- Ask questions when you do not understand. If you do not understand something, write your questions down so that you can ask at a later time. Simply formulating the questions may help you clarify your thinking.

- Always attempt to answer questions and problems before looking at the solution. This tests your understanding of the material and indicates the areas that need further study.

CHAPTER 1
Introduction: The Role, History, and Direction of Management Accounting

CHAPTER REVIEW

MANAGEMENT ACCOUNTING INFORMATION SYSTEM

☐ The **management accounting information system** has three broad objectives:
1. To provide information for costing services, products, and other objects of interest to management.
2. To provide information for planning, controlling, evaluation, and continuous improvement.
3. To provide information for decision making.

Information Needs of Managers and Other Users

☐ Accounting information can be used to:
- identify problems
- identify solutions to problems
- evaluate the effectiveness of decisions, such as continuous improvement efforts

☐ **Continuous improvement** involves searching for ways to increase overall efficiency and productivity of activities by reducing waste, increasing quality, and reducing costs. Information is needed to:
1. identify opportunities for improvement, and
2. evaluate progress made in implementing actions to create improvement.

☐ The need for greater accuracy has produced an improved management accounting information system called an *activity-based cost management information system*.

☐ **Strategic decision making** is choosing among alternative strategies with the goal of selecting one or more strategies that provide a company with a reasonable assurance of long-term growth and survival.

The Management Process

☐ The management process includes three activities:
- planning
- controlling
- decision making

❏ Managers and empowered workers participate in the management process. **Employee empowerment** authorizes operational personnel to plan, control, and make decisions without explicit authorization from middle- and higher-level management. It is based on the belief that the employee closest to the work can provide valuable input in ideas, plans, and problem solving.

❏ The management process is summarized below:

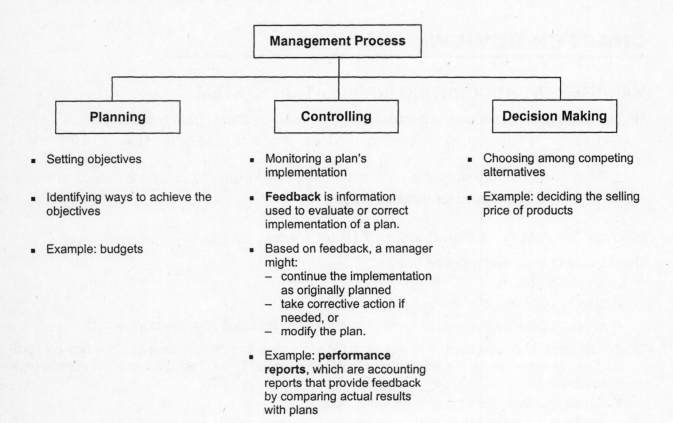

Management Process

Planning

- Setting objectives

- Identifying ways to achieve the objectives

- Example: budgets

Controlling

- Monitoring a plan's implementation

- **Feedback** is information used to evaluate or correct implementation of a plan.

- Based on feedback, a manager might:
  - continue the implementation as originally planned
  - take corrective action if needed, or
  - modify the plan.

- Example: **performance reports**, which are accounting reports that provide feedback by comparing actual results with plans

Decision Making

- Choosing among competing alternatives

- Example: deciding the selling price of products

MANAGEMENT ACCOUNTING AND FINANCIAL ACCOUNTING

❏ The accounting information system within an organization has two major subsystems:
- a management accounting system
- a financial accounting system

```
                    ┌─────────────────────────────────┐
                    │   Accounting Information System  │
                    └─────────────────────────────────┘
                                     │
                   ┌─────────────────┴─────────────────┐
        ┌──────────────────────┐         ┌──────────────────────┐
        │ Management Accounting │         │  Financial Accounting │
        │  Information System   │         │   Information System  │
        └──────────────────────┘         └──────────────────────┘
```

	Management Accounting Information System	Financial Accounting Information System
Targeted user:	internal users managers	external users shareholders and creditors
Restrictions:	no mandatory rules for preparing reports	must follow GAAP when preparing financial statements
Types of information:	financial and nonfinancial information	financial information
Time orientation:	emphasizes the future (planning and decision making)	historical orientation (reports what has already occurred)
Aggregation:	detailed information about product line, departments, etc.	information about overall firm performance
Breadth	Broad; includes theories and concepts from economics, industrial engineering, management science, etc.	Narrow; includes theory and concepts mainly from economics and finance.

❑ The accounting system should be flexible enough to supply different information for different users and different purposes. Frequently the reports of both management accounting and financial accounting are derived from the same database, which was originally established to support the reporting requirements of financial accounting. Many organizations need to redesign this database in order to satisfy more fully the needs of internal users.

CURRENT FOCUS OF MANAGEMENT ACCOUNTING

❑ Changes in the competitive environment require innovative and relevant management accounting practices.

❑ Management accounting must provide information so that managers can focus on:
- customer value
- total quality management
- time-based competition

Activity-Based Management

❑ **Activity-based management** is an approach where managers focus on *activities* with the objective of improving customer value and resulting profits.

❑ Activity-based management emphasizes:
  1. *activity-based costing (ABC)*, which improves the accuracy of cost information by tracing costs first to activities and then to products or customers that consume the activities.
  2. *process value analysis*, which focuses on:
     ▪ eliminating activities that do not add customer value, and
     ▪ performing necessary activities more efficiently.

Customer Orientation

❑ **Customer value** is the difference between what a customer receives (customer realization) and what the customer gives up (customer sacrifice). Increasing customer value means:
  ▪ increasing what the customer receives (such as product features, service, quality, training) and/or
  ▪ decreasing what the customer gives up (such as purchase cost, time to learn to use the product, postpurchase costs of using and maintaining the product).

❑ **Strategic cost management** uses cost data to identify and develop superior strategies to produce a sustainable competitive advantage. Two strategies are:
  1. cost leadership strategy—providing the same or better customer value for a *lower cost* than competitors.
  2. product differentiation strategy—providing *better customer value* for the same or lower cost than competitors.

❑ The **internal value chain** consists of activities required to design, develop, produce, market, and deliver products and services to customers. Emphasizing customer value forces managers to determine which activities add value to customers.

❑ The **industrial value chain** is the linked set of value-creating activities from basic raw materials to final disposal by end-use customers. One firm may not span the entire industrial value chain. Instead, different firms may participate in different segments of the industrial value chain.

❑ The *internal value chain* is a particular firm's portion of the *industrial value chain*.

❑ There are two types of activity linkages:
  1. **Internal linkages**—relationships of activities performed *within* a firm's portion of the industrial value chain (the internal value chain).
  2. **External linkages**—relationships of a firm's activities with activities of suppliers and customers.

❑ **Supply chain management** is the management of material flows beginning with suppliers, moving to the transformation of materials into finished goods to customers. Proper management will bring about a win-win outcome for everyone involved.

❑ The objective of successful strategic cost management is to manage these linkages better than competitors in order to create a competitive advantage.

Cross-Functional Perspective

❑ Emphasis on the value chain means that today's management accountant must understand many functions of the business, from manufacturing to marketing to distribution to customer service.

Global Perspective

❑ Globalization of business has increased competition, giving management accounting information, such as cost behaviour and estimation, a more critical role in the business environment.

Environmental Perspective

❑ Environmental awareness and regulation have created new business opportunities and a greater need for environmental cost information.

Total Quality Management

❑ The twin objectives of world-class firms are:
  1. producing products with little waste, and
  2. producing products that perform according to specifications.

❑ **Total quality management** is an environment that enables workers to manufacture zero-defect products. A management accounting system provides quality cost measurement and reporting.

Time as a Competitive Element

❑ Time is a crucial element in all phases of the value chain.

❑ Decreasing nonvalue-added time appears to go hand in hand with increasing quality.

❑ Managers need information that enables them to respond quickly and decisively to changing market conditions.

E-Business

❑ **Electronic business (e-business)** is any business transaction or information exchange that is executed using information and communication technology. It is currently in a rapid growth phase. (e.g., Buying a product with a debit card)

❑ **Electronic-commerce (e-commerce)** is buying and selling products using information and communication technology. (e.g., Buying a product over the Internet)

❑ Management accountants need to understand the risks and benefits associated with e-business.

THE ROLE OF THE MANAGEMENT ACCOUNTANT

❑ Management accountants are responsible for identifying, collecting, measuring, analyzing, preparing, interpreting, and communicating information used by management to achieve the organization's objectives.

❑ The **controller** is the chief accounting officer and has responsibility for both internal and external accounting requirements. The controller may have direct responsibility for:
  ▪ internal auditing
  ▪ cost accounting
  ▪ financial accounting (including reports to securities commissions and financial statements)

- systems accounting (including analysis, design, and internal controls)
- taxes

❏ The **treasurer** raises capital and manages cash and investments.

MANAGEMENT ACCOUNTING AND ETHICAL CONDUCT

❏ One of the major goals of management accounting is to help managers increase the profitability of their organization.

❏ However, the objective of profit maximization should be constrained by the requirement that profits be achieved through legal and ethical means.

❏ The performance evaluation and reward system should be designed so that incentives to pursue undesirable behaviour are minimized.

❏ The Standards of Ethical Conduct for Management Accountants address competence, confidentiality, integrity, and objectivity.

PROFESSIONAL DESIGNATIONS

❏ Currently, three different Canadian professional designations exist for practising accountants. They are issued by the provincial arms of national accounting organizations. Certified Management Accountant (CMA) is issued by the Society of Management Accountants, Certified General Accountant (CGA) is issued by the Certified General Accountants Association, and Charted Accountant (CA) is issued by the Institute (Ordre) of Chartered Accountants.

KEY TERMS TEST

Test your recall of the key terms as follows. Try to recall as many key terms as possible without assistance. If you need assistance, refer to the list of key terms at the end of this section.

1. A(n) _____ _____ or _____ is an accountant certified to possess the minimal professional qualifications for an external auditor. This type of accountant provides assurance concerning the reliability of a firm's financial statements.

2. _____ _____ is the process of choosing among a set of competing alternatives.

3. _____ _____ results in choices or actions that are right and proper and just.

4. _____ _____ _____ is choosing among alternative strategies with the goal of selecting one or more strategies that provide a company with a reasonable assurance of long-term growth and survival.

5. _____ involves setting objectives and identifying methods to achieve those objectives.

6. The chief accountant of an organization is called the _____.

7. _____ is monitoring a plan using feedback to ensure the plan is being implemented as expected.

8. Information that can be used to evaluate or correct steps being taken to implement a plan is called _____.

9. A(n) _____ _____ _____ _____ is an accounting information subsystem primarily concerned with producing information for external users.

10. A(n) _____ _____ _____ _____ is an information system that produces information to satisfy specific management objectives.

11. _____ _____ are reports that provide feedback to managers by comparing planned data with actual data.

12. The _____ is responsible for the finance functions of raising capital and managing cash and investments.

13. _____-_____ _____ is a system-wide integrated approach that focuses management's attention on activities with the objective of improving customer value and the profit achieved by providing this value.

14. _____ _____ is the process of searching for ways of increasing the overall efficiency and productivity of activities by reducing waste, increasing quality, and reducing costs.

15. _____ _____ is the difference between what a customer receives and what a customer gives up.

16. The _____ _____ _____ is the set of activities required to design, develop, produce, market, and deliver products and services to customers.

17. _____ _____ _____ is an approach in which manufacturers strive to create an environment that will enable workers to manufacture perfect (zero-defect) products.

18. The costs of using, maintaining, and disposing of the product are _____ _____.

19. _____ _____ involves authorizing operational personnel to plan, control, and make decisions without explicit authorization from middle- and higher-level management.

20. The _____ _____ _____ is the linked set of value-creating activities from basic raw materials to end-use customers.

21. _____ _____ are the relationships of activities performed within a firm's portion of the industrial value chain.

22. The relationships of a firm's activities within its segment of the value chain with those activities of its suppliers and customers are _____ _____.

23. A business transaction or information exchange that is performed using information and communication technology is referred to as ___-_____.

KEY TERMS

activity-based management
chartered accountant (CA)
continuous improvement
controller
controlling
customer value
decision making
e-business
employee empowerment
ethical behaviour
external linkages
feedback

financial accounting information system
industrial value chain
internal linkages
internal value chain
management accounting information system
performance reports
planning
postpurchase costs
strategic decision making
total quality management
treasurer

↻ **Compare your answers with those at the end of the chapter. Review any key terms missed. If you missed several key terms, retake the Key Terms Test after reviewing.**

CHAPTER QUIZ

Write your answers in the spaces provided.

1. Complete the following:

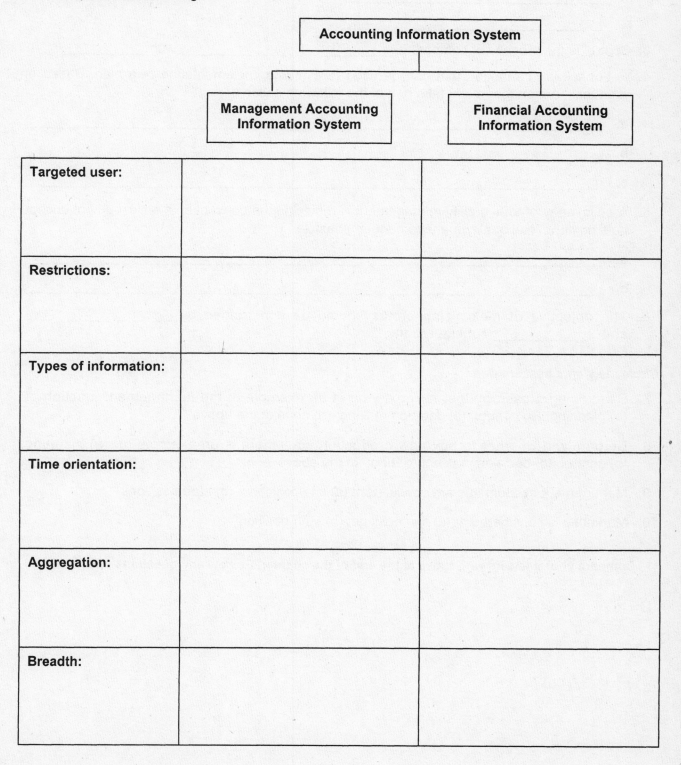

	Management Accounting Information System	Financial Accounting Information System
Targeted user:		
Restrictions:		
Types of information:		
Time orientation:		
Aggregation:		
Breadth:		

2. Managers need accounting information in order to be effective in fulfilling the management functions of:

   a. _____

   b. _____

   c. _____

3. Control is the process of comparing _____ _____ with _____.

4. Feedback is information that can be used to evaluate implementation of a plan. Based on feedback, a manager might take one of the following actions:

   a. _____

   b. _____

   c. _____

5. A philosophy of total quality management is replacing the conventional philosophy of acceptable quality. Total quality management emphasizes:

   a. _____

   b. _____

6. The objective of maximizing profits should be constrained by _____ and _____ considerations.

Circle the single best answer.

7. Developing a cash budget for next year is an example of the management function of: (a) planning; (b) control; (c) decision making; (d) none of the above

8. Determining whether to buy new production equipment is an example of: (a) planning; (b) control; (c) decision making; (d) none of the above

9. Management accountants are considered: (a) line positions; (b) staff positions

10. Marketing is considered a: (a) line position; (b) staff position

↻ **Compare your answers with those at the end of the chapter. Review any questions missed.**

ANSWERS

KEY TERMS TEST

1. chartered accountant, CA
2. Decision making
3. Ethical behaviour
4. Strategic decision making
5. Planning
6. controller
7. Controlling
8. feedback
9. financial accounting information system
10. management accounting information system
11. Performance reports
12. treasurer
13. Activity-based management
14. Continuous improvement
15. Customer value
16. internal value chain
17. Total quality management
18. postpurchase costs
19. Employee empowerment
20. industrial value chain
21. Internal linkages
22. external linkages
23. e-business

CHAPTER QUIZ

1. See page 2.
2. a. planning
   b. controlling
   c. decision making
3. actual results, plans
4. a. continue the implementation as originally planned
   b. take corrective action
   c. modify the original plan
5. a. continual improvement
   b. elimination of waste
6. legal, ethical
7. a
8. c
9. b
10. a

CHAPTER 2
Basic Management Accounting Concepts

CHAPTER REVIEW

COST ASSIGNMENT: DIRECT TRACING, DRIVER TRACING, AND ALLOCATION

☐ An objective of a management accounting information system is to assign costs to products, services, and customers. Increasing the accuracy of cost assignment produces higher-quality information for decision making.

Cost

☐ A **cost** is the cash (or cash equivalent) value sacrificed for goods or services that are expected to produce current or future benefits.

☐ Firms achieve a competitive advantage by providing the same or greater customer value for lower cost than their competitors.

☐ An **opportunity cost** is the benefit given up when one alternative is chosen over another. Opportunity costs are not usually recorded in the accounting system; however, opportunity costs should be considered when evaluating alternatives for decision making.

☐ **Expenses** are *expired* costs. Expenses are costs that are used up when generating revenue.

☐ The selling price charged must exceed the cost so that sufficient income is earned for a firm to remain in business. Therefore, managers need to know the cost of products.

Cost Objects

☐ A **cost object** is any item such as products, departments, customers, and activities for which costs are measured and assigned.

☐ An **activity** is a basic unit of work performed within an organization. Activities are cost objects. Examples of activities include equipment setup, materials handling, and product inspection.

Accuracy of Assignments

☐ Distorted cost assignments can produce erroneous decisions.

Traceability

☐ **Traceability** is the ability to assign a cost to a cost object in an economically feasible way by means of a cause-and-effect relationship.

☐ The more costs that can be traced to a cost object, the greater the accuracy of the cost assignments.

☐ **Direct costs** can be easily and accurately traced to a cost object.

☐ **Indirect costs** cannot be easily and accurately traced to a cost object.

Methods of Tracing

❏ Tracing costs to cost objects can be done using:

1. **direct tracing**, which identifies and assigns costs exclusively and physically associated with a cost object. (For example, wheels on a bicycle can be traced directly to the bicycle.)

2. **driver tracing**, which uses drivers to assign costs to cost objects. **Drivers** are factors that cause changes in resource usage; there is a cause-and-effect relationship between the driver and cost.

❏ **Allocation** is used to assign indirect costs that cannot be traced to cost objects using direct tracing or driver tracing.

❏ Methods of cost assignment are summarized below:

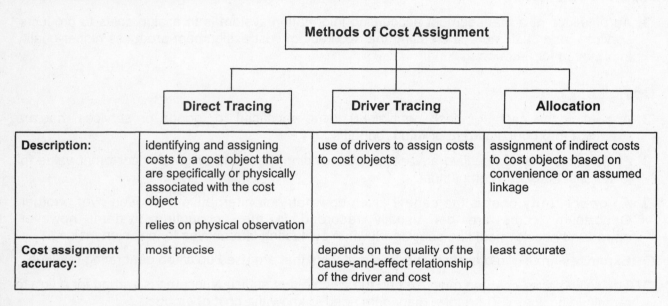

Methods of Cost Assignment		
Direct Tracing	**Driver Tracing**	**Allocation**
Description: identifying and assigning costs to a cost object that are specifically or physically associated with the cost object relies on physical observation	use of drivers to assign costs to cost objects	assignment of indirect costs to cost objects based on convenience or an assumed linkage
Cost assignment accuracy: most precise	depends on the quality of the cause-and-effect relationship of the driver and cost	least accurate

PRODUCT AND SERVICE COSTS

❏ Two types of output of organizations are summarized below:

Output of Organizations	
Goods (tangible products)	**Services**
Definition: goods produced by converting raw materials using labour and capital (plant, land, and machinery)	(1) activities performed for a customer or (2) activity performed by a customer using the organization's products or facilities
Examples: laundry detergent television bicycles	(1) accounting services dry cleaning services (2) video rental
Organization: Manufacturing organizations produce tangible products.	Service organizations produce intangible products.

Different Costs for Different Purposes

❏ **Product costs** consist of costs assigned to a product that satisfies a particular managerial objective. Since managerial objectives can differ, product cost definitions can differ—each depending on the managerial objective being served.

❏ Different cost information might be needed for internal managerial use than for external reporting.

❏ The **internal value chain** is the set of activities required to design, develop, produce, market, distribute, and service a product.

❏ A value-chain product cost consists of costs of the activities in the value chain that are assigned to the product.

Product Costs and External Financial Reporting

❏ For external product costing, costs are classified by the function they serve, as summarized below:

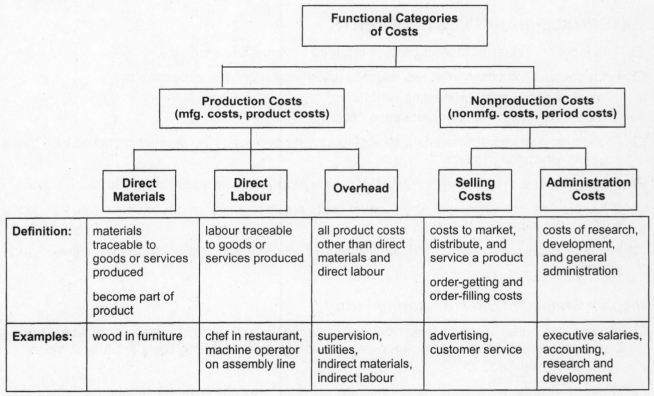

	Direct Materials	Direct Labour	Overhead	Selling Costs	Administration Costs
Definition:	materials traceable to goods or services produced become part of product	labour traceable to goods or services produced	all product costs other than direct materials and direct labour	costs to market, distribute, and service a product order-getting and order-filling costs	costs of research, development, and general administration
Examples:	wood in furniture	chef in restaurant, machine operator on assembly line	supervision, utilities, indirect materials, indirect labour	advertising, customer service	executive salaries, accounting, research and development

❏ Product costs, for external financial reporting, are manufacturing costs (direct materials, direct labour, and manufacturing overhead) that attach to the product and are first inventoried and then expensed when the product is sold.

❏ Period costs are nonproduction costs (selling and administrative) and are expensed when incurred.

Prime Costs and Conversion Costs

❐ **Prime costs** are direct materials costs and direct labour costs.

❐ **Conversion costs** are the costs of converting raw materials into a final product (direct labour costs and overhead costs).

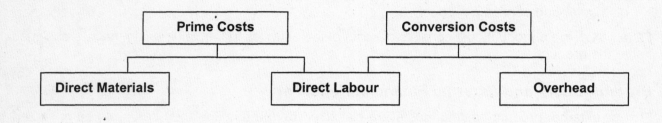

EXTERNAL FINANCIAL STATEMENTS

❐ The functional classification of costs is required for external reporting.

❐ Under absorption costing the two major functional categories of expenses are:
  1. cost of goods sold (production costs), and
  2. operating expenses (nonproduction costs).

❐ Production costs (direct materials, direct labour, and overhead) are product costs because these costs attach to the product.

❐ If the product is in inventory, the product cost is reported as inventory on the balance sheet.

❐ If the product has been sold, the product costs are recognized as an expense (cost of goods sold) on the income statement.

❐ Nonproduction costs (selling and administrative costs) are period costs that are expensed each period.

Income Statement: Manufacturing Firm

❐ Income computed using a functional classification frequently is referred to as **absorption-costing income** or **full-costing income** because all manufacturing costs are fully assigned or absorbed by the product.

❐ **Cost of goods sold** consists of the cost of direct materials, direct labour, and overhead attached to the units sold during a period.

❐ The **cost of goods manufactured** is the cost of direct materials, direct labour, and overhead attached to the units produced during a period.

❐ **Work in process** consists of all partially completed units in production.

❐ **Finished goods** are goods that are complete and ready for sale.

❐ Cost flows for a manufacturer are diagramed below:

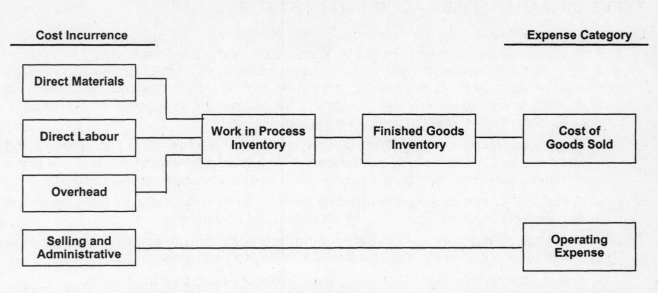

☐ As direct materials, direct labour, and manufacturing overhead are used in the production process, the associated costs are transferred to the Work in Process inventory account.

☐ As the goods in process are completed, the associated costs are transferred to the Finished Goods inventory account.

☐ As the goods are sold, the associated costs are transferred to the Cost of Goods Sold account. Thus, the product costs of direct materials, direct labour, and manufacturing overhead are not expensed until the goods are sold.

☐ A manufacturing firm might have three inventory accounts on the balance sheet:

1. Raw Materials
2. Work in Process
3. Finished Goods

Income Statement: Service Organization

☐ Cost flows for a service firm are diagramed below:

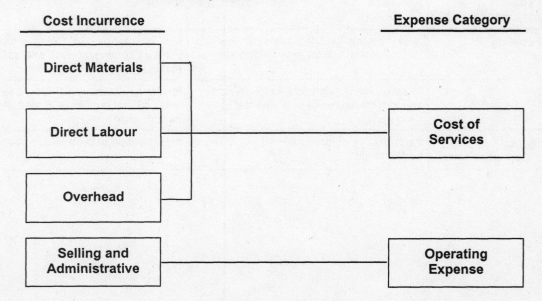

TYPES OF MANAGEMENT ACCOUNTING SYSTEMS

❑ Management accounting systems can be classified as follows:

1. **Functional-based management (FBM) accounting system** is an accounting information system that emphasizes the use of functional organizational units to assign and manage costs. Functions, such as engineering and quality control, are grouped into functional units (e.g., departments or plants). When assigning costs, costs are assigned to functional units, such as departments, and then assigned to products.

   ▪ **Functional-based costing (FBC)** assigns costs of shared resources to products and other cost objects using only **production** or **unit-level drivers** (drivers that are highly correlated with production output volume, such as direct hours or machine hours).

   ▪ **Functional-based management (FBM)** attempts to manage costs by focusing on the efficiency of functional organizational subunits, such as departments.

2. **Activity-based management (ABM) accounting system** is an accounting information system that emphasizes the use of activities for assigning and managing costs.

   ▪ **Activity-based costing (ABC)** traces costs to activities and then to products.

   ▪ **Activity-based management (ABM)** focuses on managing activities with an objective of increasing customer value and resulting profit.

❑ Functional-based and activity-based management accounting systems are compared below:

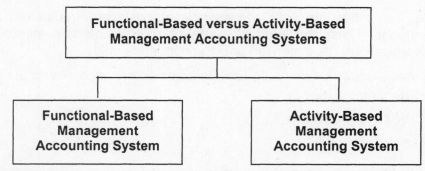

	Functional-Based Management Accounting System	**Activity-Based Management Accounting System**
Activity drivers:	unit-level drivers	unit- and nonunit-level drivers
Product cost assignment emphasis:	allocation	tracing
Product costing objective:	assign production costs to inventories and cost of goods sold for external reporting	external reporting and internal managerial use for planning, control, and decision making
Control:	focus on managing costs, emphasis on financial measures of performance	focus on managing activities, use both financial and nonfinancial measures of performance
Performance maximization emphasis:	maximization of individual unit performance	maximization of systemwide performance

KEY TERMS TEST

There are many new terms introduced in this chapter. The following is provided to assist you in reviewing the new terminology. Indicate which of the following terms best matches the statements listed below by placing the appropriate letter(s) in the blank preceding the statement.

KEY TERMS

A. activity
B. activity-based management
C. allocation
D. conversion cost
E. cost of goods manufactured
F. cost of goods sold
G. direct costs
H. direct labour
I. direct materials
J. direct tracing

K. driver tracing
L. expense
M. indirect costs
N. internal value chain
O. opportunity cost
P. overhead
Q. prime cost
R. product costs
S. service
T. work in process

DEFINITIONS

_____ 1. Materials that can be traced to the good or service being produced.

_____ 2. A cost assignment method that satisfies a well-specified managerial objective.

_____ 3. Costs that are easily traceable to a cost object.

_____ 4. Labour that is traceable to the goods or services being produced.

_____ 5. Direct labour cost plus overhead cost.

_____ 6. Direct materials cost plus direct labour cost.

_____ 7. All production costs other than direct materials and direct labour.

_____ 8. The cost of direct materials, direct labour, and overhead attached to the units sold.

_____ 9. The cost of goods completed during the current period.

_____ 10. The benefit sacrificed or foregone when one alternative is chosen instead of another.

_____ 11. An expired cost.

_____ 12. Costs that cannot be traced to a cost object.

_____ 13. A basic unit of work performed within an organization.

_____ 14. Assignment of indirect costs to cost objects.

_____ 15. Process of identifying costs that are specifically or physically associated with a cost object.

_____ 16. Use of drivers to assign costs to cost objects.

_____ 17. Set of activities required to design, develop, produce, market, distribute, and service a product.

_____ **18.** A task or activity performed for a customer or an activity performed by a customer using an organization's products or facilities.

_____ **19.** A contemporary control system that focuses on the management of activities.

_____ **20.** All partially completed units in production.

Test your recall of the remaining key terms as follows. Try to recall as many key terms as possible without assistance. If you need assistance, refer to the list of key terms at the end of this section.

21. Costs which cannot be reasonably assigned to marketing or production categories are _____ _____.

22. A(n) _____ is the cash or cash equivalent value sacrificed for goods and services expected to produce current or future benefits.

23. _____-_____ income is computed using a functional classification.

24. Any item such as products, projects, or activities for which costs are measured and assigned is a(n) _____ _____.

25. _____ _____ are costs associated with selling and general administration.

26. _____ is the ability to assign a cost directly to a cost object in an economically feasible way using a causal relationship.

27. _____ or _____-_____ _____ are drivers that are highly correlated with production output.

28. _____ are factors that cause changes in resource usage, activity usage, costs, and revenues.

29. _____ _____ are costs necessary to market and distribute a product or service.

30. _____ _____ are costs associated with the manufacture of goods or the provision of services.

31. _____ is assigning costs to a cost object using an observable measure of the cost object's resource consumption.

32. A(n) _____-_____ _____ _____ _____ emphasizes the use of functional organizational units to assign and manage costs.

33. _____-_____ _____ assigns costs of shared resources to products and other cost objects using only production or unit-level drivers.

34. _____-_____ _____ is a managerial approach that attempts to control costs by focusing on the efficiency of organizational subunits.

35. A(n) _____-_____ _____ _____ _____ emphasizes the use of activities for assigning and managing costs.

36. _____-_____ _____ traces costs to activities and then to products.

37. _____-_____ _____ are drivers other than production drivers that describe cause-and-effect relationships.

KEY TERMS

absorption costing

activity-based costing (ABC)

activity-based management accounting
    system

administrative costs

cost

cost object

drivers

functional-based costing (FBC)

functional-based management

functional-based management accounting
    system

marketing costs

nonproduction costs

nonunit-level drivers

production costs

production (unit-level) drivers

traceability

tracing

↻ **Compare your answers with those at the end of the chapter. Review any key terms missed.**

CHAPTER QUIZ

Circle the single best answer.

1. Maytag is an example of a: (a) manufacturer; (b) merchandiser; (c) service company; (d) none of the above

2. Federal Express is an example of a: (a) manufacturer; (b) merchandiser; (c) service company; (d) none of the above

3. Cost of goods sold consists of the following costs: (a) direct materials only; (b) direct materials and direct labour only; (c) direct materials, direct labour, and variable overhead; (d) direct materials, direct labour, variable overhead, and fixed overhead

4. When absorption costing is used: (a) all manufacturing costs are viewed as product costs; (b) only variable manufacturing costs are viewed as product costs; (c) manufacturing and nonmanufacturing costs are viewed as product costs; (d) only direct materials and direct labour are viewed as product costs

Use the following information to answer Questions 5 through 8:

The Flowers Company costs at 50,000 units of production are:

Direct materials...	$ 75,000
Direct labour	150,000
Overhead..	140,000
Selling and administrative costs.......................	90,000

Sales for the year totalled $700,000.

5. Total production costs equal: (a) $225,000; (b) $365,000; (c) $455,000; (d) $230,000; (e) $90,000

6. Total nonproduction costs equal: (a) $225,000; (b) $365,000; (c) $455,000; (d) $230,000; (e) $90,000

7. Gross margin is: (a) $610,000; (b) $475,000; (c) $470,000; (d) $335,000; (e) $245,000

8. The unit product cost is: (a) $4.50; (b) $7.30; (c) $9.10; (d) $4.60; (e) $1.80

9. The number of setups is a: (a) production or unit-level driver; (b) nonunit-level driver

10. Direct labour hours is a: (a) production or unit-level driver; (b) nonunit-level driver

11. Number of material moves is a: (a) production or unit-level driver; (b) nonunit-level driver

12. Machine hours is a: (a) production or unit-level driver; (b) nonunit-level driver

13. Complete the following:

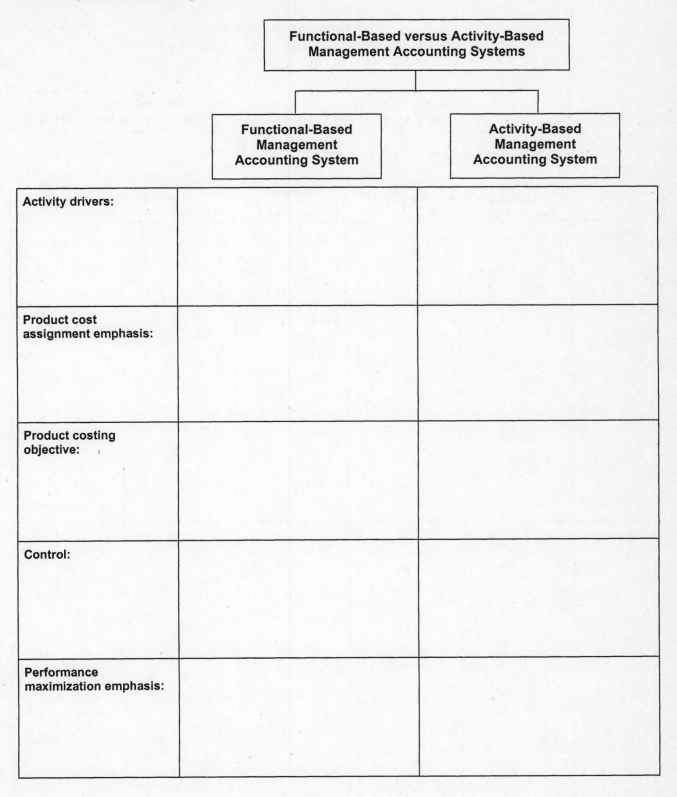

	Functional-Based Management Accounting System	Activity-Based Management Accounting System
Activity drivers:		
Product cost assignment emphasis:		
Product costing objective:		
Control:		
Performance maximization emphasis:		

14. Complete the following:

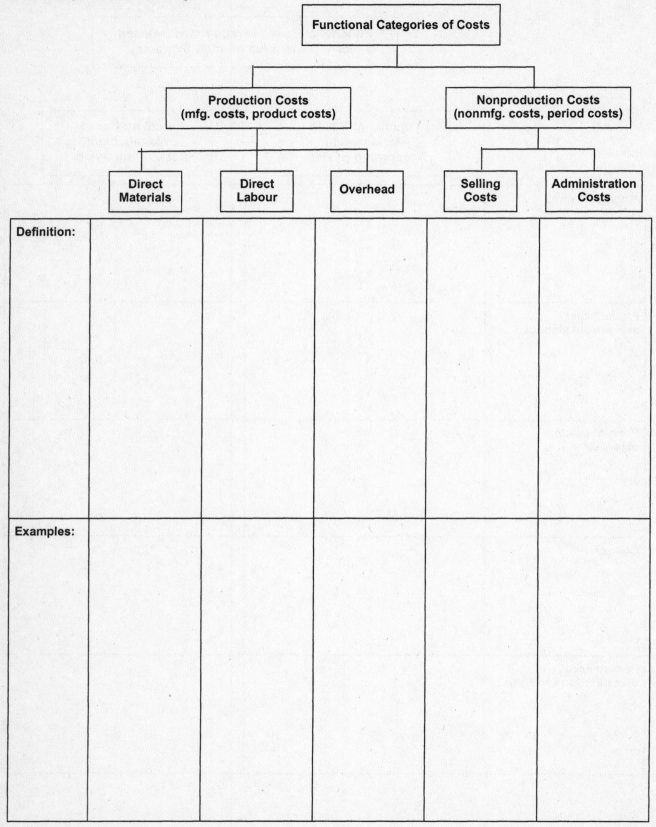

Definition:	Direct Materials	Direct Labour	Overhead	Selling Costs	Administration Costs
Examples:					

⟳ **Compare your answers with those at the end of the chapter. Review any questions missed.**

PRACTICE TEST

PROBLEM 1

Brigette & Company had the following beginning and ending inventories for the year 2000:

	Beginning	Ending
Raw materials	$80,000	$104,000
Work in process	40,000	57,200
Finished goods	30,000	54,000

During 2000, the following costs were incurred:

Purchase of raw materials	$520,000
Direct labour	400,000
Manufacturing overhead	840,000

Instructions:

Prepare a statement of cost of goods manufactured.

PROBLEM 2

The following information pertains to the York Company for the year ending December 31, 2000:

Sales	$840,000
Purchases of raw materials..............................	220,000
Indirect labour..	14,000
Indirect materials	9,000
Amortization of factory equipment....................	50,000
Amortization of factory buildings	29,000
Amortization of administrative building.............	15,000
Marketing costs	130,000
Direct labour	110,000
Raw materials inventory, 12/31/00...................	22,000
Work in process, 1/1/00	54,000
Sales returns and allowances	17,000
Raw materials inventory, 1/1/00.......................	33,000
Work in process 12/31/00	45,000
Sales discounts...	12,000
Finished goods inventory, 1/1/00	124,000
Finished goods inventory, 12/31/00	115,000

Instructions:

Prepare a statement of cost of goods manufactured and an absorption-costing income statement in good form for the York Company for the year ending December 31, 2000.

PROBLEM 2 *(Continued)*

Use this page to continue your answer.

PROBLEM 3

The Jones Company currently produces one product, a cordless phone. The cost formula for the product is as follows:

Total manufacturing cost = $400,000 + $10X$

where X is direct labour hours.

The Jones Company is considering production of another version of the cordless phone. The new version would be similar to the existing version except the new version would have a ten-number memory. The same cost formula would be used to estimate costs.

Estimates of activity for each product are as follows:

	Cordless Phone	Cordless Phone with Memory
Units of product	12,000	3,000
Direct labour hours	30,000	8,000

Instructions:

1. Estimate total manufacturing costs if only the original cordless phone is produced.

2. Estimate total manufacturing costs if both models of the cordless phone are produced.

3. Does Jones Company use a unit-level driver or a nonunit-level driver?

ANSWERS

KEY TERMS TEST

1. I.   direct materials
2. R.   product costs
3. G.   direct costs
4. H.   direct labour
5. D.   conversion cost
6. Q.   prime cost
7. P.   overhead
8. F.   cost of goods sold
9. E.   cost of goods manufactured
10. O.   opportunity cost
11. L.   expense
12. M.   indirect costs
13. A.   activity
14. C.   allocation
15. J.   direct tracing
16. K.   driver tracing
17. N.   internal value chain
18. S.   service
19. B.   activity-based management

20. T.   work in process
21.   administrative costs
22.   cost
23.   Absorption-costing
24.   cost object
25.   Nonproduction costs
26.   Traceability
27.   Production, unit-level drivers
28.   Drivers
29.   Marketing costs
30.   Production costs
31.   Tracing
32.   functional-based management accounting system
33.   Functional-based costing (FBC)
34.   Functional-based management
35.   activity-based management accounting system
36.   Activity-based costing (ABC)
37.   Nonunit-level drivers

CHAPTER QUIZ

1. a
2. c
3. d
4. a
5. b $75,000 + $150,000 + $140,000 = $365,000
6. e
7. d $700,000 − $365,000 = $335,000
8. b $365,000/50,000 units = $7.30 per unit
9. b
10. a
11. b
12. a
13. See page 16.
14. See page 13.

PRACTICE TEST
PROBLEM 1

Brigette & Company
Statement of Cost of Goods Manufactured
For the Year 2000

Direct materials:

Beginning inventory of raw materials	$ 80,000	
Add: Purchases of raw materials	520,000	
Cost of raw materials available for use	$600,000	
Less: Ending inventory of raw materials	104,000	
Direct materials used		$ 496,000
Direct labour		400,000
Manufacturing overhead		840,000
Total manufacturing costs added		$1,736,000
Add: Beginning work-in-process inventory		40,000
Total manufacturing costs		$1,776,000
Less: Ending work-in-process inventory		57,200
Cost of goods manufactured		$1,718,800

PROBLEM 2

York Company
Statement of Cost of Goods Manufactured
For the Year Ended December 31, 2000

Direct materials:		
Beginning inventory of raw materials	$ 33,000	
Add: Purchases of raw materials	220,000	
Cost of raw materials available for use	$253,000	
Less: Ending inventory of raw materials	22,000	
Direct materials used		$231,000
Direct labour		110,000
Manufacturing overhead:		
Indirect materials	$ 9,000	
Indirect labour	14,000	
Depreciation of factory equipment	50,000	
Depreciation of factory buildings	29,000	102,000
Total manufacturing costs added		$443,000
Add: Beginning work-in-process inventory		54,000
Total manufacturing costs		$497,000
Less: Ending work-in-process inventory		45,000
Cost of goods manufactured		$452,000

York Company
Income Statement
For the Year Ended December 31, 2000

Sales		$840,000
Less: Sales returns and allowances		17,000
Sales discounts		12,000
Net sales		$811,000
Cost of goods sold:		
Beginning finished goods inventory	$124,000	
Add: Cost of goods manufactured	452,000	
Cost of goods available for sale	$576,000	
Less: Ending finished goods inventory	115,000	461,000
Gross profit		$350,000
Less operating expenses:		
Selling expenses	$130,000	
General and administrative expenses	15,000	145,000
Income		$205,000

PROBLEM 3

1. Total manufacturing costs = $400,000 + ($10 \times 30,000)$
    $= \$700,000$

2. Total manufacturing costs = $400,000 + \$10(30,000 + 8,000)$
    $= \$780,000$

3. Direct labour hours is a unit-level driver.

CHAPTER 3
Activity Cost Behaviour

CHAPTER REVIEW

THE BASICS OF COST BEHAVIOUR

❏ **Cost behaviour** describes how a cost behaves or changes as output changes.

❏ Understanding cost behaviour is vital to providing cost information for budgeting, cost control, and decision making.

❏ Three cost behaviour patterns are:

1. **fixed costs**—*in total, are constant* within a relevant range as activity output changes. **Relevant range** is the range over which the fixed costs are expected to remain the same.

2. **variable costs**—*in total, vary* in direct proportion to changes in activity output.

3. **mixed costs**—have both a fixed and a variable component.

```
                          Cost Behaviour
        ┌────────────────────┼────────────────────┐
   Fixed Costs          Variable Costs          Mixed Costs
```

	Fixed Costs	Variable Costs	Mixed Costs
Description:	*in total, are constant* within the relevant range as activity output changes	*in total, vary* in direct proportion to changes in activity output	have both a fixed and a variable component
Examples:	factory rent	direct materials	lease payment of $1,000 per month plus $10 per machine hour used
Per unit:	changes as activity level changes	remains constant per unit of activity	
Formula:		**Total variable cost = Variable cost per unit × Units of activity**	**Total mixed cost = Fixed costs + Variable costs**

❏ The following two graphs illustrate how variable costs increase with activity while fixed costs remain the same.

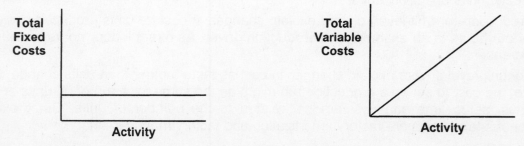

❏ Example: Assume Racing, Inc., manufactures racing bicycles. Each bicycle requires 1 handle-bar costing $10 each. The handlebars are a direct material since they become part of the finished product, and they are a variable cost because the total handlebar cost varies with the number of bicycles produced. If Racing produces 1 bicycle, the total cost for handlebars would be $10; if it manufactures 100 bicycles, the total cost for handlebars would be $1,000. See below:

Bicycles	Handlebars	Cost per Handlebar Variable Cost per Unit	Total Handlebar Cost Total Variable Cost
1	1	$10	$ 10
10	10	10	100
100	100	10	1,000
1,000	1,000	10	10,000

If Racing pays $5,000 per month to rent factory space large enough to produce up to 10,000 bicycles a month, the $5,000 rent would be classified as manufacturing overhead because it is a manufacturing cost other than direct materials or direct labour. In addition, the rent is a fixed cost because the cost will be $5,000 a month if Racing produces between 0 and 10,000 bicycles.

Bicycles	Factory Rent Total Fixed Cost	Fixed Cost per Unit
1	$5,000	$5,000
10	5,000	500
100	5,000	50
1,000	5,000	5

❏ Note that *total* variable costs vary with changes in activity while the variable cost *per unit* remains constant with changes in activity. *Total* fixed costs remain constant while fixed costs *per unit* change with changes in activity.

Classifying Costs According to Behaviour

❏ Whether a cost is fixed or variable depends upon the time horizon. For example, in the long run all costs are variable.

❏ In order to understand the behaviour of costs, it is necessary to determine the underlying activities and associated activity drivers.

❏ *Activity drivers* are causal factors that measure the amount of resources a cost object uses. Activity drivers explain changes in activity costs by measuring changes in activity use or output. For example, the activity driver for material handling costs might be the number of material moves.

❏ Two categories of activity drivers:
  1. Production (or unit-level) drivers explain changes in cost as units produced change. Direct labour hours is an example of a production driver. As direct labour hours increase, output increases.
  2. Nonunit-level drivers explain changes in cost as factors other than units change. For example, the cost to set up a production run might be the same for a run of 50 units or 500 units. Thus, setup time and cost are not related to the number of units. Other examples of nonunit-level costs are factory amortization and factory manager salary.

❏ In a functional-based cost system, unit-level drivers only describe cost behaviour.

❏ In an activity-based cost system, both unit- and nonunit-level drivers are used to describe cost behaviour.

ACTIVITIES, RESOURCE USAGE, AND COST BEHAVIOUR

❏ Capacity is the amount of activity a company can perform.

❏ **Practical capacity** is an efficient level of activity performance.

❏ Resources are economic inputs consumed in performing activities. Resources include materials, labour, and capital.

❏ **Flexible resources** are acquired from outside sources as needed and used.

❏ **Committed resources** are resources supplied in advance of usage.

❏ Characteristics of flexible and committed resources are summarized below:

	Flexible Resources	**Committed Resources**
Definition:	Resources are acquired from outside sources, and the organization is free to buy only the quantity of the resource needed.	Resources are acquired by either explicit or implicit contract to obtain a given quantity of resources, regardless of whether the quantity of the resource available is fully used or not.
Unused capacity:	No; Resource supplied = Resource usage and demand	Yes; Resource supplied ≥ Resource usage
Examples:	materials	equipment
Cost behaviour:	usually variable	Cautiously treated as fixed expenses. **Discretionary fixed expenses** are incurred for short-term capacity.

Step-Cost Behaviour

❏ A **step cost** has a constant level of cost for a range of output, then jumps to a higher level of cost, where it remains for a range of output.

❏ Step costs with narrow ranges of activity are usually treated as a variable cost.

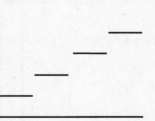

❏ Steps costs with steps that cover wide ranges of activity can be treated as fixed costs.

- ❑ Many committed resources follow a step-cost function.

- ❑ **Fixed activity rate** is based on committed resources so it is calculated as follows using capacity available:

Fixed activity rate = Total committed cost/Total capacity

- ❑ **Variable activity rate** is based on the actual capacity used because flexible resources are purchased as necessary.

Variable activity rate = Total cost of flexible resources/Capacity used

- ❑ A functional-based costing system provides information only about the cost of resources purchased, whereas an activity-based management system provides information about the amount of activity used and the cost of its usage.

METHODS FOR SEPARATING MIXED COSTS INTO FIXED AND VARIABLE COMPONENTS

- ❑ Three widely used methods for separating a mixed cost into fixed and variable components are:
    1. the high–low method
    2. the scatterplot method, and
    3. the method of least squares.

- ❑ Each method assumes a linear cost relationship.

- ❑ Mixed costs can be estimated using the following equation for a straight line:

$$Y = F + VX$$

where Y = total activity cost (the dependent variable)
F = fixed cost (the intercept parameter)
V = variable cost per unit of activity (the slope parameter)
X = activity level (the independent variable)

- ❑ Y (total cost) is called the **dependent variable** because it is dependent on the value of another variable, the activity level.

- ❑ The **intercept** of the line (where the line intersects the vertical or cost axis) is an estimate of the fixed activity cost (F).

- ❑ The **slope** of the line is an estimate of the variable cost per unit of activity (V).

- ❑ A major goal of cost behaviour analysis is to develop cost functions so that costs can be estimated at various levels of activity.

The High–Low Method

- ❑ The **high–low method** uses two points (the high activity level and the low activity level) to determine the cost formula.

- ❑ The slope or variable cost per unit of activity is calculated as:

$$\text{Variable rate} = \frac{\text{Change in cost between high point and low point}}{\text{Change in output between high point and low point}}$$

❑ Total variable costs can be calculated for different activity levels as follows:

Total variable costs = Variable rate × Output

❑ The fixed cost component can be calculated using total cost at either the high point or the low point:

Fixed costs = Total (mixed) cost at high point – (Variable rate × High output)

or

Fixed costs = Total (mixed) cost at low point – (Variable rate × Low output)

❑ The cost formula for total costs is:

Total cost = Total fixed cost + (Variable rate × Output)

❑ A weakness of the high–low method is that it uses only two observations to develop the cost formula and the two points could be outliers (points that do not represent typical cost-activity relationships). It is important that the high and low levels of activity used be representative of the general cost-activity pattern.

❑ The scatterplot method assists in determining if the high–low method produces acceptable results.

The Scatterplot Method

❑ A **scattergraph** contains a vertical axis indicating the mixed cost being analyzed (the dependent variable) and a horizontal axis indicating the activity level (the independent variable). Past cost observations are plotted on the scattergraph.

❑ The **scatterplot method** involves visually fitting a line to the points on the scattergraph by selecting two points on the scattergraph that seem to best represent the relationship between cost and activity.

❑ The slope or variable cost per unit of activity is calculated as:

$$\text{Variable rate} = \frac{\text{Change in cost between Point 1 and Point 2}}{\text{Change in output between Point 1 and Point 2}}$$

❑ Total variable costs can be calculated for different activity levels as follows:

Total variable costs = Variable rate × Output

❑ The fixed cost component is calculated as:

Fixed costs = Total (mixed) cost at Point 1 – Total variable costs at Point 1

or

Fixed costs = Total (mixed) cost at Point 2 – Total variable costs at Point 2

❑ The cost formula for total costs is:

Total cost = Total fixed cost + (Variable rate × Output)

❑ The difference between the high–low method and the scatterplot method is the way the points used are selected.

❑ One purpose of the scattergraph is to see if there is a linear relationship. Also graph may reveal points (observations) that do not seem to fit the general patte (outliers) and perhaps should be eliminated.

The Method of Least Squares

❑ The method of least squares is a statistical method for mathematically deriving a line that best fits a set of data.

❑ The **best-fitting line** is one that minimizes the differences between the cost predicted by the cost formula (the line) and actual cost observations.

❑ Deviation is the difference between the cost predicted by a cost formula and the actual cost. It measures the distance of a data point (actual cost) from the cost line (predicted cost).

❑ The formula used to predict costs is the formula for a straight line:

$$Y = F + VX$$

❑ The **method of least squares** arrives at values for F (fixed costs) and V (variable cost per unit of activity) that result in a line that fits the points (cost observations) better than any other line.

RELIABILITY OF COST FORMULAS

❑ **Goodness of fit** measures the degree of association between activity cost and activity output.

❑ The coefficient of determination is a measure of the goodness of fit.

❑ The **coefficient of determination** (R^2) measures the percentage of change in the dependent variable (cost) that is explained by the change in the independent variable (activity usage).

❑ A coefficient of determination of .92 indicates that 92 percent of the change in cost is explained by changes in activity usage. The coefficient of determination is an indication of the usefulness of the regression line. The higher the percentage of variability explained, the better the fit.

❑ The **coefficient of correlation** is the square root of the coefficient of determination. (If the correlation coefficient is known, the coefficient of determination can be calculated by squaring the correlation coefficient.)

❑ The correlation coefficient can range from −1 to +1. A correlation coefficient of +1 would indicate perfect positive correlation, while a correlation coefficient close to 0 would mean the movement of the two variables is unrelated.

❑ Positive correlation is indicated by a positive value for V. If costs decrease as activity increases, then V would be negative (indicating a downward sloping line) and the coefficient of correlation would be negative.

MULTIPLE REGRESSION

❑ **Multiple regression** uses the method of least squares and involves one dependent variable (cost) and more than one independent variable (activity). For example, multiple regression can be used when there are two variables that are related to changes in costs.

For example, multiple regression could be used to predict total factory overhead costs (the dependent variable) based on facility-level activity (the intercept) and the three independent variables of unit-level activity, batch-level activity, and product-level activity.

❑ The equation used when there are two explanatory variables is:

$$Y = F + VX + CZ$$

where X = activity level of first independent variable
          Z = activity level of second independent variable

MANAGERIAL JUDGMENT

❏ Managerial judgment can be used alone or in conjunction with the high–low, scatterplot, or least squares methods to estimate fixed and variable costs.

SUMMARY

❏ Four methods can be used to estimated the variable and fixed cost components of a mixed cost:

1. High–low method
2. Scatterplot method
3. Method of least squares
4. Managerial judgment

❏ Although the scatterplot method, the high–low method, and managerial judgment involve simpler calculations, the method of least squares produces a line which best fits the points (cost observations) on a scattergraph. (Calculators and software packages are available that perform the calculations for the method of least squares.)

KEY TERMS TEST

Test your recall of the key terms as follows. Try to recall as many key terms as possible without assistance. If you need assistance, refer to the list of key terms at the end of this section.

1. _____ _____ describes how costs change as output changes.

2. The _____ _____ depends on the value of another variable.

3. The _____-_____ _____ is a method of fitting a line to a set of data points using the high and low points in the data set. For a cost formula, the high and low points represent the high and low activity levels. This method is used to estimate the fixed and variable components of a mixed cost.

4. The _____ _____ does not depend on the value of another variable.

5. The _____ _____ is a method for fitting a line to a set of data using two points that are selected by judgment. This method is used to estimate the fixed and variable components of a mixed cost.

6. _____ _____ uses least squares analysis to determine the parameters in a linear equation involving two or more explanatory variables.

7. _____ _____ are purchased in advance of usage. These resources may or may not have unused (excess) capacity.

8. _____ _____ are purchased as used and needed. There is no unused or excess capacity for these resources.

9. The line that minimizes the differences between the cost predicted by the cost formula (the line) and actual cost observations is called the _____-_____ _____.

10. The _____ _____ _____ is the square root of the coefficient of determination, which is used to express not only the degree of correlation between two variables, but also the direction of the relationship.

11. The _____ _____ _____ is the percentage of change in a dependent variable (cost) that is explained by the change in an independent variable (activity).

12. _____ _____ _____ are costs incurred for the acquisition of short-term capacity or services.

13. _____ _____ _____ is the degree of association between Y and X (cost and activity). It is measured by how much of the total variability in Y is explained by X.

14. The _____ _____ is the point where the cost formula intercepts the vertical axis.

15. The _____ _____ _____ _____ is a statistical method for finding a line that best fits a set of data. It is used to break out the fixed and variable components of a mixed cost.

16. A(n) _____ is a plot of past cost observations at different activity levels.

17. The _____ _____ is the variable cost per unit of activity, represented by V in the cost formula $Y = F + VX$.

18. A(n) _____ _____ is a linear function, $Y = F + VX$.

19. The _____ _____ _____ is calculated as fixed activity cost divided by the total capacity of the activity driver.

20. The _____ _____ _____ is calculated as the total variable activity cost divided by the amount of the activity driver used.

21. The _____ _____ is the range of output over which the assumed cost/output relationship is valid.

22. _____ _____ is an efficient level of activity performance.

23. _____-_____ _____ explain changes in cost as factors other than units change.

24. A(n) _____ _____ displays a constant level of cost for a range of output and then jumps to a higher level of cost at some point, where it remains for a similar range of output.

KEY TERMS

best-fitting line
coefficient of correlation
coefficient of determination
committed resources
cost behaviour
cost formula
dependent variable
discretionary fixed expenses
fixed activity rate
flexible resources
goodness of fit
high–low method

independent variable
intercept parameter
method of least squares
multiple regression
nonunit-level drivers
practical capacity
relevant range
scattergraph
scatterplot method
slope parameter
step cost
variable activity rate

↻ **Compare your answers with those at the end of the chapter. Review any key terms missed.**

CHAPTER QUIZ

Circle the single best answer.

1. Cost behaviour patterns include: (a) variable costs; (b) fixed costs; (c) step costs; (d) mixed costs; (e) all of the above

2. Fixed costs: (a) remain the same in total; (b) vary per unit of activity; (c) remain constant per unit of activity; (d) vary in total; (e) a and b; (f) c and d

3. Variable costs: (a) remain the same in total; (b) vary per unit of activity; (c) remain constant per unit of activity; (d) vary in total; (e) a and b; (f) c and d

4. A car lease that specifies a $100 fee per month plus $0.30 per mile would be an example of a: (a) fixed cost; (b) variable cost; (c) mixed cost; (d) step cost

5. Supervisors' salaries of $3,000 per month would be an example of a: (a) committed resource; (b) flexible resource

6. Direct materials is an example of a: (a) committed resource; (b) flexible resource

7. The coefficient of determination indicates: (a) the percentage of change in the dependent variable explained by changes in the independent variable; (b) the percentage of change in the dependent variable caused by changes in the independent variable; (c) the percentage of change in the independent variable explained by changes in the dependent variable; (d) the percentage of change in the independent variable caused by changes in the dependent variable

8. The independent variable (activity) selected should have a high degree of correlation with the dependent variable (cost), as indicated by a coefficient of determination: (a) close to −1; (b) close to +1; (c) equal to 0; (d) none of the above

Use the following information to answer Questions 9 through 11:

The following information was collected regarding maintenance costs at different activity levels measured in machine hours:

Number of Machine Hours	Total Maintenance Costs
8,000	$600,000
10,000	640,000
11,000	800,000
9,000	700,000
14,000	900,000
12,000	870,000

9. Using the high–low method, an estimate of the variable component for maintenance costs is: (a) $50.00; (b) $52.50; (c) $64.28; (d) $75.00

10. Using the high–low method, an estimate of the fixed component for maintenance costs is: (a) $165,000; (b) $200,000; (c) $224,000; (d) $300,000

11. Using the cost formula developed using the high–low method, the estimate of maintenance costs if 13,000 machine hours are scheduled for next month would be: (a) $650,000; (b) $950,000; (c) $850,000; (d) $882,000

Use the following information to answer Questions 12 through 15:

The method of least squares produced the following computer printout using direct labour hours as the activity:

```
INTERCEPT                              20,318.00
SLOPE                                      42.00
CORRELATION COEFFICIENT                      .90
```

12. The estimate of the variable component for maintenance costs is: (a) $37.80; (b) $42.00; (c) $46.67; (d) $47.00

13. The estimate of the fixed component for maintenance costs is: (a) $18,286; (b) $20,276; (c) $20,318; (d) $20,360

14. If 5,000 machine hours are scheduled, an estimate of maintenance costs is: (a) $253,318; (b) $230,726; (c) $230,360; (d) $230,318

15. The coefficient of determination is: (a) 0.73; (b) 0.81; (c) 0.90; (d) 1.0

↻ **Compare your answers with those at the end of the chapter. Review any questions missed.**

PRACTICE TEST

PROBLEM 1

AMK, Inc., believes its electricity costs are affected by the number of machine hours worked. Machine hours and electricity costs for 2000 were as follows:

Month	Machine Hours	Electricity Cost
January	1,500	$18,400
February	1,400	18,300
March	1,300	17,800
April	1,900	22,000
May	1,700	20,200
June	1,550	18,700
July	1,200	17,600
August	1,600	19,000
September	1,100	17,510
October	2,000	22,500
November	2,100	23,000
December	2,200	24,000

Instructions:

1. Using the high–low method, develop the cost function for monthly electricity cost.

2. Estimate total electricity cost for a month in which 1,800 machine hours are worked.

3. What are the weaknesses of the high–low method?

PROBLEM 2

The Koch Company incurred the following maintenance costs during the past six months:

Month	Machine Hours	Maintenance Cost
January	120,000	$456,000
February	100,000	420,000
March	140,000	492,000
April	160,000	528,000
May	130,000	474,000
June	90,000	402,000

Instructions:

1. Using the scatterplot method, the two points that seem to best represent the relationship between cost and activity are the activity levels of 100,000 and 140,000 machine hours. Using these two points, estimate the variable and fixed components of maintenance costs.

2. Develop a cost function that the Koch Company can use to estimate maintenance cost at different volume levels.

3. Estimate maintenance costs for July if the company expects to use 110,000 machine hours.

PROBLEM 3

Max Manufacturing has five salaried accounts payable clerks responsible for processing purchase invoices. Each clerk is paid a salary of $25,000 and is capable of processing 4,000 invoices per year. When 20,000 payments are processed, Max spends $8,000 per year for forms and supplies. During the year, 18,000 invoices were processed.

Instructions:

1. **a.** Calculate the fixed activity rate.

   b. Calculate the variable activity rate.

   c. Calculate the activity rate for the purchase order activity.

2. Complete the following:

   Resources available (supplied) =   Resources used   +   Unused capacity

   _____ = _____ + _____

3. Complete the following:

   Cost of resources supplied = Cost of resources used + Cost of unused capacity

   _____ = _____ + _____

PROBLEM 4

Hentze Dental Centre currently charges $20 per dental exam. A new company that recently located near the dental centre asked if the dental center would be interested in providing dental services to their employees at a special rate of $15 per dental exam.

The dentists have agreed to offer the dental exams at the reduced fee if the $15 would cover the variable costs of the dental exam.

The dental centre's accountant provided the following information about dental exams during the first six months of the year:

Month	Number of Exams	Total Cost of Exams
January	120	$1,850
February	150	2,020
March	110	1,600
April	140	1,960
May	100	1,450
June	80	1,200

The regression results are as follows:

```
                        REGRESSION OUTPUT
    CONSTANT (INTERCEPT)                                    266
    R SQUARED                                          .955224
    X COEFFICIENT(S)                                     12.12
    STANDARD ERROR                                    75.74959
    OBSERVATIONS                                             6
```

Instructions:

1. Using the regression results, determine the variable cost per dental exam.

2. Will the $15 reduced fee cover the dental centre's variable cost of providing the dental exam?

3. Develop a cost function that can be used to estimate total exam costs at different activity levels.

PROBLEM 4 (Continued)

4. If a total of 200 exams are expected to be performed in July, what would be the total expected cost of performing the 200 exams?

5. If 50 additional exams are performed each month at the special rate:

   a. What would be the incremental revenue resulting from the 50 exams?

   b. What would be the incremental cost of providing the 50 exams?

   c. What would be the incremental profit that would result from providing the 50 exams at the reduced rate?

6. Explain the significance of R^2.

PROBLEM 5

In order to better predict setup costs, the plant manager has asked the computer centre to use the least squares method to generate a printout for use in estimating setup costs.

The following computer printout was generated and given to the plant manager:

```
INTERCEPT (CONSTANT)                                    150.00
SLOPE (X COEFFICIENT)                                    10.00
CORRELATION COEFFICIENT                                    .98
ACTIVITY                                     NUMBER OF SETUPS
```

The plant manager brought the printout to you and said, "How am I supposed to use this to estimate setup costs? This printout is worthless!"

Instructions:

1. Explain how the printout information can be used to estimate setup costs.

2. Estimate setup costs if 30 setups are expected next month.

3. What percentage change in setup costs can be explained by changes in the number of setups?

PROBLEM 6

The following information is the result of regression analysis for Felix, Inc., using factory overhead cost observations gathered during the past 18 months:

```
INTERCEPT                                        6,490
REGRESSION COEFFICIENTS:
    UNITS                                           23
    INSPECTIONS                                     15
    ENGINEERING HOURS                                3
  R²                                               .94
```

Instructions:

1. Develop a function that can be used by Felix to estimate total factory overhead costs per month.

2. How useful is this function as a predictor of factory overhead costs?

3. Estimate total factory overhead for the month, given the following budgeted activity levels for next month:

   Units.. 450
   Inspections............................... 30
   Engineering hours 120

4. Which of the activities listed in Requirement 3 above would be considered unit-level drivers? Nonunit-level drivers?

   Unit-level drivers: _____

   Nonunit-level drivers: _____

ANSWERS

KEY TERMS TEST

1. Cost behaviour
2. dependent variable
3. high–low method
4. independent variable
5. scatterplot method
6. Multiple regression
7. Committed resources
8. Flexible resources
9. best-fitting line
10. coefficient of correlation
11. coefficient of determination
12. Discretionary fixed expenses
13. Goodness of fit
14. intercept parameter
15. method of least squares
16. scattergraph
17. slope parameter
18. cost formula
19. fixed activity rate
20. variable activity rate
21. relevant range
22. Practical capacity
23. Nonunit-level drivers
24. step cost

CHAPTER QUIZ

1. e
2. e
3. f
4. c
5. a
6. b
7. a
8. b

9. a ($900,000 − $600,000)/(14,000 − 8,000)
    = $50
10. b $900,000 − ($50 × 14,000) = $200,000
11. c $200,000 + ($50 × 13,000) = $850,000
12. b
13. c
14. d $20,318 + ($42 × 5,000) = $230,318
15. b $.9^2 = 0.81$

PRACTICE TEST
PROBLEM 1

1. Variable cost per machine hour = $\dfrac{\text{Difference in total cost}}{\text{Difference in high and low levels of activity}}$

$$= \frac{\$24,000 - \$17,510}{2,200 - 1,100}$$

$$= \frac{\$6,490}{1,100}$$

$$= \$5.90$$

Total cost at high activity − Variable cost at high activity   = Fixed cost
$24,000 − ($5.90 × 2,200) = $11,020

Cost function for electricity cost = $11,020 + $5.90X
where X = machine hours

2. Total electricity cost at 1,800 machine hours = $11,020 + ($5.90 × 1,800 machine hours)
                                                                        = $11,020 + $10,620
                                                                        = $21,640

3. Weaknesses of the high–low method include:

   (1) The method uses only two points to develop the cost function, and the two points used must be representative of normal operations.

   (2) The method does not detect if the cost behaviour is curvilinear.

PROBLEM 2

1. Variable cost per machine hour = $\dfrac{\text{Difference in total cost}}{\text{Difference in levels of activity}}$

$$= \frac{\$492,000 - \$420,000}{140,000 - 100,000}$$

$$= \frac{\$72,000}{40,000}$$

$$= \$1.80 \text{ per machine hour}$$

Total cost at 140,000 machine hours – Variable cost at 140,000 machine hours = Fixed cost
$$\$492,000 - (\$1.80 \times 140,000) = \$240,000$$

2. Cost function for maintenance cost = $\$240,000 + \$1.80X$
    where X = machine hours

3. Maintenance cost at 110,000 machine hours = $\$240,000 + \$1.80X$
    $$= \$240,000 + (\$1.80 \times 110,000)$$
    $$= \$438,000$$

PROBLEM 3

1. **a.** Fixed activity rate = $(5 \times \$25,000)/20,000 = \$6.25$ per invoice

    b. Variable activity rate = $\$8,000/20,000 = \$0.40$ per invoice

    c. Activity rate = $[(5 \times \$25,000) + \$8,000]/20,000 = \$6.65$ per invoice

2. Resources available (supplied) = Resources used + Unused capacity
    20,000 invoices = 18,000 invoices + 2,000 invoices

3.

Cost of resources supplied	=	Cost of resources used	+	Cost of unused capacity
[Total fixed cost + (Variable rate × Activity usage)] =		[Activity rate × Activity usage] +		[Fixed rate × Unused capacity]
$125,000 + ($0.40 × 18,000)	=	$6.65 × 18,000	+	$6.25 × 2,000
$125,000 + $7,200	=	$119,700	+	$12,500
$132,200	=		$132,200	

PROBLEM 4

1. The slope of the regression line and an estimate of the variable cost per dental exam is $12.12.

2. Yes, the $15 reduced fee would cover the centre's variable cost of $12.12 per exam.

3. The estimate of total fixed costs is $266.
    The regression line equation is: $Y = \$266 + \$12.12X$

4. An estimate of costs for 200 dental exams would be:
    $Y = \$266 + (\$12.12 \times 200)$
    $= \$2,690$

5. **a.** Incremental revenue = Special rate × Additional exams
    $= \$15 \times 50$
    $= \$750$

    b. Incremental cost = Variable cost per exam × Additional exams
    $= \$12.12 \times 50$
    $= \$606$

    c. Incremental profit = Incremental revenue – Incremental cost
    $= \$750 - \$606$
    $= \$144$

6. R^2 (the coefficient of determination) indicates the percentage change in cost that can be explained by changes in output or activity. In this case, approximately 95 percent of the change in dental exam costs can be explained by the number of dental exams.

PROBLEM 5

1. If the intercept is within the relevant range, it is an estimate of total fixed costs.
   The slope is an estimate of variable costs.
   The printout information can be used to develop the following cost function to estimate setup costs at different activity levels.

   Total setup costs = $150 + 10X$
   where X = the number of setups

2. Total setup costs = $150 + ($10 × 30)
                       = $450

3. 96% ($.98^2$) of the change in setup costs can be explained by changes in the number of setups. This indicates that the cost function appears to be useful in estimating setup costs.

PROBLEM 6

1. Factory overhead = $6,490 + $23(Units) + $15(Inspections) + $3(Engineering hours)

2. R^2 of .94 indicates that this formula explains 94% of the variability of factory overhead costs.

3.

	Budgeted Activity	×	Regression Coefficient	=	Budgeted Overhead
Units	450		$ 23		$10,350
Inspections	30		15		450
Engineering hours	120		3		360
Fixed overhead			6,490		6,490
Total					$17,650

4. Unit-level drivers: units
   Nonunit-level drivers: inspections, engineering hours

CHAPTER 4
Activity-Based Costing

CHAPTER REVIEW

UNIT COSTS

❑ Functional-based and activity-based costing assigns costs to cost objects such as products and customers. Once costs are assigned to the cost object, the **unit cost** is calculated by dividing the total cost assigned to the units produced by the number of units produced.

❑ Unit cost information is used to:
- value inventory
- determine cost of goods sold, which affects income
- determine bids to give to potential customers
- decide whether to make or buy a product
- decide whether to accept or reject a special order
- decide whether to keep or drop a product line
- decide whether to introduce a new product

❑ Different cost information is needed for different purposes.

❑ For external reporting, product costs include direct materials, direct labour, and overhead.

❑ **Cost measurement** involves determining the dollar amount of direct materials, direct labour, and overhead used in production.

❑ Two cost measurement systems are:
- actual costing
- normal costing

❑ **Cost assignment** involves associating costs with units produced.

❑ Two cost assignment systems are:
- functional-based costing
- activity-based costing

Supplying Unit Cost Information

❑ **Actual costing** assigns *actual* costs of direct materials, direct labour, and overhead to products.

❑ Actual cost systems are rarely used because they cannot provide accurate unit cost information on a timely basis.

❑ **Normal costing** uses:
- actual costs for direct materials
- actual costs for direct labour
- a predetermined rate for manufacturing overhead

- ❑ A normal costing system can supply unit cost information on a timely basis.
- ❑ The predetermined overhead rate is calculated as:

$$\text{Predetermined overhead rate} = \frac{\text{Budgeted (estimated) overhead cost}}{\text{Estimated activity usage}}$$

- ❑ Overhead is assigned to products using the predetermined overhead rate.

FUNCTIONAL-BASED PRODUCT COSTING

- ❑ When functional-based costing is used, direct materials and direct labour are assigned to products using direct tracing.
- ❑ Overhead costs are assigned using driver tracing and allocations with unit-level activity drivers.
- ❑ **Unit-level activity drivers** are factors that cause changes in cost as the units produced change.
- ❑ Examples of unit-level drivers include:
  - units produced
  - direct labour hours
  - direct labour dollars
  - machine hours
  - direct material dollars
- ❑ An estimate for activity level can be based on:
  - **expected activity capacity**, the *expected* production level of activity for the *next* year.
  - **normal activity capacity**, the *average* activity that the firm *expects* in the *long term* (for example, average activity for the next three to five years).
  - **theoretical activity capacity**, the *maximum output* possible under perfect operating conditions.
  - **practical activity capacity**, the *output* a firm can achieve if it operates *efficiently*. Efficient operations allow for equipment breakdowns, material shortages, etc.
- ❑ Using practical or theoretical capacity avoids assigning unused capacity costs to products.
- ❑ Unit-level activity drivers assign overhead using either:
  - plantwide rates, or
  - departmental rates.

Plantwide Rates

- ❑ A plantwide overhead rate is calculated as:

$$\text{Plantwide rate} = \frac{\text{Budgeted plantwide overhead cost}}{\text{Estimated activity of unit-level driver}}$$

- ❑ Overhead cost assigned to product is calculated as:

$$\text{Applied overhead} = \text{Plantwide rate} \times \text{Actual activity used on product}$$

- ❑ The **overhead variance** is the difference between actual overhead and applied overhead.
- ❑ **Underapplied overhead** occurs when applied overhead is less than actual overhead for the period.

❏ **Overapplied overhead** occurs when applied overhead exceeds actual overhead for the period.

❏ The following T account for overhead illustrates the relationships:

Overhead

Actual overhead costs	Applied overhead
Underapplied overhead	Overapplied overhead

❏ If the overhead variance is relatively small, underapplied or overapplied overhead may be treated as an adjustment to cost of goods sold. Underapplied overhead is added to cost of goods sold, and overapplied overhead is subtracted from cost of goods sold.

Departmental Rates

❏ Departmental rates are calculated as:

$$\text{Departmental rate} = \frac{\text{Budgeted departmental overhead cost}}{\text{Estimated departmental activity}}$$

❏ Overhead cost assigned to product is calculated as:

Applied overhead = Departmental rate × Actual departmental activity used on product

❏ See the summary on the next page:

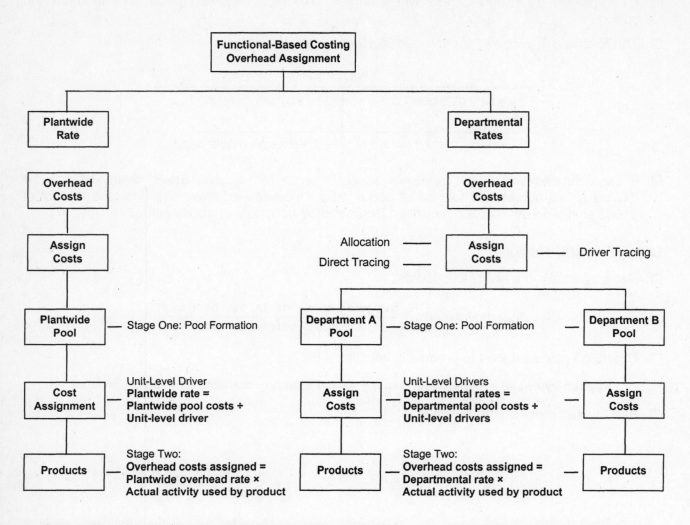

LIMITATIONS OF FUNCTIONAL-BASED COST ACCOUNTING SYSTEMS

❏ Plantwide and departmental rates may cause product cost distortions, which can be damaging for companies operating in an environment characterized by:

- firms engaged in intense competition
- continuous improvement
- total quality management
- total customer satisfaction
- sophisticated technology

❏ As firms adopt new strategies to remain competitive, the cost accounting system must change to produce more accurate product costs.

❏ Symptoms of an outdated cost system include the following:

- The outcome of bids is difficult to explain.
- Competitors' prices appear unrealistically low.
- Products that are difficult to produce show high profits.
- Operational managers want to drop products that appear profitable.
- Profit margins are hard to explain.
- The company has a highly profitable niche all to itself.

- Customers do not complain about price increases.
- The accounting department spends a lot of time on special projects.
- Some departments are using their own accounting systems.
- Product costs change because of changes in financial reporting regulations.

❏ Plantwide and departmental rates using unit-level drivers may not assign overhead costs accurately if:
   - the proportion of nonunit-level overhead costs to total overhead costs is large, and
   - the degree of product diversity is great.

Nonunit-Related Overhead Costs

❏ The main problem with the traditional approach of using plantwide and departmental overhead rates is that a product's consumption of overhead resources may not be strictly related to units produced. For example, *setup costs are related to the number of setups.*

❏ **Nonunit-level activity drivers** are factors, other than the number of units produced, that measure use of overhead resources. For example, setup costs are not driven by the number of units, but by the number of setups, a nonunit-level activity driver.

❏ Using only unit-level activity drivers to assign nonunit-related overhead costs can create distorted product costs. If nonunit-level overhead costs are only a small percentage of total overhead costs, the distortion of product costs would be small and the use of unit-level cost drivers might be acceptable.

Product Diversity

❏ **Product diversity** occurs when products consume overhead activities in different proportions.

❏ Reasons why products might consume overhead in different proportions include:
   - differences in product size
   - product complexity
   - setup time
   - size of batches

❏ **Consumption ratio** is the proportion of each activity consumed by a product.

❏ Product costs can be distorted if a unit-level cost driver is used and
   - nonunit-level overhead costs are a significant proportion of total overhead, and
   - the consumption ratios differ between unit-level and nonunit-level input categories.

ACTIVITY-BASED PRODUCT COSTING

❏ An **activity-based costing (ABC) system** traces:
   1. overhead costs to activities, and
   2. then traces costs to products.

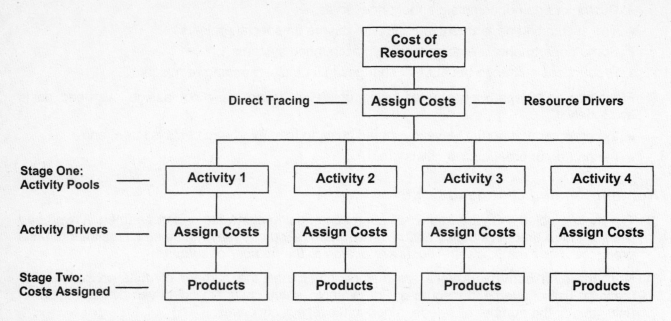

❏ Functional-based costing also involves two stages; however, overhead costs are traced to departments (instead of activities), and then traced to products.

❏ Functional-based costing and activity-based costing are compared below:

	Functional-Based Costing	**Activity-Based Costing**
First stage:	traces costs to plant or department	traces costs to activities
Second stage:	assigns costs to products	assigns costs to products
Cost tracing:	usually allocation-intensive	emphasizes direct tracing and driver tracing
Activity drivers:	unit-level	unit-level and nonunit-level

❏ Activity-based cost assignment consists of the following steps:

1. *Identify and define activities using interviews and surveys, then build an activity dictionary.* An **activity dictionary** lists activities and **activity attributes**—financial and nonfinancial information that describes the activities. Information includes:

   ▪ activity name—usually consists of an action verb and an object
   ▪ a description of the tasks that make up the activity
   ▪ classification as a **primary activity** (activity consumed by a product or customer) or a **secondary activity** (activity consumed by other primary or secondary activities)
   ▪ activity driver—a measure of activity output

2. *Assign costs to activities.* Determine the cost of resources (such as materials, labour, and capital) consumed by each activity.

   ▪ If the resource is exclusive to the activity (such as materials), use direct tracing.
   ▪ If the resource is shared by several activities, use driver tracing to assign costs to the activities. **Resource drivers** are factors that measure the consumption of resources by activities.
   ▪ The costs of secondary activities are ultimately assigned to primary activities using activity drivers.

3. *Assign costs to products.* After the cost of primary activities is calculated, assign the cost of these activities to products based on usage of the activity as measured by activity drivers. Costs assigned to products are calculated as follows:

Cost assigned to product = Predetermined activity rate × Actual usage of activity

HOMOGENEOUS POOLS OF ACTIVITIES

❐ To reduce the number of predetermined overhead activity rates, activities can be grouped into homogeneous pools.

❐ A **homogeneous cost pool** is a collection of overhead costs associated with each set of activities. Only one activity driver need be used to assign the pool's costs, thus the number of rates required can be reduced.

❐ A **pool rate** is calculated as follows:

Pool rate = Pool costs/Practical capacity of activity driver

❐ To build homogeneous sets of related activities, activities are classified into one of four general activity categories:

- **Unit-level activities** are activities performed each time a unit is produced. For example, power is used each time a unit is produced.

- **Batch-level activities** are activities performed each time a batch of products is produced. The costs of batch-level activities vary with the number of batches but are fixed with respect to the number of units in each batch. Examples include setups, inspections, production scheduling, and materials handling.

- **Product-level (sustaining) activities** are activities performed as needed to support the products. Examples include engineering changes and equipment maintenance.

- **Facility-level activities** are activities that support a factory's general manufacturing process. Examples include plant management and security.

❐ All unit-level activities that have the same cost driver would be grouped into homogeneous cost pools. For example, the unit-level category might have the following cost pools:

- labour-related overhead cost pool
- machine-related overhead cost pool
- material-related overhead cost pool

❐ All batch-level activities that use the same cost driver would be grouped into homogeneous cost pools, and all product-level activities that use the same cost driver would be grouped into homogeneous cost pools.

❐ Unit-level costs vary as the number of units change; therefore, a unit-level cost driver can be used.

❐ Batch-level and product-level costs vary in proportion to factors other than changes in the number of units; therefore, they are assigned using nonunit-level cost drivers.

❐ Facility-level activities and costs are common to several products, and it is impossible to identify individual products that consume these activities. A pure ABC system would treat facility-level costs as period costs and would not assign them to products. In practice, facility-level costs might be allocated to individual products using unit-level, batch-level, or product-level cost drivers.

Comparison with Functional-Based Costing

❑ In a functional-based cost system, the demand for overhead is assumed to be explained only by unit-level cost drivers.

❑ ABC produces more accurate product costs by more accurately tracing the consumption of overhead resources to products.

ABC CUSTOMER AND SUPPLIER COSTING

❑ ABC techniques can be used to more accurately determine the costs of customers and suppliers. For example, once you have assigned costs to customers you can determine their profitability, which will aid in the decision to keep or drop the customer.

Activity-Based Customer Costing

❑ The cost of serving different customers can affect pricing decisions and profitability.

Customer Costing versus Product Costing

❑ Customer costing involves three steps:
1. Activities, such as order entry, shipping, and sales calls, are listed in an activity inventory. Different levels include order level, customer level, and channel level.
2. Costs of resources used are assigned to activities.
3. Costs of the activities are assigned to customers.

❐ See the cost assignment summary below:

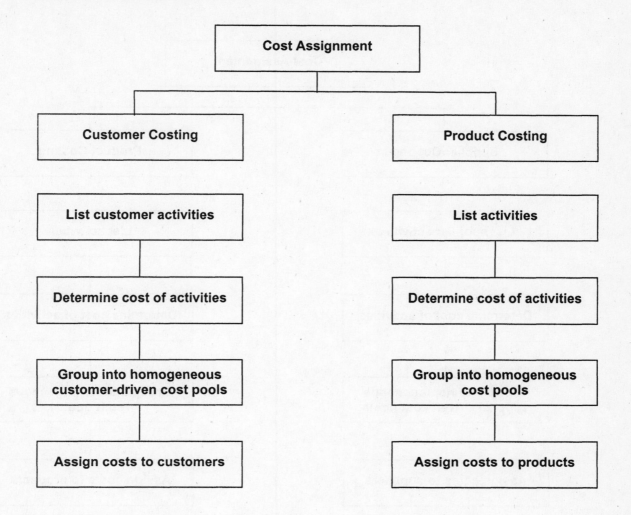

Activity-Based Supplier Costing

❐ Tracing supplier-driven costs to suppliers can enable managers to choose the true low-cost suppliers, producing a stronger competitive advantage and improved profitability.

Supplier Costing Methodology

❐ Supplier costing involves three steps:

1. Activities, such as purchasing, receiving, inspecting incoming products, reworking products and warranty work due to defective parts from suppliers, and expediting products are listed in an activity inventory.

2. Costs of resources used are assigned to activities.

3. Cost of the activities are assigned to suppliers.

❐ See the following cost assignment summary:

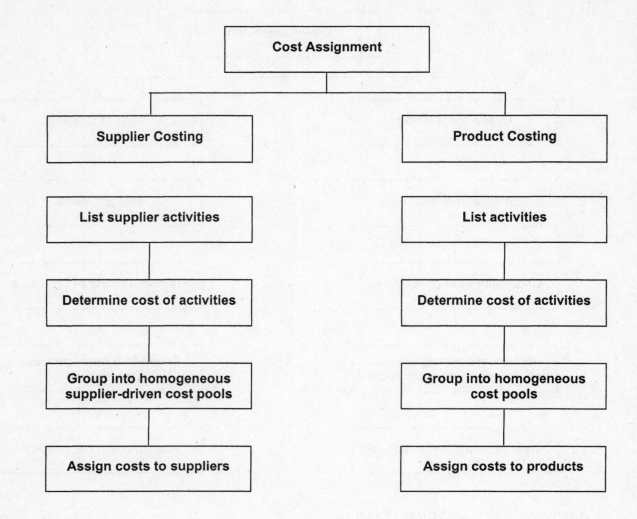

KEY TERMS TEST

Test your recall of the key terms as follows. Try to recall as many key terms as possible without assistance. If you need assistance, refer to the list of key terms at the end of this section.

1. Activities that are performed each time a batch is produced are _____-_____ _____.

2. A(n) _____ _____ is a list of activities described by specific attributes such as name, definition, classification as primary or secondary, and activity driver.

3. The proportion of an overhead activity consumed by a product is the _____ _____.

4. _____ _____ assigns actual costs of direct materials, direct labour, and overhead to products.

5. _____ _____ assigns actual costs of direct materials and direct labour to products and uses a predetermined overhead rate to assign overhead costs.

6. A(n) _____ _____ _____ is a collection of overhead costs associated with activities that have the same level and use the same cost driver to assign costs to products.

7. A(n) _____ _____ _____ is an overhead rate computed using estimated data.

8. _____-_____ _____ _____ are factors, other than the number of units produced, that measure the demands that cost objects place on activities.

9. Activities performed to enable the production of each different type of product are _____-_____ _____.

10. _____ _____ _____ or _____ permits a predetermined number of defects.

11. A cost system that first traces costs to activities and then traces costs from activities to products is a(n) _____-_____ _____ _____.

12. _____ _____ is overhead assigned to production using predetermined rates.

13. _____ _____ is the amount by which applied overhead exceeds actual overhead.

14. _____ _____ is the amount by which actual overhead exceeds applied overhead.

15. _____ _____ is the difference between actual overhead and applied overhead.

16. Activities that sustain a facility's general manufacturing process are _____-_____ _____.

17. _____ _____ involves determining the dollar amount of direct materials, direct labour, and overhead used in production

18. Two _____ _____ systems are functional-based costing and activity-based costing.

19. _____ is calculated by dividing the total cost assigned to the units produced by the number of units produced.

20. _____ _____ occurs when products consume overhead in different proportions.

21. _____-_____ _____ _____ are factors that cause changes in cost as the number of units produced changes.

22. _____ _____ are nonfinancial and financial information items that describe individual activities.

23. _____ _____ measure the consumption of activities by products and other cost objects.

24. _____-_____ _____ are performed each time a unit is produced.

25. The _____ _____ equals overhead costs for a homogeneous cost pool divided by the activity driver for the pool.

26. _____ _____ are activities consumed by products or customers.

27. _____ _____ are activities consumed by primary activities and/or other secondary activities.

KEY TERMS

acceptable quality level (AQL)
activity attributes
activity-based costing system
activity dictionary
activity drivers
actual costing
applied overhead
batch-level activities
consumption ratio
cost assignment
cost measurement
facility-level activities
homogeneous cost pool
nonunit-level activity drivers

normal costing
overapplied overhead
overhead variance
pool rate
predetermined overhead rate
primary activities
product diversity
product-level activities
secondary activities
underapplied overhead
unit cost
unit-level activities
unit-level activity drivers

◖ Compare your answers with those at the end of the chapter. Review any key terms missed.

CHAPTER QUIZ

Write your answers in the spaces provided.

1.

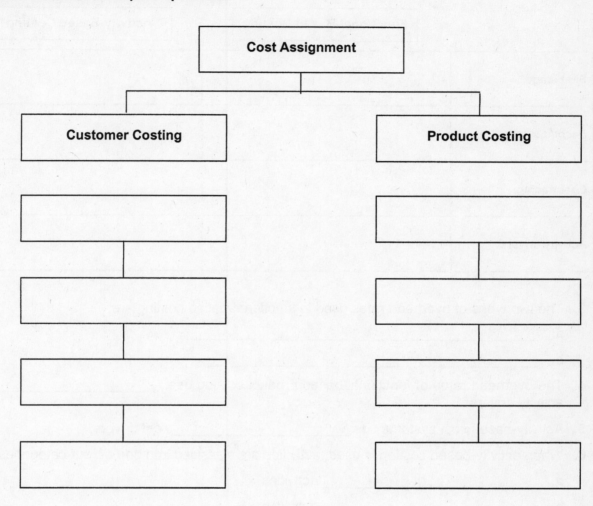

2.

Costing Systems		
	Functional-Based Costing	**Activity-Based Costing**
First stage:		
Second stage:		
Cost tracing:		
Activity drivers:		

3. The two types of overhead rates used in functional-based costing are:

    a. _____

    b. _____

4. The overhead rates of functional-based product costing use _____-_____ activity drivers.

5. Activity-based cost systems use _____-_____ cost drivers.

6. When activity-based costing is used, activities are classified into one of four categories:

    a. _____ activities

    b. _____ activities

    c. _____ activities

    d. _____ activities

7. When activity-based costing is used, the first-stage procedure involves identifying cost pools and calculating a pool rate for each cost pool. The pool rate is calculated as follows:

    Pool rate = _____ / _____

8. The second stage of activity-based costing involves tracing the costs of each overhead cost pool to products. The overhead assigned to each product is calculated as follows:

    Applied overhead = _____ × _____

Circle the single best answer.

9. Unit-level costs are assigned using: (a) unit-level activity drivers; (b) nonunit-level activity drivers

10. Batch-level costs are assigned using: (a) unit-level activity drivers; (b) nonunit-level activity drivers

11. Product-level costs are assigned using: (a) unit-level activity drivers; (b) nonunit-level activity drivers

12. A functional-based product costing system uses a two-stage procedure of (1) tracing overhead to activities, and (2) then tracing the costs to products: (a) true; (b) false

13. Customer-driven activities can be assigned to customers in much the same way as costs can be assigned to products using ABC: (a) true; (b) false

14. The use of unit-level activity drivers, such as direct labour hours or machine hours, can produce distorted product costs: (a) true; (b) false

15. A product's consumption of overhead always increases in proportion to increases in production volume: (a) true; (b) false

16. Some of the costs associated with suppliers, other than the purchase price, include sales calls, sales-order frequency, and shipping frequency: (a) true; (b) false

17. When customer costing is used, both manufacturing and nonmanufacturing costs are traced to customers to produce more accurate cost information for decision making: (a) true; (b) false

Use the following information to answer Questions 18 through 26:

The following data is available for the two products, Model E and Model Z, that Pack, Inc., manufactures:

Item	Quantity	Prime Costs	Machine Hours	Material Moves	Setups
Model E	350,000	$900,000	60,000	600,000	175
Model Z	100,000	$250,000	15,000	400,000	75
Dollar value		$1,150,000	$400,000*	$500,000	$600,000

*The cost of maintenance

Pack currently uses a functional-based costing system that assigns the costs of maintenance, material handling, and setups to the models based on machine hours, a unit-level driver. (Round numbers to two decimal places.)

18. The plantwide overhead rate is: (a) $12.00; (b) $14.67; (c) $20.00; (d) $25.00

19. Overhead assigned to Model E is: (a) $1,500,000; (b) $1,200,000; (c) $880,200; (d) $720,000

20. Overhead assigned to Model Z is: (a) $300,000 (b) $375,000; (c) $220,050; (d) $320,000

21. The unit cost of Model E is: (a) $5.40; (b) $6.00; (c) $5.50; (d) $6.86

22. The unit cost of Model Z is: (a) $4.58; (b) $5.40; (c) $6.00; (d) $5.50

23. If activity-based costing is used, overhead assigned to Model E is: (a) $1,039,800; (b) $939,800; (c) $799,800; (d) $739,800

24. If activity-based costing is used, overhead assigned to Model Z is: (a) $359,950; (b) $279,950; (c) $380,000; (d) $459,950

25. If activity-based costing is used, the unit cost of Model E is: (a) $5.26; (b) $5.54; (c) $4.31; (d) $4.86

26. If activity-based costing is used, the unit cost of Model Z is: (a) $6.30; (b) $4.28; (c) $7.10; (d) $4.60

Write your answers in the spaces provided.

Use the following information to answer Questions 27 through 32:

Classify each of the following activities as a:
- unit-level activity
- batch-level activity
- product-level activity
- facility-level activity

27. Setups: _____

28. Electricity: _____

29. Plant management: _____

30. Engineering changes: _____

31. Inspections: _____

32. Plant security: _____

PRACTICE TEST

PROBLEM 1

Paul's Plastics uses an activity-based cost system. The company produces Product X and Product Z. Information concerning the two products is given below:

	Product X	Product Z
Units produced...	50,000	75,000
Machine hours	22,000	18,000
Direct labour hours...	40,000	40,000
Material handling (number of moves)..............	10,000	15,000
Engineering labour (hours).............................	6,000	4,000
Setups..	40	20
Maintenance (hours used).............................	1,500	1,000
Kilowatt hours	16,000	14,000
Inspections...	18,000	12,000

The following overhead costs are reported:

Material handling...	$ 70,000
Maintenance	50,000
Power...	24,000
Engineering...	60,000
Setups..	75,000
Labour-related overhead................................	60,000
Machine-related overhead.............................	120,000
Inspection..	108,000

Instructions:

1. Using the format below, classify the overhead activities as unit-level activities, batch-level activities, or product-level activities.

   Unit-level activities:

   _____

   _____

   _____

   Batch-level activities:

   _____

   _____

   _____

   Product-level activities:

   _____

   _____

2. Group all overhead costs into homogeneous cost pools. Select an activity driver for each cost pool and compute a pool rate.

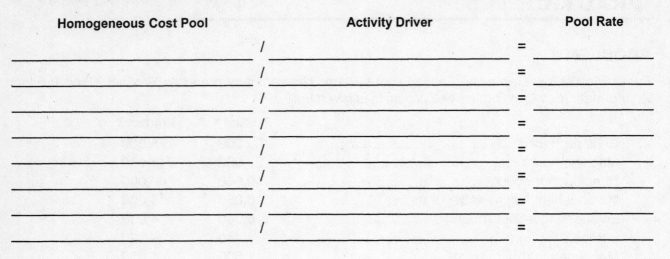

Homogeneous Cost Pool	Activity Driver	Pool Rate

PROBLEM 1 *(Continued)*

3. Using the pool rates, assign overhead costs to the two products and compute the overhead cost per unit for each. Round answers to two decimal places.

	Product X	Product Z
Unit-level activities:		
_____	_____	
_____		_____
_____	_____	
_____		_____
_____	_____	
_____		_____
Batch-level activities:		
_____	_____	
_____		_____
_____	_____	
_____		_____
_____	_____	
_____		_____
Product-level activities:		
_____	_____	
_____		_____
_____	_____	
_____		_____
Overhead cost per unit	$ _____	$ _____

PROBLEM 2

Peach, Inc., has identified the following overhead costs and cost drivers for next year:

Overhead Item	Expected Cost	Cost Driver	Expected Actual Transactions
Setup costs............................	$ 90,000	Number of setups	400
Ordering costs	50,000	Number of orders..................	4,000
Maintenance costs................	150,000	Machine hours	25,000
Power	30,000	Kilowatt hours	75,000

The following are two of the jobs completed during the year:

	Job 700	Job 701
Direct materials.................................	$1,200	$600
Direct labour	$900	$400
Units completed.................................	250	100
Direct labour hours	40	20
Number of setups	2	1
Number of orders...............................	10	4
Machine hours	50	40
Kilowatt hours	60	25

The company's practical activity is 5,000 direct labour hours.

Instructions:

1. Determine the unit cost for each job using direct labour hours to apply overhead. Round answers to two decimal places.

PROBLEM 2 *(Continued)*

2. Determine the unit cost for each job using the four activity drivers. Round answers to two decimal places.

3. Which method produces the more accurate cost assignment? Why?

PROBLEM 3

TFS Company has two types of customers: category A and category B. Category A customers tend to place small orders, more frequently with more deliveries. Category B customers order infrequently and in large quantities with few deliveries being made. TFS offers only one type of product, which costs $50 per unit to manufacture and sells for $100 per unit. The price was set the same for all customers. When the management of TFS set the price they had allocated a flat rate of $20 per unit for customer-related overhead costs, leaving TFS with a profit of $30 per unit ($100–$50–$20).

Recently, the company has noticed that they are receiving more complaints from Category B customers regarding the pricing structure. They state they can receive the same product and delivery schedules from another supplier for only $95 per unit. Ms. Avery, the controller, decided to look into the problem and gathered the following information:

	Category A	Category B
Sales Orders/ Deliveries	400	100
Sales calls	80	60
Service calls	250	50
Average order size	100	300
Manufacturing cost per unit	$50	$50

Customer Costs:	
Sales order processing and delivery costs	$2,500
Selling costs	$1,680
Servicing costs	$4,800

Instructions:

1. Select an activity driver for each cost pool and compute a pool rate.

Homogeneous Cost Pool		Activity Driver		Pool Rate
_____	/	_____	=	_____
_____	/	_____	=	_____
_____	/	_____	=	_____
_____	/	_____	=	_____

PROBLEM 3 *(Continued)*

2. Calculate the customer cost per customer type using activity-based cost assignment.

3. Should TFS consider lowering its price to Category B customers? Why or why not?

PROBLEM 4

Hanover Manufacturing has four categories of overhead. The four categories and expected overhead costs for each category for next year are listed below:

Maintenance	$200,000
Materials handling	32,000
Setups	100,000
Inspection	120,000

Currently, overhead is applied using a predetermined overhead rate based upon budgeted direct labour hours. For next year, 50,000 direct labour hours are budgeted.

The company has been asked to submit a bid for a proposed job. The plant manager thinks getting this job would result in new business in future years. Usually bids are based upon full manufacturing cost plus 20 percent.

Estimates for the proposed job (Job No. P902) are as follows:

Direct materials	$6,000
Direct labour (1,000 hours)	$10,000
Machine hours	500
Number of material moves	12
Number of setups	2
Number of inspections	10

In the past, full manufacturing cost has been calculated by allocating overhead using a volume-based cost driver (direct labour hours). The plant manager has heard of a new way of applying overhead that uses cost pools and cost drivers.

Expected activity for the four activity-based cost drivers that would be used are:

Machine hours	20,000
Material moves	1,600
Setups	2,500
Quality inspections	4,000

Instructions:

1. **a.** Determine the amount of overhead that would be allocated to the proposed job if a plant-wide rate with direct labour hours used the unit-level driver.

PROBLEM 4 *(Continued)*

    b. Determine the total cost of the proposed job.

    c. Determine the company's bid if the bid is based upon full manufacturing cost plus 20 percent.

2. a. Determine the amount of overhead that would be applied to the proposed project if activity-based drivers are used.

    b. Determine the total cost of the proposed job if activity-based costing is used.

    c. Determine the company's bid if activity-based costing is used and the bid is based upon full manufacturing cost plus 20 percent.

PROBLEM 4 *(Continued)*

3. Prepare a memorandum to the plant manager with your recommendation regarding the bid the company should submit. Include the reasons for your recommendation as well as any supporting calculations.

MEMORANDUM

DATE:

TO:

FROM:

SUBJECT:

_____

PROBLEM 5

Ortegren, Inc., has two producing departments: Assembly and Finishing. The company has been using a plantwide predetermined overhead rate based on direct labour cost. The following amounts are for the current year:

	Assembly	Finishing
Actual overhead	$220,000	$215,000
Budgeted overhead...	$240,000	$180,000
Budgeted direct labour hours	30,000	12,000
Budgeted machine hours	8,000	10,000
Actual activity in direct labour hours................	31,000	13,000
Actual activity in machine hours	9,000	11,000

Instructions:

1. **a.** Calculate a plantwide predetermined overhead rate using direct labour hours.

   b. Calculate applied overhead.

   c. Calculate the amount of underapplied or overapplied overhead.

2. **a.** Calculate separate departmental overhead rates using direct labour hours for Assembly and machine hours for Finishing.

   b. Calculate the total amount of applied overhead for each department.

   c. Calculate the amount of underapplied or overapplied overhead for each department.

ANSWERS

KEY TERMS TEST

1. batch-level activities
2. activity dictionary
3. consumption ratio
4. Actual costing
5. Normal costing
6. homogeneous cost pool
7. predetermined overhead rate
8. Nonunit-level activity drivers
9. product-level activities
10. Acceptable quality level, AQL
11. activity-based costing system
12. Applied overhead
13. Overapplied overhead
14. Underapplied overhead
15. Overhead variance
16. facility-level activities
17. Cost measurement
18. cost assignment
19. Unit cost
20. Product diversity
21. Unit-level activity drivers
22. Activity attributes
23. Activity drivers
24. Unit-level activities
25. pool rate
26. Primary activities
27. Secondary activities

CHAPTER QUIZ

1. See page 56.
2. See page 53.
3. **a.** a plantwide overhead rate
   b. departmental overhead rates
4. unit-level
5. nonunit-level
6. **a.** unit-level
   b. batch-level
   c. product-level
   d. facility-level
7. Cost pool/Activity driver
8. Pool rate × Activity driver consumed by product
9. a
10. b
11. b
12. b False Functional-based product costing uses a two-stage procedure: (1) costs are traced to the plant or departments (instead of activities), and then (2) costs are traced to products.
13. a True
14. a True
15. b False. A product's consumption of overhead does NOT always increase in proportion to increases in production volume. For example, setup costs are related to the number of setups instead of production volume.
16. b False. These are costs of customers, not suppliers.
17. a True
18. c ($400,000 + $500,000 + $600,000)/75,000 machine hours = $20.00

19. b ($20 × 60,000 machine hours) = $1,200,000
20. a ($20 × 15,000 machine hours) = $300,000
21. b ($900,000 + $1,200,000)/350,000 units = $6.00
22. d ($250,000 + $300,000)/100,000 units = $5.50
23. a Maintenance: $400,000/75,000 machine hours = $5.33/machine hour
   Materials handling: $500,000/1,000,000 moves = $0.50/move
   Setups: $600,000/250 setups = $2,400/setup

   Model E:

$5.33 × 60,000	=	$ 319,800
$0.50 × 600,000	=	$ 300,000
$2,400 × 175	=	$ 420,000
Total		$1,039,800

24. d

   Model Z:

$5.33 × 15,000	=	$ 79,950
$0.50 × 400,000	=	$200,000
$2,400 × 75	=	$180,000
Total		$459,950

25. b ($900,000 + $1,039,800)/350,000 units = $5.54
26. c ($250,000 + $459,950)/100,000 units = $7.10
27. batch-level activity
28. unit-level activity
29. facility-level activity
30. product-level activity
31. batch-level activity
32. facility-level activity

PRACTICE TEST
PROBLEM 1

1. **Unit-level activities:**   **Batch-level activities:**   **Product-level activities:**
   Labour-related overhead   Material handling   Engineering
   Machine-related overhead   Setups   Maintenance
   Power   Inspection

2.

Homogeneous Cost Pool		Activity Driver		Pool Rate
Labour-related overhead—$60,000	/	Direct labour hours—80,000	=	$0.75
Machine-related overhead—$120,000	/	Machine hours—40,000	=	$3.00
Power—$24,000	/	Kilowatt hours—30,000	=	$0.80
Material handling—$70,000	/	Number of moves—25,000	=	$2.80
Setups—$75,000	/	Number of setups—60	=	$1,250.00
Inspection—$108,000	/	Number of inspections—30,000	=	$3.60
Engineering—$60,000	/	Engineering labour hours—10,000	=	$6.00
Maintenance—$50,000	/	Maintenance hours used—2,500	=	$20.00

3.

	Product X	Product Z
Unit-level activities:		
Labour-related overhead:		
($0.75 × 40,000)/50,000 units	$0.60	
($0.75 × 40,000)/75,000 units		$0.40
Machine-related overhead:		
($3.00 × 22,000)/50,000 units	$1.32	
($3.00 × 18,000)/75,000 units		$0.72
Power:		
($0.80 × 16,000)/50,000 units	$0.26	
($0.80 × 14,000)/75,000 units		$0.15
Batch-level activities:		
Material handling:		
($2.80 × 10,000)/50,000 units	$0.56	
($2.80 × 15,000)/75,000 units		$0.56
Setups:		
($1,250 × 40)/50,000 units	$1.00	
($1,250 × 20)/75,000 units		$0.33
Inspections:		
($3.60 × 18,000)/50,000 units	$1.30	
($3.60 × 12,000)/75,000 units		$0.58
Product-level activities:		
Engineering:		
($6.00 × 6,000)/50,000 units	$0.72	
($6.00 × 4,000)/75,000 units		$0.32
Maintenance:		
($20.00 × 1,500)/50,000 units	$0.60	
($20.00 × 1,000)/75,000 units		$0.27
Overhead cost per unit	$6.36	$3.33

PROBLEM 2

1. Total overhead costs = $90,000 + $50,000 + $150,000 + $30,000
                     = $320,000

   Plantwide overhead rate = $320,000/5,000
                        = $64 per direct labour hour

	Job 700	Job 701
Direct materials	$1,200	$ 600
Direct labour	900	400
Overhead assigned:		
($64 × 40 direct labour hours)	2,560	
($64 × 20 direct labour hours)		1,280
Total cost	$4,660	$2,280
Cost per unit:		
($4,660/250 units)	$18.64	
($2,280/100 units)		$22.80

2. Activity-based overhead rates:

Setup costs:	$90,000/400 setups = $225 per setup
Ordering costs:	$50,000/4,000 orders = $12.50 per order
Maintenance costs:	$150,000/25,000 machine hours = $6 per machine hour
Power:	$30,000/75,000 kilowatt hours = $0.40 per kilowatt hour

	Job 700	Job 701
Direct materials	$1,200	$ 600
Direct labour	900	400
Overhead applied:		
($225 × 2 setups)	450	
($12.50 × 10 orders)	125	
($6.00 × 50 machine hours)	300	
($0.40 × 60 kilowatt hours)	24	
($225 × 1 setup)		225
($12.50 × 4 orders)		50
($6.00 × 40 machine hours)		240
($0.40 × 25 kilowatt hours)		10
Total cost	$2,999	$1,525
Cost per unit:		
($2,999/250 units)	$12.00	
($1,525/100 units)		$15.25

3. Activity-based costing produces the more accurate cost assignment because it uses multiple drivers that are related to overhead consumption. A product or job's consumption of overhead does not always increase in proportion to a single volume-based cost driver, such as direct labour hours.

   Setup costs are related to the number of setups, ordering costs are related to the number of orders, maintenance costs are related to the number of machine hours, and power costs are related to the number of kilowatt hours.

PROBLEM 3

1.

Homogeneous Cost Pool		Activity Driver		Pool Rate
$2,500	/	500	=	$5/order
$1,680	/	140	=	$12/sales call
$4,800	/	300	=	$16/service call

2.

	Category A	Category B
Sales orders and delivery: (400 x $5); (100 x $5)	$2,000	$500
Selling costs: (80 x $12); (60 x $12)	$960	$720
Servicing costs: (250 x $16); (50 x $16)	$4,000	$800
Total	$6,960	$2,020

3. Given the cost differential per customer category, it is likely beneficial to lower the price to the competitor's level of $95, or introduce different prices for different customer service levels. TFS should determine the unit cost under ABC of the customer service activities, if you use average order size as a proxy for number of units, customer service unit costs are $69.60 for Category A and $6.73 for Category B.

PROBLEM 4

1. a. Total overhead = $200,000 + $32,000 + $100,000 + $120,000
                        = $452,000

Overhead rate = $452,000/50,000 direct labour hours
                    = $9.04 per direct labour hour

Overhead assigned to proposed job = $9.04 × 1,000 direct labour hours
                                    = $9,040

b. Total cost of proposed job:

Direct materials	$ 6,000
Direct labour	10,000
Overhead applied	9,040
Total cost	$25,040

c. Company's bid = Full manufacturing cost × 120%
                    = $25,040 × 120%
                    = $30,048

2. a. Maintenance: $200,000/20,000 machine hours = $10 per machine hour
Materials handling: $32,000/1,600 material moves = $20 per move
Setups: $100,000/2,500 setups = $40 per setup
Inspection: $120,000/4,000 inspections = $30 per inspection

Overhead assigned to proposed job:

Maintenance ($10 × 500)	$5,000
Materials handling ($20 × 12)	240
Setups ($40 × 2)	80
Inspections ($30 × 10)	300
Total overhead assigned to job	$5,620

b. Total cost of proposed project:

Direct materials	$ 6,000
Direct labour	10,000
Overhead applied	5,620
Total cost	$21,620

c. Company's bid = Full manufacturing cost × 120%
   = $21,620 × 120%
   = $25,944

3. Your memorandum should contain the following:

   (a) A brief introductory sentence to inform the reader of the purpose of the memorandum.
       Example: This memorandum regards the recommended bid price for proposed Job No. P902.

   (b) A concise and specific recommendation.
       Example: I recommend that Hanover Manufacturing submit a bid of $25,944 for Job No. P902.

   (c) A discussion of the reasons why your recommendation should be followed.
       Example: This bid price was developed using activity-based costing (ABC) because ABC produces more accurate product costs and more competitive bids.

   (d) Supporting calculations included in the body of the memorandum or attached on a separate page.
       Example: The bid price of $25,944 was determined as follows:

Direct materials		$ 6,000
Direct labour		10,000
Overhead assigned:		
Maintenance ($10 × 500)	$5,000	
Materials handling ($20 × 12)	240	
Setups ($40 × 2)	80	
Inspections ($30 × 10)	300	
Total overhead assigned to job		5,620
Total cost		$21,620
Markup		× 120%
Bid price		$25,944

   (e) A closing sentence.
       Example: If you have any questions, please contact me at Extension 76.

PROBLEM 5

1. a. Plantwide rate = Budgeted plant overhead/Budgeted direct labour hours
      = ($240,000 + $180,000)/(30,000 + 12,000)
      = $10 per direct labour hour

   b. Applied overhead = Plantwide overhead rate × Actual activity
      = $10 × (31,000 + 13,000)
      = $440,000

   c.
   Overhead

Actual overhead	Applied overhead
$220,000	$440,000
215,000	
	$ 5,000 overapplied

2. a. Assembly departmental rate = $240,000/30,000 direct labour hours
      = $8.00 per direct labour hour

      Finished departmental rate = $180,000/10,000 machine hours
      = $18.00 per machine hour

   b. Applied overhead: Assembly = $8.00 × 31,000 direct labour hours
      = $248,000

      Applied overhead: Finishing = $18.00 × 11,000 machine hours
      = $198,000

   c.

Overhead: Assembly		**Overhead: Finishing**	
Actual overhead	Applied overhead	Actual overhead	Applied overhead
$220,000	$248,000	$215,000	$198,000
	$ 28,000 overapplied		$ 17,000 underapplied

CHAPTER 5
Job-Order Costing

CHAPTER REVIEW

UNIT COST IN THE JOB-ORDER ENVIRONMENT

☐ Unit cost information is needed for:
1. the financial reporting requirements of costing inventory and determining income, and
2. decision making, such as product pricing.

☐ Different cost information is needed for different purposes.

☐ Two cost assignment systems are:
1. job-order costing, and
2. process costing.

Job-Order Production and Costing

☐ A **job-order costing system** accumulates manufacturing costs by job.

☐ Such a system is used when separate jobs are identifiable, such as in a construction company.

☐ Unit costs in a job-order system are calculated by dividing the total manufacturing cost of the job by the number of units produced in the job.

Process Production and Costing

☐ A **process-costing system** is used where similar or homogeneous units are mass produced, such as in the manufacturing of paint or bricks.

☐ In a process-costing system, production costs are accumulated by process or by department for a given period of time.

☐ Unit costs are calculated by dividing the processing department's costs by the output for the period.

☐ A comparison of job-order and process costing follows:

Job-Order Costing	Process Costing
1. Wide variety of distinct products	1. Homogenous products
2. Costs accumulated by job	2. Costs accumulated by process or department
3. Unit cost is computed by dividing total job costs by the units produced.	3. Unit cost is computed by dividing process costs of the period by the units produced in the period.

Calculating Unit Cost with Job-Order Costing

☐ Using a normal costing system, the total cost of a job is calculated using:
- actual costs for direct materials
- actual costs for direct labour
- a predetermined rate to apply overhead

☐ Overhead can be assigned using:
- a single, unit-level activity driver, or
- multiple activity drivers.

☐ Unit-level systems can be used effectively whenever one of three conditions is met: (1) the nonunit-level overhead is a small percentage of the total overhead, (2) the products produced in the job environment have the same overhead consumption ratios, or (3) the cost of using both unit-level and nonunit-level drivers exceeds the benefits.

KEEPING TRACK OF JOB COSTS WITH SOURCE DOCUMENTS

☐ A job cost system's success depends upon tracking costs to specific jobs.

☐ A **job-order cost sheet** is used to accumulate the manufacturing costs (direct materials, direct labour, and overhead) associated with a job.

☐ The job-order cost sheets are the subsidiary ledgers to the Work in Process account. Work in Process is the total of all incomplete job costs.

☐ The **materials requisition form** is the source document used to record direct materials on the job-cost sheet. Materials requisition forms are used to make requests for materials from inventory. They contain information such as quantity, raw material type, and, most importantly, the job number.

☐ Indirect materials are included in manufacturing overhead and assigned to jobs using the predetermined overhead rate.

☐ **Time tickets** indicate the direct labour time worked on each job. Information on the time tickets is used to post direct labour costs to the job-order cost sheets for individual jobs.

☐ Indirect labour costs are included in overhead and assigned to jobs using the predetermined overhead rate.

☐ Completed job cost sheets are the subsidiary ledgers for finished goods inventory.

THE FLOW OF COSTS THROUGH THE ACCOUNTS (INCLUDING APPENDIX MATERIAL – JOURNAL ENTRIES)

Accounting for Materials

☐ The materials account is used to account for:
1. purchases of materials and supplies, and
2. issuance of materials to production.

☐ The entry to record the purchase of materials would be:

Debit: Raw Materials
  Credit: Accounts Payable

❏ The entry to record the issuance of direct materials for use in production would be:

Debit: Work in Process
　Credit: Raw Materials

Accounting for Direct Labour Cost

❏ The entry to record direct labour costs would be:

Debit: Work in Process
　Credit: Wages Payable

❏ The job-order cost sheets are updated to indicate the direct labour costs associated with each job.

Accounting for Overhead

❏ Overhead is applied to specific jobs using a predetermined overhead rate established at the beginning of the period.

ABC and Job-Order Costing

❏ ABC establishes activity-based overhead rates by estimating:
1. a budgeted cost for each activity pool, and
2. expected demand for the activity driver for each pool. Examples of activity drivers include direct labour hours, machine hours, purchase orders, number of setups, etc.

❏ Activity-based rates are calculated as follows:

$$\text{Activity-based rate} = \frac{\text{Budgeted cost for activity pool}}{\text{Expected demand for activity driver}}$$

❏ Overhead is assigned to specific jobs by multiplying the activity-based rate by the actual activity for the specific job.

$$\text{Applied overhead} = \text{Activity-based rate} \times \text{Activity for job}$$

❏ The summary entry to record total overhead applied would be:

Debit: Work in Process
　Credit: Overhead Control

❏ Overhead applied to specific jobs would be recorded on the job-cost sheet for the particular job.

Applying Overhead Using Functional Approaches

❏ Overhead can also be applied using:
- a plantwide rate (usually based on direct labour hours)
- departmental rates (usually based on unit-level drivers, such as direct labour hours or machine hours)

❏ The predetermined overhead rate is calculated as follows:

$$\text{Predetermined overhead rate} = \frac{\text{Budgeted overhead costs}}{\text{Budgeted activity}}$$

❑ Overhead is assigned or applied to each job by multiplying the activity for that particular job by the predetermined rate. For example, if a firm selected direct labour hours as the activity, overhead would be applied by multiplying the number of hours worked on the particular job by the predetermined rate.

Applied overhead = Predetermined overhead rate × Actual activity

❑ Differences between functional and activity-based costing are summarized below:

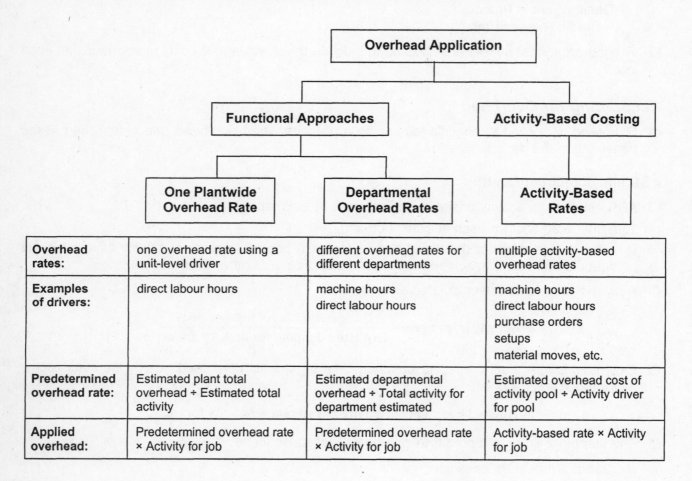

	One Plantwide Overhead Rate	Departmental Overhead Rates	Activity-Based Rates
Overhead rates:	one overhead rate using a unit-level driver	different overhead rates for different departments	multiple activity-based overhead rates
Examples of drivers:	direct labour hours	machine hours direct labour hours	machine hours direct labour hours purchase orders setups material moves, etc.
Predetermined overhead rate:	Estimated plant total overhead ÷ Estimated total activity	Estimated departmental overhead ÷ Total activity for department estimated	Estimated overhead cost of activity pool ÷ Activity driver for pool
Applied overhead:	Predetermined overhead rate × Activity for job	Predetermined overhead rate × Activity for job	Activity-based rate × Activity for job

Accounting for Actual Overhead Costs

❑ Actual overhead costs are recorded in the Overhead Control account.

❑ Actual overhead costs include:

1. indirect materials
2. indirect labour, overtime premium, and idle time
3. invoices received from outside suppliers for utilities, rent, repairs, property taxes, etc. The entry to record these costs would be:

    Debit: Overhead Control
       Credit: Accounts Payable

4. internal transfers of costs, such as amortization and the expiration of prepaid insurance. The entry to record such items would be:

> Debit: Overhead Control
>   Credit: Accumulated Amortization—Building
>   Credit: Accumulated Amortization—Equipment
>   Credit: Prepaid Insurance

Overhead		Work in Process	
Actual overhead costs	Applied overhead		
(Debit)	(Credit)		
		Applied overhead	

Overhead Variance

❑ The overhead variance is the difference between actual overhead and applied overhead.

❑ Underapplied overhead results when applied overhead is less than actual overhead for the period.

❑ Overapplied overhead results when applied overhead exceeds actual overhead for the period.

❑ If immaterial, underapplied or overapplied overhead may be treated as an adjustment to cost of goods sold.

Accounting for Finished Goods

❑ When a job is completed, the cost of the job is transferred from the Work in Process account to the Finished Goods account. The entry to record the transfer would be:

> Debit: Finished Goods
>   Credit: Work in Process

❑ At the end of the period, the Work in Process account will have a balance only if there is uncompleted work in the factory.

Accounting for Cost of Goods Sold

❑ As goods are sold, the associated costs are transferred from the Finished Goods account to the Cost of Goods Sold account. The entry to record the transfer would be:

> Debit: Cost of Goods Sold
>   Credit: Finished Goods

❑ The entry to record the sale would be:

> Debit: Accounts Receivable
>   Credit: Sales Revenue

❑ If the overhead variance is immaterial, it is treated as an adjustment to cost of goods sold at the end of the year. The entry to close overapplied overhead to cost of goods sold would be:

> Debit: Cost of Goods Sold
>   Credit: Overhead Control

❑ **Normal cost of goods sold** is the amount of cost of goods sold before adjustment for an overhead variance.

❑ **Adjusted cost of goods sold** is normal cost of goods sold after adjustment for an overhead variance.

Summary of Manufacturing Cost Flows

- ❏ The diagram on the next page summarizes the flow of manufacturing costs.

- ❏ Because Cost of Goods Sold is an expense, it appears on the company's income statement.

- ❏ Raw Materials, Work in Process, and Finished Goods would appear in the current assets section of the company's balance sheet.

- ❏ Work in Process would also appear in the schedule of cost of goods manufactured, while Finished Goods would also appear in the cost of goods sold section of the income statement.

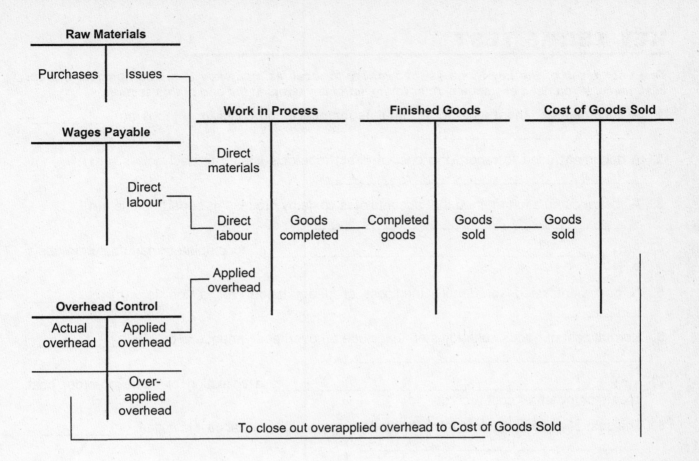

Accounting for Nonmanufacturing Costs

❑ Selling and general administrative costs (nonmanufacturing costs) are considered period costs and are not assigned to the product.

❑ The entry to record selling and general administrative costs would be:

    Debit: Selling Expense Control
    Debit: Administrative Expense Control
       Credit: Accounts Payable
       Credit: Wages Payable
       Credit: Accumulated Depreciation

❑ Selling and administrative expenses appear on the income statement.

KEY TERMS TEST

Test your recall of the key terms as follows. Try to recall as many key terms as possible without assistance. If you need assistance, refer to the list of key terms at the end of this section.

1. A document or record used to accumulate manufacturing costs for a job is a(n) _____-_____ _____ _____.

2. A document used to record the cost of direct materials issued to each job is a(n) _____ _____ _____.

3. A cost accumulation method that accumulates costs by process or department is a(n) _____-_____ _____.

4. A(n) _____-_____ _____ _____ accumulates manufacturing costs by job.

5. A document used to identify the cost of direct labour for a job is a(n) _____ _____.

6. Normal cost of goods sold adjusted to include an overhead variance is called _____ _____ _____ _____.

7. A(n) _____-_____-_____ _____ is a collection of open job-order cost sheets or job-order cost records.

8. The cost of goods sold amount calculated using per-unit normal cost is called _____ _____ _____ _____ _____.

KEY TERMS

adjusted cost of goods sold   normal cost of goods sold
job-order cost sheet   process-costing system
job-order costing system   time ticket
materials requisition form   work-in-process file

↻ **Compare your answers with those at the end of the chapter. Review any key terms missed.**

CHAPTER QUIZ

Circle the single best answer.

1. Material requisitions are used for recording: (a) materials purchased; (b) materials issued and used in production; (c) materials on hand in the storeroom; (d) none of the above

2. A department that is equipment intensive would most likely use a predetermined departmental overhead rate based on which of the following cost drivers: (a) machine hours; (b) direct labour hours; (c) direct labour cost; (d) units of direct material used

3. The overhead costs of a given period might appear in all of the following accounts except: (a) Raw Materials; (b) Work in Process (c) Finished Goods; (d) Cost of Goods Sold

4. A job-order cost system associates costs with particular jobs: (a) true; (b) false

5. A job-order cost system is especially appropriate for situations where basically homogeneous units flow through production on a fairly continuous basis: (a) true; (b) false

6. Time tickets indicate the direct labour time worked on each job: (a) true; (b) false

7. The Work in Process account will have a balance only if there is uncompleted work in the factory: (a) true; (b) false

8. Finished Goods is an expense account: (a) true; (b) false

9. Raw Materials, Work in Process, and Cost of Goods Sold would appear in the assets section of the balance sheet: (a) true; (b) false

10. Most firms use actual costing because it provides product cost information on a timely basis: (a) true; (b) false

11. A single, unit-level driver usually results in a more accurate cost assignment for overhead than activity-based costing: (a) true; (b) false

Use the following information to answer Questions 12 through 14:

Estimated overhead	$320,000
Actual overhead costs incurred	$344,400
Estimated direct labour hours..........................	40,000
Actual direct labour hours worked	42,000

12. The predetermined overhead rate for applying overhead would be: (a) $7.62; (b) $8.00; (c) $8.20; (d) $8.61

13. If the predetermined overhead rate is used to apply overhead, applied overhead would be: (a) $321,000; (b) $328,000; (c) $336,000; (d) $344,400

14. The amount of the overhead variance would be: (a) $24,400 overapplied; (b) $24,400 underapplied; (c) $8,400 overapplied; (d) $8,400 underapplied

☉ **Compare your answers with those at the end of the chapter. Review any questions missed.**

PRACTICE TEST

PROBLEM 1

Strief Industries identified the following budgeted overhead activities and drivers:

Activity Pools		Activity Drivers	
Machining	$80,000	Machine hours	10,000
Setups	$15,000	Number of setups	5,000
Purchasing	$10,000	Purchase orders	2,000

Data associated with Job 786 follows:

Direct materials	$1,000
Direct labour	$3,500
Machine hours	300
Number of setups	50
Purchase orders	20

Instructions:

1. **a.** Calculate a unit-level overhead rate based on machine hours.

   b. What is the total cost of Job 786 using this rate?

2. **a.** Calculate activity-based overhead rates.

PROBLEM 1 *(Continued)*

b.   What is the total cost of Job 786 using the three activity rates?

3. Which method of overhead application (activity-based rates or one plantwide rate) is more accurate?

PROBLEM 2

The Paine Company uses a predetermined overhead rate to apply overhead to production. The rate is based on direct labour hours.

Estimates for the year 2000 are given below:

Estimated overhead	$500,000
Estimated direct labour hours.........	50,000

During 2000, the Paine Company used 60,000 direct labour hours.

At the end of 2000, the Paine Company records revealed the following information:

Raw materials inventory	$ 40,000
Work-in-process inventory..............	100,000
Finished goods inventory	200,000
Cost of goods sold	700,000
Overhead	510,000

Instructions:

1. Calculate the predetermined overhead rate for 2000.

PROBLEM 2 (Continued)

2. Determine the amount of underapplied or overapplied overhead for 2000.

3. If underapplied or overapplied overhead is treated as an adjustment to cost of goods sold, determine the cost of goods sold amount that would appear on the company's income statement.

PROBLEM 3

Getz, Inc., has two producing departments: Assembly and Finishing. The company has been using a plantwide predetermined overhead rate based on direct labour cost.

The following estimates were made for the current year:

	Assembly	Finishing	Total
Overhead............................	$240,000	$160,000	$400,000
Direct labour cost.................	$300,000	$500,000	$800,000
Machine hours	15,000	10,000	25,000

Instructions:

1. Calculate a plantwide predetermined overhead rate for the current year based on direct labour cost.

PROBLEM 3 *(Continued)*

2. Calculate separate departmental overhead rates based upon direct labour cost for Assembly and machine hours for Finishing.

PROBLEM 4

Cornell Industries uses a job-order costing system and applies overhead on the basis of direct labour hours. At the beginning of 2000, management estimated that 200,000 direct labour hours would be worked and $600,000 of overhead costs would be incurred.

During the year, the company actually worked 220,000 direct labour hours and incurred the following production costs:

Indirect labour	$140,000
Indirect materials..	100,000
Insurance	50,000
Utilities	90,000
Repairs and maintenance	80,000
Amortization...	180,000
Direct materials used in production	540,000
Direct labour..	700,000

Instructions:

1. Calculate the predetermined overhead application rate for 2000.

PROBLEM 4 *(Continued)*

2. Determine the amount of overhead applied to work in process during 2000.

3. Determine the amount of underapplied or overapplied overhead for the year.

PROBLEM 4 *(Continued)*

4. If goods with a cost of $1,500,000 were completed and transferred to finished goods during 2000, determine the cost of goods in process at the end of the period.

5. Prepare the journal entry to close underapplied or overapplied overhead to cost of goods sold. (appendix)

PROBLEM 5

Voellenger, Incorporated, uses a job-order costing system and a predetermined overhead rate based on machine hours.

At the beginning of the year, Voellenger estimated overhead for the year would be $50,000 and 8,000 machine hours would be used.

The following information pertains to December of the current year:

	Job No. 77	Job No. 79	Job No. 73	Totals
Work in process, December 1..............	$6,000	$2,500	$1,500	$10,000
December production activity:				
Materials requisitioned	$1,200	$800	$650	$2,650
Direct labour costs	$1,000	$400	$250	$1,650
Machine hours	300	200	100	600

Actual overhead costs incurred in December were $5,000, of which $1,000 was amortization on the factory building and $500 was amortization on the production equipment.

Instructions:

1. Compute the predetermined overhead rate.

2. Prepare the journal entries to record the activity for the month of December. (appendix)

PROBLEM 5 *(Continued)*

3. Determine the cost associated with each job.

4. If Job No. 77 was completed during December, what is the balance of the Work in Process account at December 31?

5. If there was no balance in the Overhead Control account on December 1, what is the balance at December 31?

6. Prepare the journal entry to close underapplied or overapplied overhead to cost of goods sold. (appendix)

PROBLEM 6 (APPENDIX)

Thompson Industries uses a job-order costing system and a predetermined overhead rate based on direct labour cost.

Estimated overhead for 2000 was $540,000 and estimated direct labour costs were $900,000.

On January 1, 2000, the company had the following inventories:

Raw materials............................	$ –0–
Work in process (Job No. 96)......	16,000
Finished goods...........................	–0–

The following information pertains to the company's activities for the month of January 2000:

a. Purchased $150,000 of materials on account.

b. Job Nos. 97 and 98 were started during the month.

c. Materials requisitioned for production totalled $144,000, of which $6,000 was for indirect materials.

Job No. 96	$46,000
Job No. 97	70,000
Job No. 98	22,000

d. Factory payroll for the month totalled $100,000, of which $15,000 was for indirect labour. The direct labour was distributed as follows:

Job No. 96	$20,000
Job No. 97	35,000
Job No. 98	30,000

e. The company made adjusting entries at the end of January to record the following expenses:

Amortization................................	$5,000
Expired insurance	1,000

f. Other manufacturing costs not yet paid totalled $30,650.

g. Overhead was applied using the predetermined overhead rate based upon direct labour cost.

h. Job Nos. 96 and 97 were completed during the month.

i. Job No. 96 was sold on account during the month at a selling price of 120% of manufacturing cost.

Instructions:

1. Prepare journal entries to record the manufacturing activities of the company for January and post to job-cost sheets, where appropriate. (appendix)

PROBLEM 6 *(Continued)*

Use this page to continue your answer.

PROBLEM 6 *(Continued)*

2. Prepare T accounts for Raw Materials, Manufacturing Overhead Control, Work in Process, Finished Goods, and Cost of Goods Sold. Enter beginning balances, where appropriate, and post the transactions for January. (appendix)

3. Prepare the journal entry to dispose of the underapplied or overapplied overhead if the underapplied or overapplied overhead is immaterial. (appendix)

PROBLEM 7

AEU Industries uses a job-order costing system. There are two production departments: Machining and Assembly. A predetermined overhead rate is used in each department.

The Machining Department bases its rate on machine hours, and the Assembly Department bases its rate on direct labour hours.

The company made the following estimates at the beginning of the current year:

	Machining	Assembly
Machine hours......................	20,000	15,000
Direct labour hours...............	7,000	40,000
Overhead cost......................	$200,000	$800,000

The following information was available for Job No. 12-5, which was started and completed during December.

JOB NO. 12-5

	Machining	Assembly
Direct materials	$2,000	$–0–
Direct labour cost	$1,200	$5,500
Direct labour hours................	30	200
Machine hours......................	150	50

Instructions:

1. Calculate the predetermined overhead rate used by each producing department.

2. Compute the total cost of Job No. 12-5.

ANSWERS

KEY TERMS TEST

1. job-order cost sheet
2. materials requisition form
3. process-costing system
4. job-order costing system

5. time ticket
6. adjusted cost of goods sold
7. work-in-process file
8. normal cost of goods sold

CHAPTER QUIZ

1. b
2. a
3. a
4. a   True
5. b   False. Process costing would be appropriate for situations where basically homogeneous units flow through production on a fairly continuous basis.
6. a   True
7. a   True
8. b   False. Of the six control accounts, Cost of Goods Sold is the only expense account. Finished Goods is an inventory account that would appear in the current assets section of the balance sheet.

9. b   False. The three inventory accounts are Raw Materials, Work in Process, and Finished Goods. Cost of goods sold appears on the income statement.
10. b   False. Most firms do not use actual costing because actual costs cannot be determined until the end of the period.
11. b   False. Multiple activity drivers used in activity-based costing usually result in a more accurate cost assignment than a single, unit-level driver.
12. b $320,000/40,000 = $8.00
13. c $8 × 42,000 = $336,000
14. d $344,400 − $336,000 = $8,400 underapplied

PRACTICE TEST

PROBLEM 1

1. a. Unit-level overhead rate:

$$= \frac{\text{Total overhead costs}}{\text{Activity}}$$

$$= \frac{(\$80,000 + \$15,000 + \$10,000)}{10,000 \text{ machine hours}}$$

$$= \frac{\$105,000}{10,000 \text{ machine hours}}$$

$$= \$10.50 \text{ per machine hour}$$

b. Job 786 total cost:

Direct materials	$1,000
Direct labour	3,500
Overhead (300 machine hours × $10.50)	3,150
	$7,650

2. a. Activity-based overhead rates:

Machining rate: $80,000/10,000 machine hours = $8 per machine hour
Setup rate: $15,000/5,000 setups = $3 per setup
Purchasing rate: $10,000/2,000 purchase orders = $5 per purchase order

b. Job 786 total cost:

Direct materials	$1,000
Direct labour	3,500
Overhead (300 machine hours × $8.00)	2,400
Setups (50 setups × $3.00)	150
Purchasing (20 purchase orders × $5.00)	100
	$7,150

3. Activity-based rates

PROBLEM 2

1. Predetermined overhead rate:

$$= \frac{\text{Estimated total overhead}}{\text{Estimated total activity}}$$

$$= \frac{\$500,000}{50,000 \text{ direct labour hours}}$$

= $10 per direct labour hour

2. Overapplied overhead for 2000:

Overhead Control

Actual overhead	Applied overhead
$510,000	$600,000 (60,000 DLH × $10)
	$ 90,000 overapplied

3. Adjusted cost of goods sold:

Cost of goods sold	$700,000
Overapplied overhead	(90,000)
Adjusted cost of goods sold	$610,000

Since overhead was overapplied, cost of goods sold is reduced.

PROBLEM 3

1. Plantwide rate $= \dfrac{\text{Overhead}}{\text{Direct labour cost}}$

$$= \frac{\$400,000}{\$800,000}$$

= 50% of direct labour cost

2. Departmental rates:

Assembly application rate $= \dfrac{\text{Overhead}}{\text{Direct labour cost}}$

$$= \frac{\$240,000}{\$300,000}$$

= 80% of direct labour cost

Finishing application rate $= \dfrac{\text{Overhead}}{\text{Machine hours}}$

$$= \frac{\$160,000}{10,000 \text{ hours}}$$

= $16 per machine hour

PROBLEM 4

1. Predetermined overhead rate $= \dfrac{\text{Estimated overhead}}{\text{Estimated activity}}$

$$= \frac{\$600,000}{200,000 \text{ direct labour hours}}$$

= $3.00 per direct labour hour

2. Overhead applied to work in process during 2000:

> = Actual activity × Predetermined rate
> = 220,000 direct labour hours × $3 per direct labour hour
> = $660,000

3. Overapplied overhead for 2000:

Overhead Control

(Actual costs)		(Applied)	
Indirect labour	$140,000		
Indirect materials	100,000		
Insurance	50,000		
Utilities	90,000		
Repairs and maintenance	80,000		
Amortization	180,000		
		Overhead applied	$660,000
		Overapplied	$ 20,000

4.

Work in Process

Direct materials	$540,000		
Direct labour	700,000		
Overhead applied	660,000		
		Goods completed	$1,500,000
Ending balance	$400,000		

5. Journal entry to close overapplied overhead to Cost of Goods Sold:

Manufacturing Overhead Control	20,000	
Cost of Goods Sold		20,000

Since overhead was overapplied, Cost of Goods Sold is reduced by $20,000.

PROBLEM 5

1. Predetermined overhead rate = $\dfrac{\$50,000}{8,000 \text{ machine hours}}$

> = $6.25 per machine hour

2. Journal entries to record the activity for the month of December:

Entry to record issuance of direct materials for production:

Work in Process	2,650	
Raw Materials		2,650

Entry to record direct labour used in production:

Work in Process	1,650	
Wages Payable		1,650

Entry to record actual overhead costs incurred during December:

Overhead Control	5,000	
Accounts Payable		3,500
Accumulated Amortization—Building		1,000
Accumulated Amortization—Equipment		500

Entry to record overhead applied during December:

Work in Process	3,750*	
Overhead Control		3,750

*($6.25 × 600)

3.

	Job No. 77	Job No. 79	Job No. 73
Work in process, December 1	$ 6,000	$2,500	$1,500
December production activity:			
Materials	1,200	800	650
Direct labour..	1,000	400	250
Overhead:			
$6.25 × 300 machine hours	1,875		
$6.25 × 200 machine hours		1,250	
$6.25 × 100 machine hours			625
Totals	$10,075	$4,950	$3,025

4. If Job No. 77 was completed during December, Work in Process at December 31 would have a balance of $7,975. (The Job No. 79 balance would be $4,950, and the Job No. 73 balance would be $3,025.)

5. The balance in the Overhead Control account at December 31 could be calculated as follows:

Overhead Control

(Actual costs)	(Applied)
$5,000	$3,750
Underapplied $1,250	

6. Journal entry to close underapplied overhead to cost of goods sold:

Cost of Goods Sold..	1,250	
Manufacturing Overhead Control...........................		1,250

Since overhead was underapplied, Cost of Goods Sold is increased by the entry.

PROBLEM 6

1. Journal entries to record manufacturing activities for January:

a. Purchased materials on account:

Raw Materials	150,000	
Accounts Payable..		150,000

b. No entry required.

c. Materials requisitioned for production:

Work in Process...	138,000	
Overhead Control	6,000	
Raw Materials..		144,000

d. Factory payroll for January:

Work in Process...	85,000	
Overhead Control	15,000	
Wages Payable		100,000

e. Expenses recorded with adjusting entries:

Overhead Control	6,000	
Accumulated Amortization		5,000
Prepaid Insurance		1,000

f. Other manufacturing costs not yet paid:

Overhead Control	30,650	
Accounts Payable..		30,650

g. Overhead applied using a predetermined overhead rate:

$$\text{Predetermined overhead rate} = \frac{\text{Estimated total overhead}}{\text{Estimated total direct labour cost}}$$

$$= \frac{\$540,000}{\$900,000}$$

$$= 60\% \text{ of direct labour cost}$$

Entry to apply manufacturing overhead in January:

Work in Process	51,000*	
Overhead Control		51,000

*(60% × $85,000)

h. Job Nos. 96 and 97 were completed and transferred to finished goods. (See the job-order cost sheets on page 102 for how the amounts were determined.)

Finished Goods	220,000*	
Work in Process		220,000

*(Job No. 96 at $94,000 and Job No. 97 at $126,000)

i. Job No. 96 was sold during the month. (See the job-order cost sheets below for how the amount was determined.)

Cost of Goods Sold	94,000	
Finished Goods		94,000
Accounts Receivable	112,800*	
Sales Revenue		112,800

*($94,000 × 120%)

Job No. 96		**Job No. 97**		**Job No. 98**	
Balance	$16,000	Balance	$ –0–	Balance	$ –0–
DM	46,000	DM	70,000	DM	22,000
DL	20,000	DL	35,000	DL	30,000
OH	12,000[1]	OH	21,000[2]	OH	18,000[3]
Total	$94,000	Total	$126,000	Total	$70,000

[1]($20,000 × 60%)
[2]($35,000 × 60%)
[3]($30,000 × 60%)

2. T accounts for the inventory accounts, Cost of Goods Sold, and Overhead Control:

Raw Materials			**Work in Process**			**Finished Goods**			**Cost of Goods Sold**	
$150,000		Bal.	$ 16,000						$94,000	
	$144,000	DM	138,000							
		DL	85,000							
		OH	51,000							
				$220,000		$220,000				
							$94,000			
$ 6,000			$ 70,000			$126,000			$94,000	

Overhead Control			
(Actual costs)		(Applied)	
Indirect materials	$ 6,000		
Indirect labour	15,000		
Amortization and insurance	6,000		
Other costs	30,650		
		Overhead applied	$51,000
Underapplied	$ 6,650		

3. Underapplied overhead is closed to Cost of Goods Sold:

Cost of Goods Sold.. 6,650
     Manufacturing Overhead Control............................   6,650

PROBLEM 7

1. Machining overhead rate = $\dfrac{\text{Estimated overhead}}{\text{Estimated machine hours}} = \dfrac{\$200,000}{20,000 \text{ machine hours}}$ = \$10 per machine hour

    Assembly predetermined overhead rate = $\dfrac{\text{Estimated overhead}}{\text{Estimated DLH}} = \dfrac{\$800,000}{40,000 \text{ DLH}}$ = \$20 per DLH

2.   **JOB NO. 12-5**

Direct materials—Machining	$ 2,000
Direct labour—Machining	1,200
Direct labour—Assembly	5,500
Overhead—Machining ($10 × 150 machine hours)	1,500
Overhead—Assembly ($20 × 200 direct labour hours)	4,000
Total	$14,200

CHAPTER 6
Process Costing

CHAPTER REVIEW

CHARACTERISTICS OF PROCESS MANUFACTURING

❏ Cost accounting systems should be designed to fit the nature of the manufacturing operation.

❏ *Process costing* works well whenever relatively homogeneous products pass through a series of processes and receive *similar* amounts of manufacturing costs.

❏ A process is a series of operations performed on the product, such as mixing, molding, or packaging.

❏ *Job-order costing* works well whenever products pass through a series of processes that deal out *different* amounts of manufacturing costs.

❏ The manufacture of nearly any product requires three types of cost:
  1. Direct materials
  2. Direct labour
  3. Manufacturing overhead

❏ The job-order costing system is designed to trace costs to a job.

❏ A process-costing system traces the costs to the process, instead of the job.

❏ **Operation costing** is a costing method that uses job-order costing to assign material costs and process costing to assign conversion costs (direct labour and manufacturing overhead).

❏ The same accounts are used in the process-costing system as in a job-order costing system with the exception of the number of Work in Process accounts. A different Work in Process account is required for each processing department.

❏ The major differences between process costing and job-order costing are summarized as follows:

Process Costing	Job-Order Costing
1. Homogeneous units pass through a series of similar processes.	1. Unique jobs are worked on during a time period.
2. Costs are accumulated by processing department.	2. Costs are accumulated by individual job.
3. Unit costs are computed by dividing the processing departments' costs by output. In addition, output is measured in equivalent units, not in units produced.	3. Unit costs are determined by dividing the total costs on the job-order cost sheet by the number of units in the job.
4. The production report provides the detail for the Work in Process account for each processing department.	4. The job-order cost sheet provides the detail for the Work in Process account.

Types of Process Manufacturing

❑ In a process-manufacturing firm, units produced pass through a series of manufacturing steps or processes.

❑ The product may flow through the processing departments in different ways.

❑ The product may flow through the factory's processing departments using:

1. sequential processing, or
2. parallel processing.

❑ **Sequential processing** is a method of process manufacturing in which units pass from one process to another in a sequential pattern and each unit is processed using the same series of steps.

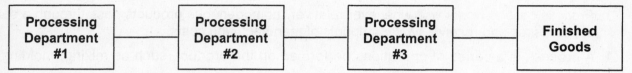

❑ Two examples of **parallel processing** are as follows:

1. Two different products emerge from a common process, and then each flows through its own separate series of processes for completion.

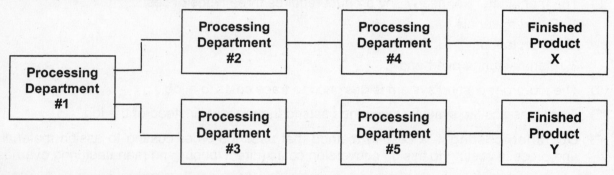

2. The products flow through their separate series of processes and then eventually flow through a common department.

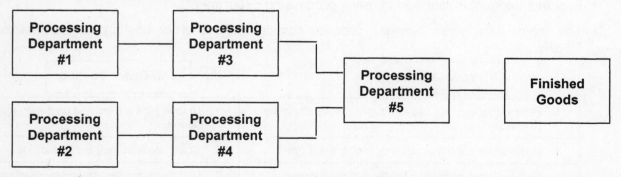

❑ No matter what the product flow, a unit cost is determined for each process, and the cost of the finished product is the total of the unit costs accumulated as the product passes through the processing departments.

How Costs Flow Through the Accounts in Process Costing

- ☐ As raw materials are purchased, the cost of the materials is recorded in a Raw Materials inventory account.

- ☐ As used, raw materials, direct labour, and manufacturing overhead are recorded in the Work in Process account.

- ☐ When goods are completed, their cost is transferred from the Work in Process account to the Finished Goods account.

- ☐ As goods are sold, their cost is transferred from the Finished Goods account to the Cost of Goods Sold account.

- ☐ In process costing, each processing department has its own Work in Process account.

- ☐ Costs transferred from a prior process to a subsequent process are called **transferred-in costs**.

Accumulating Costs in the Production Report

- ☐ The **production report** summarizes the manufacturing activity for a processing department during a period.

- ☐ The production report is divided into two main sections:
  1. Unit information
     a. Units to account for
     b. Units accounted for
  2. Cost information
     a. Costs to account for
     b Costs accounted for

Service and Manufacturing Organizations

- ☐ Process costing can be used for any product or service that is basically homogeneous and repetitively produced, including service organizations, manufacturing organizations using JIT, and traditional manufacturing organizations.

THE IMPACT OF WORK-IN-PROCESS INVENTORIES ON PROCESS COSTING

- ☐ **Equivalent units of output** is the expression of a processing department's activity in terms of fully completed units.

- ☐ For example, two units that are 50 percent complete are the equivalent of one unit fully completed.

- ☐ Work done on partially completed units in beginning work-in-process inventory represents prior period work. Manufacturing costs assigned to these units represent prior period costs.

- ☐ Two approaches used for dealing with prior period output and prior period costs found in beginning work in process are:
  1. weighted average method, and
  2. first-in, first-out (FIFO) method.

❒ Both the weighted average method and the FIFO method use the following general pattern to determine the cost of production:

1. Analysis of the flow of physical units
2. Calculation of equivalent units
3. Computation of unit costs
4. Valuation of inventories
   a. Cost of units transferred out, and
   b. Cost of units in ending work in process
5. Cost reconciliation

WEIGHTED AVERAGE COSTING

❒ The **weighted average costing method** combines the partially completed units in beginning work-in-process inventory with units produced in the current period to determine a weighted average equivalent units of production.

❒ Equivalent units of output using the weighted average method is calculated as:

> **Units completed and transferred out***
> **+ Equivalent units of production in ending work in process**
> **= Equivalent production**

*Note that the weighted average method includes the partially completed units in beginning inventory with the units that were started and completed in the current period.

❒ The weighted average method also merges prior-period costs with current-period costs by adding manufacturing costs in beginning work in process to manufacturing costs incurred during the current period.

❒ The major advantage of the weighted average method is simplicity.

Five Steps in Preparing a Production Report

Step One: Physical Flow Analysis

Units to account for:

       Units in beginning work in process

   + Units started during the period

   = Total units to account for

Units accounted for:

       Units completed and transferred out

   + Units in ending work in process

   = Total units accounted for

Step Two: Calculation of Equivalent Units (Weighted Average)

       Units completed and transferred out

   + Units in ending work in process × Fraction complete

   = Equivalent units of output

Step Three: Computation of Unit Cost

Costs to account for:

       Beginning work in process

   + Costs added (incurred) during the period

   = Total costs to account for

Cost per equivalent unit = Total costs to account for/Total equivalent units

---

Step Four: Valuation of Inventories

Costs accounted for:

       Goods transferred out (unit cost × equivalent units)

   + Goods in ending work in process (unit cost × equivalent units)

   = Total costs accounted for

Step Five: Cost Reconciliation

Compare total costs to account for with total costs accounted for to determine that they are equal.

MULTIPLE INPUTS AND MULTIPLE DEPARTMENTS

Nonuniform Application of Manufacturing Inputs

❏ Equivalent units must be calculated for *each* category of manufacturing input.

❏ Equivalent units are calculated for:
1. each type of material
2. transferred-in costs (if any), and
3. conversion costs.

❏ For example, if ending work in process contained 1,000 units and materials were 100% complete but conversion was only 40% complete, equivalent units would be calculated as follows:

Equivalent units for materials = 1,000 × 100% = 1,000
Equivalent units for conversion = 1,000 × 40% = 400

❏ A unit cost for materials and a unit cost for conversion would be calculated based upon the equivalent units for each.

APPENDIX: PRODUCTION REPORT—FIFO COSTING

❏ FIFO costing excludes the equivalent units and costs in beginning work in process (prior-period costs) from the current-period unit cost calculations.

❏ Only current-period work and current-period costs are used to compute FIFO unit costs.

❏ If the costs of the manufacturing inputs remain fairly stable, the weighted average and FIFO methods will produce very similar results.

❏ If the costs of the manufacturing inputs fluctuate from period to period, the FIFO method may be more useful for cost control, pricing decisions, and performance evaluation because the FIFO method concentrates on the current period's activity.

KEY TERMS TEST

Test your recall of the key terms as follows. Try to recall as many key terms as possible without assistance. If you need assistance, refer to the list of key terms at the end of this section.

1. _____ _____ involves determining whether the costs assigned to units transferred out and to units in ending work in process are equal to the costs in beginning work in process plus the manufacturing costs incurred in the current period.

2. The _____ _____ _____ is a process-costing method that separates units in beginning inventory from those produced during the current period.

3. A method of process manufacturing in which subunits pass through different sequential processes before being brought together in a final process is called _____ _____.

4. A method of process manufacturing in which units flow from one process to another in a set order is called _____ _____.

5. The _____ _____ _____ _____ combines prior-period work and costs with current-period work and costs.

6. The expression of a processing department's activity in terms of fully completed units is called _____ _____ _____ _____.

7. _____ _____ uses job-order costing to assign material costs and process costing to assign conversion costs.

8. The _____ _____ summarizes the manufacturing activity for a department during a period and discloses physical flow, equivalent units, total costs to account for, unit cost computation, and costs assigned to goods transferred out and to units in ending work in process.

9. _____-_____ _____ are the costs of a prior process.

10. A(n) _____ _____ _____ is a schedule that accounts for all units flowing through a department during a period.

KEY TERMS

cost reconciliation
equivalent units of output
FIFO costing method
operation costing
parallel processing

physical flow schedule
production report
sequential processing
transferred-in costs
weighted average costing method

↻ **Compare your answers with those at the end of the chapter. Review any key terms missed.**

CHAPTER QUIZ

Write your answers in the spaces provided.

1. Cost accounting systems should be designed to fit the nature of the manufacturing operation. _____ costing works well whenever relatively homogeneous products pass through a series of processes and receive similar amounts of manufacturing costs.
   _____-_____ costing works well whenever products pass through a series of processes that deal out different amounts of manufacturing costs.

2. The manufacture of nearly any product requires the following three types of costs:

   a._____

   b._____

   c._____

3. In a process-manufacturing firm, units pass through a series of processes. The product may flow through the processing departments using:

   a. _____ processing, or

   b. _____ processing.

4. Equivalent production is the expression of all activity of a processing department in terms of _____ _____ units.

5. Equivalent units using the weighted average method is calculated as:

   _____

   + _____

   = Equivalent units of output

6. Cost per equivalent unit using the weighted average method is calculated as:

   Cost per equivalent unit = _____ / _____

7. List the five sections of the cost of production report.

   a. _____

   b. _____

   c. _____

   d. _____

   e. _____

Circle the single best answer.

8. In a process-costing system, costs are accumulated by jobs: (a) true; (b) false

9. In a process-costing system, a cost of production report contains the detail for the Work in Process account: (a) true; (b) false

10. In a job-order costing system, unit costs are determined by dividing the total costs on the job-order cost sheet by the number of units in the job: (a) true; (b) false

11. The FIFO method is more useful for cost control purposes because the FIFO method concentrates on the current period's activity: (a) true; (b) false

12. Job-order costing works well whenever relatively homogeneous products are produced on a continuous basis: (a) true; (b) false

13. Operation costing is a costing method that uses job-order costing to assign material costs and process costing to assign conversion costs: (a) true; (b) false

14. Costs transferred in from a prior process are handled in the same manner as materials: (a) true; (b) false

15. As raw materials are purchased, the cost of the materials is recorded in the Work in Process account: (a) true; (b) false

16. When using FIFO costing, work done on partially completed units in beginning work-in-process inventory is considered current-period work: (a) true; (b) false

17. The major advantage of the weighted average method is simplicity: (a) true; (b) false

Use the following information to answer Questions 18 through 23:

The Jones Company manufactures medicated shampoo. It passes through two processes: (1) mixing, where ingredients are added and blended together, and (2) packaging, where the shampoo is put into bottles and packed for shipment.

The following information pertains to the Mixing Department for September 2000:

	Units (Pounds)
Work in process, September 1 (80% complete, materials; 70% complete, labour and overhead)	10,000
Started during September	120,000
Work in process, September 30 (60% complete, materials; 40% complete, labour and overhead)	12,000

The costs of work in process at September 1 for the Mixing Department were as follows:

	Mixing Department
Work in process, September 1:	
Materials	$ 60,000
Direct labour	40,000
Overhead	25,000
Total	$125,000

Costs added by the Mixing Department during September were as follows:

	Mixing Department
Materials	$ 880,000
Direct labour	520,500
Overhead	208,600
Total costs added	$1,609,100

Using the weighted average costing method, calculate the following for the Mixing Department for September:

18. The equivalent units of production for materials is: (a) 118,000; (b) 125,200; (c) 130,000; (d) 142,000

19. The unit cost for materials is: (a) $5.69; (b) $7.07; (c) $7.23; (d) $7.51

20. The equivalent units of production for conversion is: (a) 112,000; (b) 118,000; (c) 122,800; (d) 130,000

21. The unit cost for conversion costs is: (a) $4.23; (b) $5.94; (c) $6.26; (d) $6.47

22. Cost of goods transferred out is: (a) $1,649,640; (b) $1,652,000; (c) $1,716,744; (d) $1,817,400

23. Cost of ending work in process is: (a) $77,640; (b) $82,632; (c) $85,128; (d) $90,120

↻ **Compare your answers with those at the end of the chapter. Review any questions missed.**

PRACTICE TEST

PROBLEM 1

Jax, Inc., manufactures a product that passes through two processes: assembly and finishing. All manufacturing costs are added uniformly for both processes.

Information for the Assembly Department for the month of November follows:

Work in process, November 1:
Direct materials...	$10,000
Direct labour	$15,000
Overhead..	$8,000
Number of units (20% complete)......................	6,000

During November, 20,000 units were completed and transferred to the Finishing Department. The following costs were incurred by the Assembly Department during November:

Direct materials..	$35,000
Direct labour	50,000
Overhead..	28,280

On November 30, 2,000 units that were 60% complete remained in assembly.

Instructions:

On the following page, complete the production report for the Assembly Department for November using the weighted average method.

PROBLEM 1 *(Continued)*

Jax, Inc.
Assembly Department - Production Report for November 2000
(Weighted Average Method)

UNIT INFORMATION

Units to account for:

Units in beginning work in process .... _____

Units started during the period............................ _____

Total units to account for .... _____

	Equivalent Units		
	Physical Flow	**Materials**	**Conversion Cost**
Units completed	_____	_____	_____
Units in ending work in process	_____	_____	_____
Total equivalent units	_____	_____	_____

COST INFORMATION

Calculation of Unit Costs

	Materials	**Conversion Cost**	**Total**
Costs to account for:			
Beginning work in process.............................	_____	_____	_____
Costs incurred during the period	_____	_____	_____
Total costs to account for	_____	_____	_____
Cost per equivalent unit	_____	_____	_____

Costs Transferred Out and Cost of Ending Inventory

	Transferred Out	**Ending Work in Process**	**Total**
Costs accounted for:			
Goods transferred out (total unit cost × units)	_____		_____
Goods in ending work in process:			
Materials (unit cost for materials × equivalent units)		_____	_____
Conversion (unit cost for conversion × equivalent units)		_____	_____
Total costs accounted for..........................	_____	_____	_____

PROBLEM 2

Jim's Paint Products manufactures house paint. The ingredients are combined in the Mixing Department, then put in gallon cans in the Packaging Department.

The following information pertains to the Mixing Department for May 2000:

	Units (Gallons)
Work in process, May 1 (100% complete, materials; 60% complete, labour and overhead)	5,000
Started during May	80,000
Work in process, May 31 (100% complete, materials; 35% complete, labour and overhead)	9,000

The costs of the Mixing Department's work in process at May 1 were as follows:

	Mixing Department
Work in process, May 1:	
Materials	$34,000
Direct labour	23,000
Overhead	15,000
Total	$72,000

The costs added by the Mixing Department during May were as follows:

	Mixing Department
Materials	$ 680,000
Direct labour	293,600
Overhead	182,875
Total costs added	$1,156,475

Instructions:

On the following page prepare a production report for the Mixing Department for May using the weighted average method. The report should include the following:

1. Physical flow of units

2. Equivalent units

3. Calculation of unit costs

4. Costs accounted for showing costs transferred out and cost of ending work in process

PROBLEM 2 *(Continued)*

Use this page for your answer.

PROBLEM 3

The following information pertains to the Packaging Department of Jim's Paint Products for May 2000:

	Units (Gallons)
Work in process, May 1 (20% converted)......................	2,000
Transferred in from Mixing Department	76,000
Work in process, May 31 (70% converted)	8,000

The costs of the Packaging Department's work in process at May 1 were as follows:

	Packaging Department
Work in process, May 1:	
Costs transferred in from Mixing Department.........	$25,900
Direct labour	17,040
Manufacturing overhead	22,120
Total..	$65,060

The costs added by the Packaging Department during May were as follows:

	Packaging Department
Direct labour	$240,000
Manufacturing overhead	560,000
Total..	$800,000

Instructions:

Using the information from Problem 2 and the above information, on the following page prepare a production report for the Packaging Department for May using the weighted average method. The report should include the following:

1. Physical flow of unit

2. Calculation of equivalent units

3. Calculation of unit costs

4. Costs accounted for showing costs transferred out and the cost of ending work in process

PROBLEM 3 *(Continued)*

Use this page for your answer.

PROBLEM 4 (Appendix)

Instructions:

Using the information from Problems 2 and 3, prepare a production report for the Mixing Department for May 2000 using the first-in, first-out method.

(Round unit costs to four decimal places and round other amounts to dollars.)

PROBLEM 5

Instructions:

1. Refer to the information presented in Problems 2 and 3 regarding Jim's Paint Products. Prepare journal entries to summarize the activities in the Mixing and Packaging Departments for May 2000 using the weighted average method.

2. Prepare T accounts for work in process for the Mixing and Packaging Departments of Jim's Paint Products.

ANSWERS

KEY TERMS TEST

1. Cost reconciliation
2. FIFO costing method
3. parallel processing
4. sequential processing
5. weighted average costing method
6. equivalent units of output
7. Operation costing
8. production report
9. Transferred-in costs
10. physical flow schedule

CHAPTER QUIZ

1. Process, Job-order
2. a. Direct materials
   b. Direct labour
   c. Manufacturing overhead
3. a. sequential
   b. parallel
4. fully completed
5. Units completed and transferred out + Units in ending work in process × Fraction complete
6. Total costs to account for/Equivalent units
7. a. Physical flow of units
   b. Equivalent units
   c. Calculation of unit cost
   d. Costs accounted for (calculation of costs transferred out and cost of ending work in process inventory)
   e. Cost reconciliation
8. b False. A job-order costing system accumulates costs by jobs while a process-costing system accumulates costs by processing department.
9. a True
10. a True
11. a True
12. b False. Process costing works well whenever relatively homogeneous products are produced on a continuous basis.
13. a True
14. a True
15. b False. As raw materials are purchased, the cost is recorded as inventory. As raw materials are used in production, the cost is transferred to work in process.
16. b False. The FIFO method does not include prior-period costs in the current-period unit cost.
17. a True
18. b (10,000 + 120,000 − 12,000) = 118,000 units completed; [118,000 units completed + (12,000 units in ending inventory × 60%)] = 125,200
19. d (60,000 + 880,000)/125,200 EUP = $7.51
20. c [118,000 units completed + (12,000 units in ending inventory × 40%)] = 122,800
21. d ($40,000 + $25,000 + $520,500 + $208,600)/122,800 = $6.47
22. a [118,000 × ($7.51 + $6.47)] = $1,649,640
23. c [(7,200 × $7.51) + (4,800 × $6.47)] = $85,128

PRACTICE TEST
PROBLEM 1

Jax, Inc.
Assembly Department
Production Report for November 2000
(Weighted Average Method)

UNIT INFORMATION

Units to account for:

Units in beginning work in process............................	6,000
Units started during the period	16,000
Total units to account for	22,000

	Equivalent Units		
	Physical Flow	Materials	Conversion Cost
Units completed	20,000	20,000	20,000
Units in ending work in process.....................................	2,000	1,200	1,200
Total equivalent units	22,000	21,200	21,200

COST INFORMATION

Calculation of Unit Costs

	Materials	Conversion Cost	Total
Costs to account for:			
Beginning work in process.....................................	$10,000	$ 23,000	$ 33,000
Costs incurred during the period	35,000	78,280	113,280
Total costs to account for....................................	$45,000	$101,280	$146,280
Cost per equivalent unit	$2.123	$4.777	$6.90

Costs Transferred Out and Cost of Ending Inventory

	Transferred Out	Ending Work in Process	Total
Costs accounted for:			
Goods transferred out ($6.90 × 20,000)	$138,000.00		$138,000.00
Goods in ending work in process:			
Materials ($2.123 × 1,200)		$2,547.60	2,547.60
Conversion ($4.777 × 1,200)		5,732.40	5,732.40
Total costs accounted for	$138,000.00	$8,280.00	$146,280.00

PROBLEM 2

Jim's Paint Products
Mixing Department
Production Report for May 2000
(Weighted Average Method)

UNIT INFORMATION

Units to account for:

Units in beginning work in process.............................	5,000	
Units started during May..	80,000	
Total units to account for...	85,000	

	Physical Flow	Materials	Conversion Cost
	Equivalent Units		
Units completed	76,000	76,000	76,000
Units in ending work in process:			
Materials (100% × 9,000)	9,000	9,000	
Conversion (35% × 9,000)......................................			3,150
Total equivalent units..	85,000	85,000	79,150

COST INFORMATION

Calculation of Unit Costs

	Materials	Conversion Cost	Total
Costs to account for:			
Beginning work in process......................................	$ 34,000	$ 38,000	$ 72,000
Costs incurred during the period............................	680,000	476,475	1,156,475
Total costs to account for	$714,000	$514,475	$1,228,475
Cost per equivalent unit..	$8.40	$6.50	$14.90

Costs Transferred Out and Cost of Ending Inventory

	Transferred Out	Ending Work in Process	Total
Costs accounted for:			
Goods transferred out ($14.90 × 76,000).................	$1,132,400		$1,132,400
Goods in ending work in process:			
Materials ($8.40 × 9,000)		$75,600	75,600
Conversion ($6.50 × 3,150)...................................		20,475	20,475
Total costs accounted for.................................	$1,132,400	$96,075	$1,228,475

PROBLEM 3

**Jim's Paint Products
Packaging Department
Production Report for May 2000
(Weighted Average Method)**

UNIT INFORMATION

Units to account for:

Units in beginning work in process.............................	2,000		
Units started during May (transferred in from Mixing)	76,000		
Total units to account for	78,000		

		Equivalent Units	
	Physical Flow	**Transferred In**	**Conversion Cost**
Units completed	70,000	70,000	70,000
Units in ending work in process:			
Materials (100% × 8,000)	8,000	8,000	
Conversion (70% × 8,000)	_____	_____	5,600
Total equivalent units..	78,000	78,000	75,600

COST INFORMATION

Calculation of Unit Costs

	Transferred In	**Conversion Cost**	**Total**
Costs to account for:			
Beginning work in process......................................	$ 25,900	$ 39,160	$ 65,060
Costs incurred during the period	1,132,400	800,000	1,932,400
Total costs to account for...................................	$1,158,300	$839,160	$1,997,460
Cost per equivalent unit	$14.85	$11.10	$25.95

Costs Transferred Out and Cost of Ending Inventory

	Transferred Out	**Ending Work in Process**	**Total**
Costs accounted for:			
Goods transferred out ($25.95 × 70,000)	$1,816,500		$1,816,500
Goods in ending work in process:			
Materials ($14.85 × 8,000)		$118,800	118,800
Conversion ($11.10 × 5,600)	_____	62,160	62,160
Total costs accounted for	$1,816,500	$180,960	$1,997,460

PROBLEM 4 (APPENDIX)

Jim's Paint Products
Mixing Department
Production Report for May 2000
(FIFO Method)

UNIT INFORMATION

Units to account for:			
Units in beginning work in process.............................	5,000		
Units started during May...	80,000		
Total units to account for..	85,000		

	Equivalent Units		
	Physical Flow	**Materials**	**Conversion Cost**
Units started and completed	71,000	71,000	71,000
Units completed from beginning work in process...........	5,000		2,000
Units in ending work in process:			
Materials (100% × 9,000)	9,000	9,000	
Conversion (35% × 9,000)...			3,150
Total equivalent units...	85,000	80,000	76,150

COST INFORMATION

Calculation of Unit Costs

	Materials	**Conversion Cost**	**Total**
Costs to account for:			
Beginning work in process......................................	$ 34,000	$ 38,000	$ 72,000
Costs incurred during the period............................	680,000	476,475	1,156,475
Total costs to account for	$714,000	$514,475	$1,228,475
Cost per equivalent unit (Cost added/Equivalent units).................................	$8.50	$6.2571	$14.7571

Costs Transferred Out and Cost of Ending Inventory

	Transferred Out	**Ending Work in Process**	**Total**
Costs accounted for:			
Units in beginning work in process:			
From prior period..	$ 72,000		$ 72,000
From current period ($6.2571 × 2,000)	12,514		12,514
Units started and completed ($14.7571 × 71,000)..	1,047,754		1,047,754
Goods in ending work in process:			
Materials ($8.50 × 9,000)		$76,500	76,500
Conversion ($6.2571 × 3,150).............................		19,710	19,710
Total costs accounted for...................................	$1,132,268	$96,210	$1,228,478*

*Difference due to rounding

PROBLEM 5

1. Journal entries for the Mixing and Packaging Departments:

Entry to record materials used in production:

Work in Process—Mixing	680,000	
Raw Materials		680,000

Entry to record direct labour:

Work in Process—Mixing	293,600	
Wages Payable..		293,600

Entry to record manufacturing overhead:

Work in Process—Mixing	182,875	
Manufacturing Overhead Control...........................		182,875

Entry to record transfer of costs from the Mixing Department to the Packaging Department:

Work in Process—Packaging	1,132,400	
Work in Process—Mixing		1,132,400

Entry to record direct labour and manufacturing overhead costs in the Packaging Department in May:

Work in Process—Packaging	800,000	
Wages Payable..		240,000
Manufacturing Overhead Control...........................		560,000

Entry to record the transfer of costs from the Packaging Department to finished goods:

Finished Goods...	1,816,500	
Work in Process—Packaging		1,816,500

2. T account for the Mixing Department:

Work in Process—Mixing Department

Beginning balance	$ 72,000		
Materials	680,000		
Direct labour	293,600	Transferred out to	
Overhead	182,875	Packaging	$1,132,400
Ending balance	$ 96,075*		

*Agrees with costs assigned to ending work in process in Problem 2 ($75,600 + $20,475 = $96,075).

T account for the Packaging Department:

Work in Process—Packaging Department

Beginning balance	$ 65,060		
Transferred in costs	1,132,400		
Direct labour	240,000	Transferred out to	
Overhead	560,000	Finished Goods	$1,816,500
Ending balance	$ 180,960*		

*Agrees with costs assigned to ending work in process in Problem 3 ($118,800 + $62,160 = $180,960).

CHAPTER 7
Support Department Cost Allocation

CHAPTER REVIEW

- ❏ Allocation is a means of assigning a portion of a pool of costs to various subunits, such as departments or products.

- ❏ Cost allocation can affect bid prices, profitability of products, and managers' behaviour.

AN OVERVIEW OF COST ALLOCATION

- ❏ A **common cost** is the cost of a resource used in the output of two or more services or products. Common costs must be assigned to products or services produced.

Types of Departments

- ❏ When using allocations, costs are allocated or assigned to cost objects.

- ❏ If departments are the cost objects, departments are classified as either producing departments or support departments.

	Producing Departments	**Support Departments**
Definition:	responsible for creating the products or services sold to customers	provide support services for producing departments
Examples:	assembly department, finishing department	maintenance, personnel, security

- ❏ Although support departments do not work directly on the products of an organization, the costs of providing these support services are part of the total product cost.

- ❏ Three steps in allocating costs are:
    1. trace all overhead costs to a support or producing department
    2. allocate support-department costs to the producing departments, and
    3. allocate overhead costs to units of individual products using a predetermined overhead rate. The predetermined overhead rate is calculated as follows:

$$\text{Predetermined overhead rate} = \frac{\text{Budgeted overhead}}{\text{Budgeted activity}}$$

- ❏ Note that a producing department's overhead consists of two parts:
    - overhead directly associated with the producing department
    - overhead allocated to the producing department from the support departments

Types of Allocation Bases

- ❏ **Causal factors** are variables or activities within a producing department that cause the incurrence of service costs.

❏ In general, causal factors should be used as the basis for allocating service costs.

❏ For example, if power costs were to be allocated, kilowatt hours would be the causal factor that could be used as the allocation base.

❏ Using causal factors results in more accurate product costs, and if causal factors are known, managers are better able to control the consumption of services.

Objectives of Allocation

❏ The major objectives associated with the allocation of support-department costs to producing departments and ultimately to specific products are:
  ■ to obtain a mutually agreeable price
  ■ to compute product-line profitability
  ■ to predict economic effects for planning and control purposes
  ■ to value inventory (GAAP requires both direct and indirect manufacturing costs to be assigned to inventory for external reporting purposes)
  ■ to motivate managers

ALLOCATING ONE DEPARTMENT'S COSTS TO ANOTHER DEPARTMENT

❏ A charging rate is used to allocate the costs of a support department to user departments.

A Single Charging Rate

❏ If a single charging rate is used, fixed costs and variable costs are combined and then divided by estimated activity.

$$\text{Single charging rate} = \frac{\text{(Fixed costs + Variable costs)}}{\text{Total estimated usage}}$$

❏ The amount charged to producing departments is calculated as follows:

Single charging rate × Producing department usage

Budgeted versus Actual Usage

❏ Budgeted, not actual, costs should be allocated so that support departments' efficiencies or inefficiencies are not passed on to the producing departments.

❏ Two reasons for allocating support-department costs are:
  1. to determine the cost of units produced, and
  2. for performance evaluation.

❏ For product costing, the allocation is made at the beginning of the year based on budgeted usage so that a predetermined overhead rate can be computed to cost products during the year.

❏ For performance evaluation purposes, the allocation is made at the end of the period based on actual usage.

	Product Costing	Performance Evaluation
Usage:	Budgeted usage	Actual usage
Service department allocation:	**Budgeted rate × Budgeted usage**	**Budgeted rate × Actual usage**

CHOOSING A SUPPORT DEPARTMENT COST ALLOCATION METHOD

❏ Three methods used to allocate support-department costs to producing departments are:

1. direct method
2. sequential method, and
3. reciprocal method.

Direct Method of Allocation

❏ The **direct method** allocates support-department costs directly to the producing departments based on relative use.

❏ This method ignores reciprocal services (services provided by one support department to another support department). For example, this method would ignore service provided by the data processing department to other support departments, such as personnel or maintenance.

❏ If a firm has two support departments (maintenance and data processing) and two producing departments (assembly and finishing), the allocation of support-department costs using the direct method could be diagrammed as follows:

Maintenance   Data Processing   Assembly   Finishing

Sequential Method of Allocation

❏ The **sequential (or step) method** allocates support-department costs to the producing departments *and* to some support departments. Thus, the sequential method partially recognizes reciprocal services.

❏ The sequential method is applied in the following manner:

1. Select a support department and allocate its costs to the producing departments and support departments to which it provides services. (The support department with the greatest total costs is allocated first.)
2. Select another support department and allocate its cost to the producing departments and the remaining support departments.
3. Proceed in this manner until all of the support-department costs have been allocated to the producing departments.

❏ Notice that once the costs of a support department are allocated, no further allocations are made to that support department.

❏ The allocation of support-department costs under the sequential method can be diagrammed as follows:

Maintenance   Data Processing   Assembly   Finishing

Reciprocal Method of Allocation

❑ The **reciprocal method** fully recognizes the reciprocal services provided by support departments to other support departments.

❑ The reciprocal method requires the use of simultaneous equations.

❑ The total cost of a support department is calculated:

Total cost of support department = Direct costs + Allocated costs of other support departments

❑ The allocation of support-department costs under the reciprocal method can be diagrammed as follows:

Maintenance	Data Processing	Assembly	Finishing

DEPARTMENTAL OVERHEAD RATES AND PRODUCT COSTING

❑ Support-department costs are allocated to the producing departments, and then the support-department costs are included in the producing departments' overhead application rates.

❑ The flow of costs could be diagramed as follows:

Support Department Costs	Producing Department Overhead Costs	Units of Product
	$400,000	
$200,000 ———	$200,000	
	$600,000 ———	

❑ The $600,000 of producing department overhead would be allocated to units of product using a cost driver such as direct labour hours or machine hours.

SUMMARY

❑ To summarize, the four steps involved in support-department allocation are as follows:

1. Prepare departmental budgets for producing and support departments.
2. Select an allocation base for use in allocating the support-department costs.
3. Allocate the budgeted support-department costs to the producing departments using either the direct, sequential, or reciprocal method.
4. Calculate a predetermined overhead application rate for each producing department to apply total overhead costs to units of product produced.

KEY TERMS TEST

Test your recall of the key terms as follows. Try to recall as many key terms as possible without assistance. If you need assistance, refer to the list of key terms at the end of this section.

1. A unit within an organization responsible for producing the products or services that are sold to customers is called a(n) _____ _____.

2. A unit within an organization that provides essential support services for producing departments is called a(n) _____ _____.

3. The _____ _____ simultaneously allocates service costs to all user departments. It gives full consideration to interactions among support departments.

4. The _____ _____ is a method of allocating service costs that ignores any interactions that may exist among support departments.

5. _____ _____ are activities or variables that cause the incurrence of service costs.

6. The _____ _____ is a method of allocating support-department costs that gives partial consideration to interactions among support departments.

7. The costs of a resource used in the output of two or more services or products are _____ _____.

KEY TERMS

causal factors
common costs
direct method
producing department

reciprocal method
sequential (or step) method
support department

↺ **Compare your answers with those at the end of the chapter. Review any key terms missed.**

CHAPTER QUIZ

Circle the single best answer.

1. The direct method of allocating support-department costs partially recognizes services that support departments provide to each other: (a) true; (b) false

2. The reciprocal method of allocating support-department costs fully recognizes services that support departments provide to each other: (a) true; (b) false

3. Producing departments are responsible for producing the products sold to customers: (a) true; (b) false

4. Support departments are responsible for providing services directly to customers: (a) true; (b) false

5. Accounting in an automobile factory is an example of a producing department: (a) true; (b) false

6. Maintenance is an example of a support department: (a) true; (b) false

7. The company cafeteria is an example of a producing department: (a) true; (b) false

8. Packaging is an example of a support department: (a) true; (b) false

9. One of the main objectives of allocation is to motivate managers: (a) true; (b) false

10. One of the main objectives of allocation is to value inventory: (a) true; (b) false

11. One of the main objectives of allocation is to compute product line profitability: (a) true; (b) false

12. Actual costs should always be used when allocating support-department costs: (a) true; (b) false

13. Support-department costs should be allocated directly to units of product: (a) true; (b) false

14. If the allocation is for performance evaluation, support-department costs should be allocated based on the actual rate and actual usage: (a) true; (b) false

15. If the allocation is for product costing, variable support-department costs should be allocated based on the budgeted rate and budgeted usage: (a) true; (b) false

Use the following information to answer Questions 16 through 22:

Mollet, Inc., often bids on jobs using a cost-plus basis; therefore, in order to be competitive, it is important to determine costs as accurately as possible. The company operates two support departments (Department A and Department B) and two producing departments (Department C and Department D).

Budgeted costs and normal activity levels are given below:

	Support Departments		Producing Departments	
	A	B	C	D
Overhead costs	$120,000	$160,000	$300,000	$240,000
Number of employees	8	12	40	60
Maintenance hours	3,000	400	8,000	2,000
Machine hours	—	—	12,000	15,000
Direct labour hours	—	—	1,800	15,000

The costs of Department A are allocated on the basis of number of employees, and the costs of Department B are allocated on the basis of maintenance hours.

Assume the direct method is used for Questions 16 through 20.

16. If the direct method is used, Department A costs allocated to Department C would be: (a) $48,000; (b) $96,000; (c) $72,000; (d) $120,000

17. If the direct method is used, Department B costs allocated to Department C would be: (a) $192,000; (b) $160,000; (c) $128,000; (d) $80,000

18. If Department C uses machine hours to allocate overhead to units of product, the overhead rate per machine hour for Department C would be: (a) $35.67; (b) $29.00; (c) $32.66; (d) $39.67

19. If Department D uses direct labour hours to allocate overhead to units of product, the overhead rate per direct labour hour for Department D would be: (a) $22.93; (b) $18.13; (c) $16.80; (d) $16.00

20. Estimates relating to a job that Mollet, Inc., plans to bid on are as follows:

Direct materials	$1,000
Direct labour	$600
Machine hours in Department C	20
Direct labour hours in Department D	30

The estimate for the cost of the job would be: (a) $2,393; (b) $2,288; (c) $1,481; (d) $3,081

21. If the sequential method is used and the costs of the support department with the greatest total cost are allocated first, Department B costs allocated to Department D would be: (a) $36,923; (b) $30,463; (c) $24,615; (d) $21,450

22. If the sequential method is used, Department A costs allocated to Department C would be: (a) $60,649; (b) $62,769; (c) $62,980; (d) $69,280

○ **Compare your answers with those at the end of the chapter. Review any questions missed.**

PRACTICE TEST

PROBLEM 1

Husmann Company has three support departments and two producing departments. Information for each department for 2000 is as follows:

	Support Departments			Producing Departments	
	Plant Administration	Plant Maintenance	Plant Cafeteria	Machining	Assembly
Budgeted overhead cost........	$120,000	$100,000	$50,000	$200,000	$400,000
Direct labour hours	6,000	10,000	4,000	20,000	30,000
Square feet occupied.............	2,000	3,000	5,000	35,000	65,000
Number of employees	5	6	3	15	25

Plant administration costs are allocated based on direct labour hours, plant maintenance costs are allocated based on square footage occupied, and plant cafeteria costs are allocated based on the number of employees.

The company uses a single charging rate. Predetermined overhead rates for the producing departments are based on direct labour hours.

Instructions:

Allocate the support-department costs using the direct method. Then calculate the predetermined overhead rates the producing departments would use to apply overhead to units of product.

	Support Departments			Producing Departments	
	Plant Administration	Plant Maintenance	Plant Cafeteria	Machining	Assembly
Budgeted overhead cost	$120,000	$100,000	$50,000	$200,000	$400,000

PROBLEM 2

Instructions:

Using the information from the previous problem, allocate the support-department costs using the sequential method, starting with the support department with the greatest total cost. Then, calculate the predetermined overhead rates the producing departments would use to apply overhead to units of product.

	Support Departments			Producing Departments	
	Plant Administration	Plant Maintenance	Plant Cafeteria	Machining	Assembly
Budgeted overhead cost	$120,000	$100,000	$50,000	$200,000	$400,000

PROBLEM 3

Taylor Bus Lines provides school bus service to two area school districts—Unit 1 and Unit 2.

Taylor has one support centre that is responsible for service, maintenance, and cleanup of its buses. The costs of the support centre are allocated to each operating unit on the basis of total miles driven.

During the first month of the year, the support centre was expected to incur fixed costs of $25,000 and variable costs of $0.30 per mile. During the month, the support centre incurred actual variable costs of $105,000 and actual fixed costs of $20,000.

The estimated and actual miles logged by each unit are given below:

	Unit 1	Unit 2
Estimated activity (miles)......................	170,000	80,000
Actual activity (miles)............................	175,000	90,000

Instructions:

1. Calculate a single charging rate per mile driven for support centre services.

2. Calculate the support centre costs that would be allocated at the end of the month to each district if a single charging rate is used.

PROBLEM 3 *(Continued)*

3. Based on the fixed and variable amounts budgeted, how much should it have cost the support centre for the actual number of miles driven?

4. Is the amount in Requirement 3 different from the cost allocated in Requirement 2? Why?

ANSWERS

KEY TERMS TEST

1. producing department
2. support department
3. reciprocal method
4. direct method

5. Causal factors
6. sequential method (or step method)
7. common costs

CHAPTER QUIZ

1. b False. The step method partially recognizes reciprocal services.
2. a True
3. a True
4. b False. Support departments provide support services to the producing departments.
5. b False. Accounting is an example of a support department.
6. a True
7. b False. The company cafeteria would be an example of a support department.
8. b False. Since packaging would work directly with the product, packaging would be considered a producing department.
9. a True
10. a True
11. a True
12. b False. Budgeted costs, not actual costs, should be allocated.
13. b False. First, support-department costs are allocated to the producing departments. Then producing department overhead (including the allocated support-department costs) is allocated to units of product.
14. b False. If the allocation is for performance evaluation, variable support-department costs should be allocated based on the budgeted rate and actual usage.
15. a True
16. a $120,000 × 40/100 = $48,000
17. c $160,000 × 8,000/10,000 = $128,000
18. d ($300,000 + $48,000 + $128,000)/12,000 = $39.67
19. a ($240,000 + $72,000 + $32,000)/15,000 = $22.93
20. d $1,000 + $600 + ($39.67 × 20) + ($22.93 × 30) = $3,081
21. c $160,000 × (2,000/13,000) = $24,615
22. b $160,000 × (3,000/13,000) = $36,923; ($120,000 + $36,923) × (40/100) = $62,769

PRACTICE TEST

PROBLEM 1

	Support Departments			Producing Departments	
	Plant Administration	Plant Maintenance	Plant Cafeteria	Machining	Assembly
Budgeted overhead cost	$ 120,000	$ 100,000	$ 50,000	$200,000	$400,000
Allocate plant administration (20,000/50,000; 30,000/50,000)	(120,000)			48,000	72,000
Allocate plant maintenance (35,000/100,000; 65,000/100,000) ...		(100,000)		35,000	65,000
Allocate plant cafeteria (15/40; 25/40)			(50,000)	18,750	31,250
Total producing department overhead to apply				$301,750	$568,250
Divided by direct labour hours				÷ 20,000	÷ 30,000
Predetermined overhead rate				$15.0875	$18.9417

PROBLEM 2

	Support Departments			Producing Departments	
	Plant Administration	Plant Maintenance	Plant Cafeteria	Machining	Assembly
Budgeted overhead cost	$ 120,000	$ 100,000	$ 50,000	$200,000	$400,000
Allocate plant administration (10/64; 4/64; 20/64; 30/64)	(120,000)	18,750	7,500	37,500	56,250
Total cost in plant maintenance		$ 118,750			
Allocate plant maintenance (5/105; 35/105; 65/105)		(118,750)	5,655	39,583	73,512
Total cost in plant cafeteria			$ 63,155		
Allocate plant cafeteria (15/40; 25/40)			(63,155)	23,683	39,472
Total producing department overhead to apply				$300,766	$569,234
Divided by direct labour hours.............				÷ 20,000	÷ 30,000
Predetermined overhead rate...............				$15.0383	$18.9745

PROBLEM 3

1. Single charging rate per mile driven would be calculated as follows:

Variable costs ($0.30 × (170,000 + 80,000)).........................	$ 75,000
Fixed costs	25,000
Total estimated costs	$100,000

Single charging rate = Total estimated costs/Number of estimated miles
= $100,000/(170,000 + 80,000)
= $0.40 per mile

2. Support centre costs that would be allocated to each district if a single charging rate is used would be calculated as follows:

District	Miles Driven	Charge per Mile	Total Charges
Unit 1............................	175,000	$0.40	$ 70,000
Unit 2............................	90,000	0.40	36,000
Total	265,000		$106,000

3. Based on budgeted fixed and variable costs, the support department should have incurred the following costs for the actual number of miles driven:

Variable costs ($0.30 × 265,000 miles driven)......................	$ 79,500
Fixed costs	25,000
Total costs..	$104,500

4. Yes, the support centre costs allocated to the districts total $106,000. However, the total cost budgeted for 265,000 miles driven is only $104,500. This difference of $1,500 is due to treating the $25,000 of fixed costs as a variable cost for allocation purposes. The $25,000 fixed cost is divided by 250,000 budgeted miles to arrive at a fixed cost per mile of $0.10 for allocation purposes. If the actual number of miles driven differs from the budgeted miles of 250,000 used to calculated the fixed cost per mile, then there will be a resulting difference between total costs budgeted versus total costs allocated. This is a disadvantage of using a single charging rate that combines variable and fixed costs.

CHAPTER 8
Variable Costing: Segmented Reporting and Performance Evaluation

CHAPTER REVIEW

VARIABLE COSTING AND ABSORPTION COSTING: AN ANALYSIS AND COMPARISON

❒ Two product costing methods are:

1. absorption costing
2. variable costing

❒ **Absorption costing** is required for *external* financial reporting and income tax purposes.

❒ **Variable costing** is used for *internal* reporting to management because it provides information that is useful for planning, control, and decision making.

❒ The main difference between the two methods relates to how fixed manufacturing overhead is recorded.

   ▪ When using absorption costing, fixed manufacturing overhead is considered a product cost, included in inventory and expensed when the inventory is sold.

   ▪ When using variable costing, fixed manufacturing overhead is *not* included in inventory but is expensed in the period it is incurred.

❒ The ending finished goods inventory values for absorption and variable costing will differ by the amount of fixed manufacturing costs included in ending inventory.

❒ Product and period costs under absorption and variable costing are summarized below:

	Absorption Costing	**Variable Costing**
Product costs:	direct materials (DM) direct labour (DL) variable overhead (VOH) fixed overhead (FOH)	direct materials (DM) direct labour (DL) variable overhead (VOH)
Period costs:	variable selling expenses fixed selling expenses variable administrative expenses fixed administrative expenses	fixed overhead (FOH) variable selling expenses fixed selling expenses variable administrative expenses fixed administrative expenses

❐ The following diagram illustrates the flow of manufacturing costs using absorption costing:

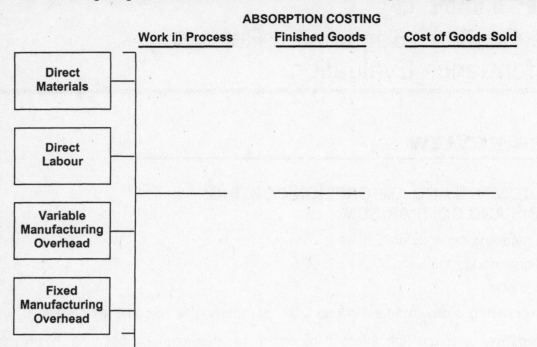

ABSORPTION COSTING

❐ The following diagram illustrates the flow of manufacturing costs using variable costing:

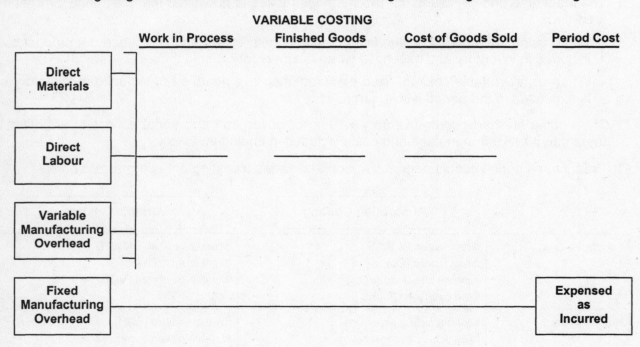

VARIABLE COSTING

Income Statements: Analysis and Reconciliation

❐ Under absorption costing, costs are classified by *function* as:
   1. manufacturing costs (both fixed and variable)
   2. selling and administrative costs (both fixed and variable)

❏ The format used when costs are classified by function for absorption costing is:

> **Sales**
> **– Cost of goods sold (Manufacturing costs)**
> **= Gross margin**
> **– Selling and administrative expenses**
> **= Net income**

❏ When variable costing is used, costs are classified by *behaviour* as:

1. variable costs
   - variable manufacturing
   - variable selling and administrative
2. fixed costs
   - fixed manufacturing
   - fixed selling and administrative

❏ The format used for a variable-costing income statement follows:

> **Sales**
> **– Variable expenses:**
>   Variable cost of goods sold
>   Variable selling and administrative
> **= Contribution margin**
> **– Fixed expenses:**
>   Fixed overhead
>   Fixed selling and administrative
> **= Net income**

Production, Sales, and Income Relationships

❏ When sales equal production, income is the same under variable and absorption costing.

❏ When production exceeds sales, absorption-costing income will generally exceed variable-costing income. This occurs because under variable costing, all fixed manufacturing costs are expensed, while under absorption costing, the part of *fixed manufacturing costs associated with unsold units is deferred in inventory*.

❏ When sales exceed production, variable-costing income will generally exceed absorption-costing income. This occurs because as the unit balance in ending absorption inventory decreases, *fixed manufacturing costs deferred from prior years are now expensed*.

❏ Production, sales, and income relationships are summarized below:

If	*Then*
Production > Sales	**Absorption net income > Variable net income**
Production < Sales	**Absorption net income < Variable net income**
Production = Sales	**Absorption net income = Variable net income**

❏ The difference between absorption-costing income and variable-costing income results from differences in the *timing* of the recognition of fixed manufacturing overhead costs as an expense. Variable costing always recognizes the period's fixed overhead as an expense.

❏ Absorption costing recognizes as an expense only the fixed overhead *attached* to the units sold.

❏ The difference in variable cost net income can be reconciled to absorption costing net income as follows: variable costing net income minus FOH included in beginning inventory under absorption costing plus FOH included in ending inventory under absorption costing equals absorption costing net income. The textbook implies you need only calculate the change in the number of units of inventory and multiply this amount by the FOH rate to reconcile the difference between the two costing methods' net incomes; however, this will only work if the FOH rate is constant from one period to the next.

The Treatment of Fixed Factory Overhead in Absorption Costing

❏ Under absorption costing, fixed factory overhead is:

1. assigned to units produced, and
2. expensed when the units to which it is attached are sold (FOH will show up in Cost of Goods Sold).

❏ Applied fixed overhead is the fixed manufacturing overhead assigned to production using a predetermined fixed overhead rate.

❏ The difference between applied fixed overhead and actual fixed overhead equals over- or under-applied fixed overhead.

Over- or underapplied fixed overhead = Applied fixed overhead – Actual fixed overhead

❏ If applied fixed overhead exceeds actual fixed overhead, fixed overhead is overapplied.

❏ If applied fixed overhead is less than actual fixed overhead, fixed overhead is underapplied.

❏ If over- or underapplied fixed overhead is immaterial in amount, it is closed to Cost of Goods Sold.

❏ Over- or underapplied variable overhead is treated in the same fashion.

VARIABLE COSTING AND PERFORMANCE EVALUATION OF MANAGERS

❏ A manager's performance is often evaluated based on the profit of the organizational units he or she controls. In general, if a manager's performance is evaluated based on income, then managers have the right to expect the following (assuming all other things are equal):

1. If sales revenue *increases*, income should *increase*.
2. If sales revenue *decreases*, income should *decrease*.
3. If sales revenue remains the *same*, income should remain the *same*.

❏ Variable costing always results in the expected association between sales and income.

❏ Absorption income is affected by the level of inventory and does not always result in the expected association between sales and income.

VARIABLE COSTING AND SEGMENTED REPORTING

❑ A **segment** is a subunit of an organization and can be a division, product line, sales territory, or plant.

❑ **Segmented reporting** is the process of preparing financial performance reports for segments within a firm.

❑ Segment reports can be prepared for any level of the organization: division, product line, plants within a division, and so on.

❑ Segmented reports prepared using variable costing produce better evaluations and decisions than those prepared on an absorption-costing basis.

Segmented Reporting: Variable-Costing Basis

❑ A comparison of the formats for a variable-costing income statement and a segmented income statement using variable costing follows:

Variable-Costing Income Statement	Variable-Costing Segmented Income Statement
Sales	**Sales**
− **Variable expenses:**	− **Variable expenses:**
Variable cost of goods sold	Variable cost of goods sold
Variable selling and administrative	Variable selling and administrative
= **Contribution margin**	= **Contribution margin**
	− **Direct fixed expenses:**
	Direct fixed overhead
	Direct selling and administrative
− **Fixed expenses:**	= **Segment margin**
Fixed overhead	− **Common fixed expenses:**
Fixed selling and administrative	Common fixed overhead
	Common selling and administrative
= **Net income**	= **Net income**

❑ **Direct fixed expenses** are fixed costs that are *directly traceable to a particular segment* and arise because of the existence of that segment.

❑ Direct fixed expenses are *avoidable* because they would be eliminated or avoided if the segment is eliminated.

❑ **Common fixed expenses** are fixed costs that *benefit more than one segment* and are not directly traceable to a particular segment. An example of a common fixed cost would be the corporate president's salary.

❑ Common fixed costs continue to be incurred even if one of the segments is eliminated.

❑ The segment contribution margin (sales less variable costs) provides information useful in making short-run operating decisions such as accepting or rejecting orders at special prices.

❑ **Segment margin** is the segment contribution margin remaining after covering the direct fixed costs of the segment. Segment margin is the amount the segment contributes toward covering the firm's common fixed costs and generating profit. Thus, variable costing enables management to evaluate each segment's contribution to overall firm performance.

❑ The segment margin (sales less variable costs less direct fixed costs) provides information useful in assessing the long-run profitability of a segment.

❐ If a segment does not affect the sales of other segments, the segment margin is the amount by which the firm's profits would change if the segment were eliminated.

Customer Profitability

❐ Customer profitability can be assessed by treating each customer group as a segment and determining activities associated with each group.

❐ Steps in determining customer profitability include:
- Identify the customer.
- Determine which customer groups are most profitable (considering product, marketing, and administrative activities used to serve each class of customer).
- Eliminate the unprofitable customers.
- Retain and add to the base of profitable customers.

VARIABLE COSTING FOR PLANNING AND CONTROL

❐ Management may wish to look at several different levels of sales in order to assess the possibilities facing the firm. Because fixed costs do not vary with volume changes, a distinction between fixed and variable costs is critical for planning costs at different sales and production volumes.

❐ Management controls operations by comparing actual performance with plans. When controlling operations, a knowledge of cost behaviour is important.

KEY TERMS TEST

Test your recall of the key terms as follows. Try to recall as many key terms as possible without assistance. If you need assistance, refer to the list of key terms at the end of this section.

1. _____ _____ is calculated as revenue less variable costs and direct fixed costs.

2. _____ _____ is the product-costing method that assigns only variable manufacturing costs to a product: direct materials, direct labour, and variable overhead. Fixed overhead is treated as a period cost.

3. _____ _____ is the product-costing method that assigns all manufacturing costs to a product: direct materials, direct labour, variable overhead, and fixed overhead.

4. _____ _____ _____ are directly traceable to a given segment and would be avoided if the segment is eliminated.

5. _____ _____ _____ are not directly traceable to a particular segment and are unaffected by the elimination of any one segment.

6. _____ _____ is the process of preparing financial performance reports for segments within a firm.

KEY TERMS

absorption costing
common fixed expenses
direct fixed expenses

segment margin
segmented reporting
variable costing

↻ **Compare your answers with those at the end of the chapter. Review any key terms missed.**

CHAPTER QUIZ

Write your answers in the spaces provided.

1. Two product costing methods are absorption costing and variable costing. _____ costing is used for internal reporting to management because it provides information that is useful for planning, control, and decision making. _____ costing is required for external financial reporting and income tax purposes.

2. The main difference between absorption costing and variable costing relates to how _____ _____ is treated.

3. When absorption costing is used, the costs considered product costs are:

   1. _____

   2. _____

   3. _____

   4. _____

4. When absorption costing is used, the costs considered period costs are:

   1. _____

   2. _____

   3. _____

   4. _____

5. When variable costing is used, the costs considered product costs are:

   1. _____

   2. _____

   3. _____

6. When variable costing is used, the costs considered period costs are:

   1. _____

   2. _____

   3. _____

   4. _____

   5. _____

7. The income statement used for absorption costing classifies costs by _____.

8. A variable-costing income statement classifies costs by _____ as either _____ costs or _____ costs.

Circle the single best answer.

9. Variable costing may be used for internal or external reporting: (a) true; (b) false

10. When using absorption costing, all manufacturing costs (direct materials, direct labour, variable overhead, and fixed overhead) are considered product costs: (a) true; (b) false

11. The income statement used for variable costing usually classifies costs by function (manufacturing costs vs. selling and administrative costs): (a) true; (b) false

12. Contribution margin equals sales minus variable manufacturing costs: (a) true; (b) false

13. When sales equal production, net income is the same under the two methods: (a) true; (b) false

14. When sales exceed production, absorption-costing income will generally exceed variable-costing income: (a) true; (b) false

15. The difference between absorption-costing income and variable-costing income can be calculated as the change in the number of units in inventory multiplied by the fixed overhead rate per unit (assuming the FOH rate remains unchanged): (a) true; (b) false

16. The segment margin provides information useful in assessing the long-run profitability of a segment: (a) true; (b) false

Use the following information to answer Questions 17 through 24:

Selected data for the Christie Company's past year of operations are presented below:

	Product A	Product B
Production (units)	160,000	300,000
Sales (units)	100,000	250,000
Selling price	$6.00	$5.00
Direct labour hours	60,000	90,000
Manufacturing costs:		
Direct materials	$ 80,000	$270,000
Direct labour	240,000	540,000
Variable overhead	24,000	30,000
Fixed overhead:		
Direct	80,000	50,000
Common[a]	25,000	25,000
Nonmanufacturing costs:		
Variable selling	$ 40,000	$ 75,000
Direct fixed selling	50,000	65,000
Common fixed selling[b]	30,000	30,000

[a]Common overhead totals $50,000 and is divided equally between the two products.
[b]Common fixed selling totals $60,000 and is divided equally between the two products.

Budgeted fixed overhead for the year of $180,000 equalled actual fixed overhead. Fixed overhead is assigned to products using a plantwide rate based on expected direct labour hours, which were 150,000. The company had 5,000 of Product B in inventory at the beginning of the year. These units had the same unit cost as the units produced during the year. (Round amounts to two decimal places.)

17. The unit product cost for Product A using variable costing is: (a) $2.00; (b) $2.15; (c) $2.45; (d) $2.60

18. The unit product cost for Product A using absorption costing is: (a) $2.15; (b) $2.45; (c) $2.60; (d) $2.80

19. The unit product cost for Product B using variable costing is: (a) $2.15; (b) $2.45; (c) $2.80; (d) $3.04

20. The unit product cost for Product B using absorption costing is: (a) $3.16; (b) $2.80; (c) $2.60; (d) $2.45

21. Variable cost of goods sold for the year is: (a) $700,000; (b) $915,000; (c) $1,025,000; (d) $1,072,000

22. Variable-costing net income for the year is: (a) $938,000; (b) $763,000; (c) $648,000; (d) $465,000

23. Using absorption costing, cost of goods sold for the year is: (a) $1,050,000; (b) $912,000; (c) $797,000; (d) $760,000

24. Absorption-costing net income for the year is: (a) $840,000; (b) $648,000; (c) $510,000; (d) $488,000

25. Complete the following:

	Product Costing Methods	
	Absorption Costing	**Variable Costing**
Product costs:		
Period costs:		

↻ **Compare your answers with those at the end of the chapter. Review any questions missed.**

PRACTICE TEST

PROBLEM 1

Barth Industries began operations on January 1, 2004. The company sells a single product for $10 per unit. During 2004, 60,000 units were produced and 50,000 units were sold. There was no work in process inventory at December 31, 2004.

Barth uses an actual cost system for product costing and actual costs for 2004 were as follows:

	Fixed Costs	Variable Costs
Direct materials	–0–	$2.00 per unit produced
Direct labour	–0–	$1.00 per unit produced
Manufacturing overhead	$60,000	$0.50 per unit produced
Selling and administrative expense	$40,000	$0.80 per unit sold

Instructions:

1. What is the product cost per unit under each of the following?

   a. variable costing

   b. absorption costing

PROBLEM 1 *(Continued)*

2. What is the finished goods inventory cost at December 31, 2004, under each of the following?

   a. variable costing

   b. absorption costing

3. Prepare income statements for 2004 under each of the following:

   a. variable costing

   b. absorption costing

PROBLEM 1 *(Continued)*

4. Reconcile the difference between variable-costing income and absorption-costing income.

PROBLEM 2

Griffiths Manufacturing uses an actual cost system for product costing. The company's income statement for 2004 is presented below:

Griffiths Manufacturing
Income Statement
For the Year Ending December 31, 2004

Sales (10,000 units @ $20)		$200,000
Cost of goods sold:		
Finished goods inventory, January 1	$ –0–	
Cost of goods manufactured (12,000 units @ $15)	180,000	
Goods available for sale	$180,000	
Finished goods inventory, December 31 (2,000 units @ $15)	30,000	
Cost of goods sold		150,000
Gross margin		$ 50,000
Operating expenses:		
Selling	$ 20,000	
Administrative	20,000	
Total selling and administrative		40,000
Net income		$ 10,000

The following additional information is available:

Variable costs per unit:

Direct materials	$4
Direct labour	5
Manufacturing overhead	2
Selling expense	1

Fixed costs for the period:

Manufacturing overhead	$48,000
Selling	10,000
Administrative	20,000

PROBLEM 2 *(Continued)*

Instructions:

1. When absorption costing was used, how much fixed manufacturing overhead was deferred in finished goods inventory?

2. Recast the income statement for 2004 using variable costing.

PROBLEM 2 *(Continued)*

3. Reconcile variable-costing income and absorption-costing income.

PROBLEM 3

The Snow Company began the year 2004 with no inventories of work in process or finished goods. The company produces a single product, and cost data for the product are given below:

Variable costs:

Direct materials	$10	per unit
Direct labour	15	per unit
Manufacturing overhead	6	per unit
Selling expenses	4	per unit

Fixed costs:

Manufacturing overhead	$50,000	per month
Selling and administrative	20,000	per month

During the first three months of 2004, production and sales in units were as follows:

	Production	Sales
January	10,000	10,000
February	10,000	8,000
March	10,000	12,000
Total	30,000	30,000

The company uses an actual cost system. The selling price of the product is $50 per unit. There were no work in process inventories at the end of each month.

Instructions:

1. Determine the unit cost of production each month under each of the following:

   a. variable costing

	January	February	March

PROBLEM 3 *(Continued)*

b. absorption costing

	January	February	March

2. Prepare income statements for the three months for each of the following:

a. variable costing

	January	February	March	Total

PROBLEM 3 *(Continued)*

b. absorption costing

	January	February	March	Total

3. If selling prices and costs do not change significantly, what can be said about the relationship of income under absorption costing and variable costing for each of the following?

   a. Sales equal production.

   b. Sales are less than production.

   c. Sales are greater than production.

PROBLEM 4

Belmont, Inc., has just completed its first year of operations. The unit costs on a normal costing basis are as follows:

Manufacturing costs:
Direct materials (3 lbs. @ $2)....................	$ 6.00 per unit
Direct labour (2 hrs. @ $8).......................	16.00 per unit
Variable overhead (2 hrs. @ $1.75).........	3.50 per unit
Fixed overhead	?
Total...	$?

Selling and administrative costs:
Variable..	$4.00 per unit
Fixed..	$100,000

During the year, the company had the following activity:

Units produced...	20,000
Units sold..	16,000
Unit selling price	$50
Direct labour hours worked	40,000

Actual fixed overhead was $170,000 for the year, and actual variable overhead was $72,000. Budgeted fixed overhead was $180,000, and the company used an expected activity level of 40,000 direct labour hours to compute the predetermined overhead rates. Any overhead variances are closed to Cost of Goods Sold.

Instructions:

1. Compute the unit cost using each of the following:

   a. absorption costing

   b. variable costing

PROBLEM 4 *(Continued)*

2. Prepare an absorption-costing income statement.

PROBLEM 4 *(Continued)*

3. Prepare a variable-costing income statement.

4. Reconcile the difference between the two income statements.

PROBLEM 5

Lawson Industries produces two products, Product X and Product Y. Information relating to the products for 2004 is as follows:

	Product X	Product Y
Units produced and sold	20,000	50,000
Selling price per unit	$15	$10
Variable expenses per unit	$8	$4

Lawson's fixed costs totaled $350,000, of which $60,000 can be avoided if Product X is dropped and $120,000 can be avoided if Product Y is dropped.

PROBLEM 5 *(Continued)*

Instructions:

1. Prepare a segmented income statement using variable costing and segregating direct and common fixed costs.

2. What would be the effect on Lawson's profit if Product X is dropped?

3. What would be the effect on Lawson's profit if Product Y is dropped?

4. Would you recommend that Lawson drop Product X or Product Y? Why or why not?

ANSWERS

KEY TERMS TEST

1. Segment margin
2. Variable costing
3. Absorption costing
4. Direct fixed expenses
5. Common fixed expenses
6. Segmented reporting

CHAPTER QUIZ

1. Variable, Absorption
2. fixed overhead
3. 1. direct materials
   2. direct labour
   3. variable manufacturing overhead
   4. fixed manufacturing overhead
4. 1. variable selling expenses
   2. fixed selling expenses
   3. variable administrative expenses
   4. fixed administrative expenses
5. 1. direct materials
   2. direct labour
   3. variable manufacturing overhead
6. 1. fixed manufacturing overhead
   2. variable selling expenses
   3. fixed selling expenses
   4. variable administrative expenses
   5. fixed administrative expenses
7. function (manufacturing, selling and administrative)
8. behaviour, variable, fixed
9. b False. Absorption costing is required for external financial reporting and income tax purposes.
10. a True
11. b False. When variable costing is used, a contribution margin format is usually used. The contribution margin format classifies costs by behaviour (variable costs vs. fixed costs).
12. b False. Contribution margin equals sales minus all variable costs (variable manufacturing and variable selling and administrative costs).
13. a True
14. b False
15. a True
16. a True
17. b

Direct materials ($80,000/160,000)	$0.50
Direct labour ($240,000/160,000)	1.50
Variable overhead ($24,000/160,000)	0.15
Variable cost per unit	$2.15

18. c

Direct materials ($80,000/160,000)	$0.50
Direct labour ($240,000/160,000)	1.50
Variable overhead ($24,000/160,000)	0.15
Variable cost per unit	$2.15
Fixed overhead [(60,000 DLH × $1.20[a])/160,000]	0.45
Absorption cost per unit	$2.60

[a]Fixed overhead rate = $180,000/150,000 = $1.20

19. c

Direct materials ($270,000/300,000)	$0.90
Direct labour ($540,000/300,000)	1.80
Variable overhead ($30,000/300,000)	0.10
Variable cost per unit	$2.80

20. a

Direct materials ($270,000/300,000)	$0.90
Direct labour ($540,000/300,000)	1.80
Variable overhead ($30,000/300,000)	0.10
Variable cost per unit	$2.80
Fixed overhead [(90,000 DLH × $1.20)/300,000]	0.36
Absorption cost per unit	$3.16

21. b (100,000 × $2.15) + (250,000 × $2.80) = $915,000

22. d

Sales (100,000 × $6) + (250,000 × $5)	$1,850,000
Variable cost of goods sold	(915,000)
Variable selling ($40,000 + $75,000)	(115,000)
Fixed overhead	(180,000)
Fixed selling	(175,000)
Net income	$ 465,000

23. a (100,000 × $2.60) + (250,000 × $3.16) = $1,050,000

24. c

Sales	$ 1,850,000
Cost of goods sold	(1,050,000)
Selling expenses	(290,000)
Net income	$ 510,000

25. See page 275.

PRACTICE TEST
PROBLEM 1

1. a. Cost per unit using variable costing:

Direct materials	$2.00
Direct labour	1.00
Variable manufacturing overhead	0.50
Cost per unit	$3.50

   b. Cost per unit using absorption costing:

Direct materials	$2.00
Direct labour	1.00
Variable manufacturing overhead	0.50
Fixed manufacturing overhead ($60,000/60,000 units)	1.00
Cost per unit	$4.50

2. a. Finished goods inventory cost at December 31, 2004, under variable costing: 10,000 units × $3.50 = $35,000

   b. Finished goods inventory cost at December 31, 2004, under absorption costing: 10,000 units × $4.50 = $45,000

3. a.

Barth Industries
Income Statements
For the Year Ending December 31, 2004
Variable Costing

Sales (50,000 × $10)		$500,000
Less variable expenses:		
Variable cost of goods sold (50,000 × $3.50)	$175,000	
Variable selling (50,000 × $0.80)	40,000	
Total variable expenses		215,000
Contribution margin		$285,000
Less fixed expenses:		
Fixed overhead	$ 60,000	
Fixed selling and administrative	40,000	
Total fixed expenses		$100,000
Net income		$185,000

b.

Absorption Costing

Sales (50,000 × $10)		$500,000
Cost of goods sold[a]		225,000
Gross profit		$275,000
Selling and administrative expenses:		
Fixed	$ 40,000	
Variable	40,000	
Total selling and administrative expenses		80,000
Net income		$195,000
[a]Beginning inventory	$ –0–	
Cost of goods manufactured (60,000 × $4.50)	270,000	
Goods available for sale	$270,000	
Ending inventory (10,000 × $4.50)	45,000	
Cost of goods sold	$225,000	

4. The difference in incomes results from the difference in the treatment of fixed manufacturing overhead costs.

Difference in income	=	Absorption-costing income	– Variable-costing income
	=	$195,000	– $185,000
	=	$10,000	

Difference in income	=	Change in inventory in units	× Fixed overhead rate per unit
	=	10,000	× $1
	=	$10,000	

When absorption costing is used, $10,000 of fixed overhead costs are deferred in finished goods inventory, resulting in a $10,000 higher income.

PROBLEM 2

1. Fixed overhead cost per unit = $48,000/12,000 units = $4 per unit

   Fixed overhead deferred in finished goods inventory = 2,000 units × $4 per unit = $8,000

2.

Variable Costing		
Sales (10,000 × $20)...		$200,000
Less variable expenses:		
Variable cost of goods sold[a]	$110,000	
Variable selling (10,000 × $1)..	10,000	
Total variable expenses..		120,000
Contribution margin		$ 80,000
Less fixed expenses:		
Fixed overhead..	$ 48,000	
Fixed selling..	10,000	
Fixed administrative..	20,000	
Total fixed expenses..		$ 78,000
Net income		$ 2,000
[a]Beginning inventory...		$ –0–
Cost of production (12,000 × $11).....................................		132,000
Goods available for sale..		$132,000
Ending inventory (2,000 × $11)		22,000
Variable cost of goods sold		$110,000

3. Difference in income = Absorption-costing income – Variable-costing income
   = $10,000 – $2,000
   = $8,000

   Difference in income = Change in inventory in units × Fixed overhead rate per unit
   = 2,000 × $4
   = $8,000

PROBLEM 3

1. **a.** Unit cost of production under variable costing:

	January	February	March
Direct materials	$10	$10	$10
Direct labour...	15	15	15
Variable manufacturing overhead	6	6	6
Total variable manufacturing cost per unit	$31	$31	$31

   b. Unit cost of production under absorption costing:

	January	February	March
Direct materials	$10	$10	$10
Direct labour...	15	15	15
Variable manufacturing overhead	6	6	6
Fixed manufacturing overhead ($50,000/10,000)	5	5	5
Total variable manufacturing cost per unit	$36	$36	$36

   Basic unit information:

	January	February	March	Total
Beginning inventory in units	–0–	–0–	2,000	–0–
Units produced..	10,000	10,000	10,000	30,000
Units sold	10,000	8,000	12,000	30,000
Ending inventory in units..	–0–	2,000	–0–	–0–

2. a.

Variable-Costing Income Statements				
	January	February	March	Total
Sales	$500,000	$400,000	$600,000	$1,500,000
Less variable expenses:				
Beginning inventory	–0–	–0–	62,000	–0–
Cost of production (10,000 × $31)	310,000	310,000	310,000	930,000
Goods available for sale	$310,000	$310,000	$372,000	$ 930,000
Ending inventory	–0–	62,000	–0–	–0–
Cost of goods sold	$310,000	$248,000	$372,000	$ 930,000
Selling expenses ($4 per unit)	40,000	32,000	48,000	120,000
Total variable expenses	$350,000	$280,000	$420,000	$1,050,000
Contribution margin	$150,000	$120,000	$180,000	$ 450,000
Less fixed expenses:				
Fixed manufacturing	$ 50,000	$ 50,000	$ 50,000	$ 150,000
Fixed selling and administrative...............	20,000	20,000	20,000	60,000
Total fixed expenses	$ 70,000	$ 70,000	$ 70,000	$ 210,000
Net income..	$ 80,000	$ 50,000	$110,000	$ 240,000

b.

Absorption-Costing Income Statements				
	January	February	March	Total
Sales	$500,000	$400,000	$600,000	$1,500,000
Cost of goods sold:				
Beginning inventory	–0–	–0–	72,000	–0–
Cost of production (10,000 × $36)	360,000	360,000	360,000	1,080,000
Goods available for sale	$360,000	$360,000	$432,000	$1,080,000
Ending inventory	–0–	72,000	–0–	–0–
Cost of goods sold	$360,000	$288,000	$432,000	$1,080,000
Gross profit..	$140,000	$112,000	$168,000	$ 420,000
Selling and administrative............................	60,000	52,000	68,000	180,000
Net income..	$ 80,000	$ 60,000	$100,000	$ 240,000

3. a. If sales equal production, income under the two methods should be the same.

b. If sales are less than production, absorption-costing income will be greater than variable-costing income because some fixed manufacturing overhead will be deferred in ending inventory.

c. If sales are greater than production, absorption-costing income will be less than variable-costing income because some fixed manufacturing overhead deferred from a prior period will be expensed in the current period when the units are sold.

PROBLEM 4

Note that Problems 1, 2, and 3 of this chapter used an actual cost system while this problem uses a normal cost system. Recall that a normal cost system uses actual costs for direct materials and direct labour and predetermined overhead rates to apply overhead. Because applied overhead and actual overhead usually differ, overapplied or underapplied overhead often exists when a normal cost system is used.

1. a. Unit cost using absorption costing:

Direct materials (3 lbs. @ $2)...	$ 6.00
Direct labour (2 hrs. @ $8)..	16.00
Variable overhead (2 hrs. @ $1.75)....................................	3.50
Fixed overhead (2 hrs. @ $4.50[a]).....................................	9.00
Total	$34.50

[a]Predetermined fixed overhead rate = $\dfrac{\text{Budgeted fixed overhead}}{\text{Budgeted activity}}$

= $180,000/40,000 direct labour hours = $4.50/direct labour hour

b. Unit cost using variable costing:

Direct materials (3 lbs. @ $2)...	$ 6.00
Direct labour (2 hrs. @ $8)..	16.00
Variable overhead (2 hrs. @ $1.75)....................................	3.50
Total	$25.50

2. Both variable and fixed overhead were applied on the basis of direct labour hours. Since 40,000 hours were worked, total applied fixed overhead amounts to $180,000. Actual fixed overhead was $170,000.

Fixed Overhead

Applied fixed overhead (40,000 hours worked × $4.50/DLH)....................	$180,000
Actual fixed overhead...	170,000
Overapplied fixed overhead	$ 10,000

Variable Overhead

Applied variable overhead (40,000 hours worked × $1.75/DLH)..............	$70,000
Actual variable overhead...	72,000
Underapplied variable overhead	$ (2,000)

Belmont, Inc.
Absorption-Costing Income Statement

Sales (16,000 @ $50)...		$800,000
Cost of goods sold (16,000 @ $34.50)	$552,000	
Less: Overapplied overhead ($10,000 – $2,000).................................	8,000	544,000
Gross margin..		$256,000
Less: Selling and administrative expenses ($100,000 + (16,000 × $4))		164,000
Net income		$ 92,000

3.
Belmont, Inc.
Variable-Costing Income Statement

Sales (16,000 @ $50)...		$800,000
Variable cost of goods sold (16,000 @ $25.50)..................................	$408,000	
Add: Underapplied variable overhead...	2,000	(410,000)
Variable selling expense (16,000 @ $4)		(64,000)
Contribution margin..		$326,000
Less fixed expenses:		
Fixed factory overhead...	$170,000	
Fixed selling and administrative	100,000	270,000
Net income		$ 56,000

Note that *actual* fixed factory overhead, not applied fixed factory overhead, is expensed on the income statement.

4. Absorption income – Variable income = Fixed overhead rate per unit × (Production – Sales)

$$\$92,000 - \$56,000 = \$9 \times (20,000 - 16,000)$$
$$\$36,000 = \$9 \times 4,000$$
$$\$36,000 = \$36,000$$

PROBLEM 5

1.
Lawson Industries
Segmented Income Statement
For the Year Ended December 31, 2004

	Product X	Product Y	Total
Sales	$300,000	$500,000	$800,000
Less: Variable expenses	160,000	200,000	360,000
Contribution margin	$140,000	$300,000	$440,000
Less: Direct fixed expenses	60,000	120,000	180,000
Product margin	$ 80,000	$180,000	$260,000
Less: Common fixed expenses			170,000
Net income			$ 90,000

2. If Product X is dropped, Lawson's profit would decrease by $80,000, the amount of Product X's product margin.

3. If Product Y is dropped, Lawson's profit would decrease by $180,000, the amount of Product Y's product margin.

4. Based on the information presented, Lawson should not drop Product X nor Product Y because dropping either product would reduce total profit.

CHAPTER 9
Cost–Volume–Profit Analysis:
A Managerial Planning Tool

CHAPTER REVIEW

❏ Cost–volume–profit analysis enables a firm to determine the sales (in units or dollars) necessary to attain a desired level of profit. CVP analysis is useful in assessing the effect of operating changes (such as changes in selling price or operating costs) upon profit.

BREAKEVEN POINT IN UNITS

❏ The **breakeven point** is the point where total revenues equal total expenses, the point where profit equals zero. This can be expressed as:

Total revenue – Total variable cost – Total fixed cost = $0

or

Total revenue = Total variable cost + Total fixed cost

Shortcut to Calculating Breakeven Units

❏ To determine how many units must be sold in order to break even, solve for *X* (the number of units) in the following equation:

Total revenue = Variable cost + Fixed cost

(Selling price per unit)(*X*) = (Variable cost per unit)(*X*) + Fixed cost

$$X = \frac{\text{Fixed cost}}{\text{Selling price per unit} - \text{Variable cost per unit}}$$

$$X = \frac{\text{Fixed cost}}{\text{Contribution margin per unit}}$$

❏ **Contribution margin** per unit is calculated as:

Contribution margin per unit = Selling price per unit – Variable cost per unit

❏ **Operating income** is income or profit *before* income taxes.

Unit Sales Needed to Achieve Targeted Profit

❏ In order to earn a desired profit, total revenues must equal variable costs, fixed costs, *and* desired profit.

Total revenue = Total variable cost + Total fixed cost + Desired profit

❑ To determine how many units must be sold in order to earn a desired profit, solve for X (the number of units) in the following equation:

Total revenue = Total variable cost + Total fixed cost + Desired profit

(Selling price per unit)(X) = (Variable cost per unit)(X) + Total fixed cost + Desired profit

$$X = \frac{\text{Fixed cost + Desired profit}}{\text{Selling price per unit − Variable cost per unit}}$$

$$X = \frac{\text{Fixed cost + Desired profit}}{\text{Contribution margin per unit}}$$

❑ After fixed costs are covered, the contribution margin per unit above breakeven volume is profit per unit.

After-Tax Profit Targets

❑ If a firm knows desired after-tax profit, desired before-tax profit can be calculated as follows:

Before-tax desired profit × (1 − Tax rate) = After-tax desired profit

$$\text{Before-tax desired profit} = \frac{\text{After-tax desired profit}}{1 - \text{Tax rate}}$$

❑ By substituting [(After-tax profit)/(1 − Tax rate)] for before-tax profit into the equation for CVP analysis, the equation becomes:

$$X = \frac{\text{Fixed cost + [(After-tax profit) / (1 − Tax rate)]}}{\text{Contribution margin per unit}}$$

BREAKEVEN POINT IN SALES DOLLARS

❑ Instead of using units sold, managers might prefer to use sales revenue as the measure of sales activity.

❑ Breakeven in units can be converted to breakeven in sales revenue as follows:

Breakeven sales = (Selling price per unit × Unit sales at break-even)

❑ Also, breakeven in sales dollars can be calculated using the following equation:

$$\text{Breakeven sales} = \frac{\text{Fixed cost}}{\text{Contribution margin ratio}}$$

❑ **The contribution margin ratio** is the proportion of each sales dollar available to cover fixed costs and provide for profit.

❑ The contribution margin ratio can be calculated in three different ways:

1. **Contribution margin ratio = Total contribution margin/Total revenue**
2. **Contribution margin ratio = Contribution margin per unit/Selling price per unit**
3. **Contribution margin ratio = 1 − Variable cost ratio**

❐ The **variable cost ratio** is the proportion of each sales dollar that must be used to cover variable costs.

Variable cost ratio = Variable cost/Sales revenue

Profit Targets and Sales Revenue

❐ Sales dollars necessary to earn a desired profit can be calculated as:

$$\text{Sales revenue} = \frac{\textbf{Fixed cost + Desired profit}}{\textbf{Contribution margin ratio}}$$

MULTIPLE-PRODUCT ANALYSIS

Breakeven Point in Units

Sales Mix and CVP Analysis

❐ When CVP analysis is used by firms that manufacture more than one product, the sales mix (the proportion in which the various products are expected to be sold) must be considered.

❐ When CVP analysis is used for a multiple-product firm, the product is defined as a package of products. For example, if the sales mix is 3:1 for Products A and B, the package would consist of 3 units of Product A and 1 unit of Product B.

❐ The contribution margin per package is calculated as:

(Contribution margin per unit of A × Sales mix for A)
+ (Contribution margin per unit of B × Sales mix for B)
= Package contribution margin

❐ Breakeven in packages for a multiple-product firm is then calculated as:

$$\text{Breakeven packages} = \frac{\textbf{Fixed cost}}{\textbf{Package contribution margin}}$$

Sales Dollars Approach

❐ Breakeven in sales dollars for a multiple-product firm is calculated as:

$$\text{Breakeven sales} = \frac{\textbf{Fixed cost}}{\textbf{Contribution margin ratio}}$$

❐ The contribution margin ratio is calculated as:

Contribution margin ratio = Total contribution margin/Total sales

GRAPHICAL REPRESENTATION OF CVP RELATIONSHIPS

The Profit–Volume Graph

❐ The **profit–volume graph** portrays the relationship between profits and sales volume.

❐ The profit–volume graph is the graph of the operating income equation:

Operating income = (Price × Units) – (Unit variable cost × Units) – Fixed cost

The Cost–Volume–Profit Graph

❑ The **cost–volume–profit graph** depicts the relationships among cost, volume, and profits.

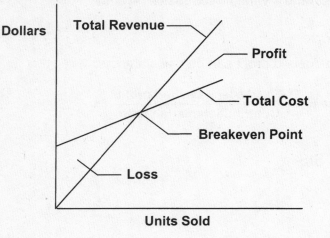

❑ The point where the total revenue line and the total cost line intersect is the breakeven point.

Assumptions of Cost–Volume–Profit Analysis

❑ Limitations of CVP analysis include:

- The analysis assumes a linear revenue function and a linear cost function.
- The analysis assumes that price, total fixed costs, and unit variable costs can be accurately identified and remain constant over the relevant range.
- The analysis assumes that units produced are sold.
- For multiple-product analysis, the sales mix is assumed to be known.
- The selling prices and costs are assumed to be known with certainty.

CHANGES IN THE CVP VARIABLES

Introducing Risk and Uncertainty

Margin of Safety

❑ The **margin of safety** is a measure of how far sales can drop until the breakeven point is reached.

❑ The margin of safety expressed in dollars is the difference between budgeted sales and break-even sales.

Margin of safety = Expected sales – Sales at breakeven

❑ The margin of safety can be viewed as a crude measure of risk.

Operating Leverage

❑ **Operating leverage** is concerned with the mix of fixed costs and variable costs.

❑ For example, if a firm chooses to automate its operations, fixed costs increase, variable costs (direct labour) decrease, and operating leverage increases.

❑ The **degree of operating leverage (DOL)** is a measure of the sensitivity of profit changes to changes in sales volume. DOL measures the percentage of change in profit that results from a percentage of change in sales.

Degree of operating leverage = Contribution margin/Profit

❏ The higher the degree of operating leverage, the greater the change in profit when sales change.

Percentage change in profit = DOL × Percentage change in sales

Sensitivity Analysis and CVP

❏ **Sensitivity analysis** is a "what if" technique that examines the impact of changes on an answer. For example, computer spreadsheets are used to analyze changes in prices, variable costs, and fixed costs on expected profits.

CVP ANALYSIS AND ACTIVITY-BASED COSTING

❏ Conventional cost–volume–profit analysis assumes that costs can be classified as:

1. variable costs—costs that vary, in total, with sales volume, and
2. fixed costs—costs that do not vary, in total, with sales volume.

❏ There are many costs that do not vary with volume but vary with changes in other cost drivers.

❏ In an activity-based costing system, CVP analysis divides costs into:

- unit-based costs
- nonunit-based costs (batch-level and product-level costs)
- fixed costs

KEY TERMS TEST

Test your recall of the key terms as follows. Try to recall as many key terms as possible without assistance. If you need assistance, refer to the list of key terms at the end of this section.

1. The _____ _____ _____ is calculated as variable costs divided by sales revenue.

2. The _____ _____ _____ is a measure of how far sales can drop until breakeven is reached.

3. The _____ _____ _____ is calculated as contribution margin divided by sales revenue.

4. The point where total sales revenue equals total costs is called the _____-_____ _____. It is the point of zero profits.

5. _____ _____ _____ _____ measures the percentage change in profits resulting from a percentage change in sales.

6. The relative combination of products (or services) sold by an organization is called _____ _____.

7. _____ _____ is achieved by increasing fixed costs while lowering variable costs.

8. A(n) _____-_____-_____ _____ depicts the relationships among costs, volume, and profits.

9. _____ _____ is sales revenue minus total variable cost.

10. _____ _____ is income or profit before taxes.

11. The _____ _____ is the range of volume for which the linear cost and revenue relationships are valid.

12. _____ _____ is a "what if" technique that examines the impact of changes in underlying assumptions on an answer.

KEY TERMS

breakeven point
contribution margin
contribution margin ratio
cost–volume–profit graph
degree of operating leverage
margin of safety

operating income
operating leverage
relevant range
sales mix
sensitivity analysis
variable cost ratio

↻ **Compare your answers with those at the end of the chapter. Review any key terms missed.**

CHAPTER QUIZ

Write your answers in the spaces provided.

1. Cost–volume–profit analysis enables a firm to determine _____ necessary to attain a desired level of _____.

2. Variable-costing income is calculated as follows:

    Sales

    – Variable costs

    = _____

    – _____

    = Operating income

3. Breakeven in units = _____ / _____

4. Sales revenue at breakeven = _____ / _____

5. Before-tax profit = _____ / _____

6. The margin of safety, a crude measure of risk, indicates how far sales can drop until break-even is reached. The margin of safety is calculated as follows:

    Margin of safety = _____ – _____

7. Operating leverage magnifies increases in profit as sales increase and magnifies reductions in profit as sales decrease. The degree of operating leverage is calculated as follows:

    Degree of operating leverage = _____ / _____

8. The higher the degree of operating leverage, the greater the change in profit when sales change. The percentage change in profit is calculated as follows:

    Percentage change in profit = _____ × _____

Circle the single best answer.

9. Breakeven is the point where: (a) revenue equals variable manufacturing costs; (b) revenue equals variable manufacturing and variable selling and administrative costs; (c) revenue equals variable and fixed manufacturing costs; (d) revenue equals all variable and fixed costs

10. The contribution margin ratio equals: (a) revenue minus variable costs; (b) variable costs divided by revenue; (c) contribution margin divided by revenue; (d) variable costs divided by contribution margin

11. Limitations of CVP analysis include all of the following except: (a) a nonlinear revenue function and a nonlinear cost function; (b) what is produced is sold; (c) selling prices and costs are known with certainty; (d) costs can be separated into fixed and variable components

Use the following information to answer Questions 12 through 17:

Selling price per unit $100
Variable manufacturing costs per unit $20
Fixed manufacturing costs per unit $30
Variable selling costs per unit $25
Fixed selling costs per unit $10
Expected production and sales .... 1,000 units

12. Contribution margin per unit is: (a) $15; (b) $50; (c) $55; (d) $80

13. The contribution margin ratio is: (a) 15%; (b) 45%; (c) 50%; (d) 55%

14. Breakeven for the product (rounded to the nearest whole unit) is: (a) 727 units; (b) 888 units; (c) 1,000 units; (d) 1,500 units

15. If the firm wants to earn $70,000 in before-tax profit, sales revenue must equal: (a) $60,500; (b) $110,000; (c) $200,000; (d) $244,444

16. If the firm wants to earn $70,000 in before-tax profit, contribution margin must equal: (a) $98,000; (b) $110,000; (c) $125,000; (d) $155,000

17. If the tax rate is 40 percent, how many units must be sold to earn an after-tax profit of $60,000? (a) 4,000 units; (b) 1,500 units; (c) 2,640 units; (d) 2,546 units

☼ **Compare your answers with those at the end of the chapter. Review any questions missed.**

PRACTICE TEST

PROBLEM 1

AAH, Inc., manufactures a product that sells for $50. The variable costs per unit are:

Direct materials	$15
Direct labour..	5
Variable manufacturing overhead.....................	4

During 2000, the budgeted fixed manufacturing overhead is estimated to be $500,000, and budgeted fixed selling, general, and administrative costs are expected to be $300,000. Variable selling costs are $6 per unit.

Instructions:

1. Determine the breakeven point in units.

2. Determine the number of units that must be sold to earn $100,000 in profit before taxes.

PROBLEM 1 *(Continued)*

3. What dollar amount of sales must be attained in order to earn $300,000 in profit before taxes?

4. If there is a 40% tax rate, determine the sales level in dollars that must be attained in order to generate an after-tax profit of $300,000.

PROBLEM 2

The Anton Company has developed the following income statement using a contribution margin format:

Anton Company
Projected Income Statement
For the Year Ending December 31, 2004

Revenues...		$200,000
Less variable costs:		
Variable manufacturing..	$60,000	
Variable selling..	20,000	
Total variable costs..		80,000
Contribution margin...		$120,000
Less fixed costs:		
Fixed manufacturing...	$80,000	
Fixed selling, general, and administrative............	25,000	
Total fixed costs		105,000
Net income..		$ 15,000

The projected income statement was based upon sales of 10,000 units. Anton has the capacity to produce 15,000 units during the year.

Instructions:

Each of the following questions is independent of the others.

1. Determine the breakeven point in units.

PROBLEM 2 *(Continued)*

2. Calculate the margin of safety in dollars.

3. The sales manager believes the company could increase sales by 1,000 units if advertising expenditures are increased by $16,000. Should the company increase advertising expenditures?

PROBLEM 2 (Continued)

4. What is the maximum amount the company could pay for advertising if the advertising would increase sales by 1,000 units?

5. Management believes that by lowering the selling price to $17 per unit, the company can increase sales by 2,000 units. Based upon these estimates, would it be profitable for the company to lower its selling price?

PROBLEM 3

The Laurel Company produces two types of food processors. Information about the two product lines for 2004 is as follows:

	Regular	Deluxe
Selling price per unit	$75	$100
Variable costs per unit	50	50
Contribution margin per unit....................	$25	$ 50

The company expects fixed costs to be $150,000 in 2004. The firm expects 80% of its sales (in units) to be Regular model food processors.

Instructions:

1. Determine the breakeven point in units.

2. Determine sales in units of Regular and Deluxe models necessary to generate a before-tax profit of $90,000.

PROBLEM 3 *(Continued)*

3. Determine sales in units of Regular and Deluxe models necessary to generate an after-tax profit of $90,000 if the tax rate is 40%.

PROBLEM 4

The Matt Company produces two models of garage door openers, Standard and Supreme.

The company expects to sell 900 units of the Standard model and 300 units of the Supreme model (a sales mix of 3:1).

A projected income statement for the firm as a whole for 2004 follows:

The Matt Company
Projected Income Statement
For the Year Ending December 31, 2004

Revenues	$300,000
Less: Variable costs	120,000
Contribution margin	$180,000
Less: Total fixed costs	60,000
Profit	$120,000

Instructions:

1. Determine the breakeven point in sales dollars for 2004.

2. Determine sales revenue necessary to generate a before-tax profit of $150,000.

3. Determine sales revenue necessary to generate an after-tax profit of $210,000 if the tax rate is 30%.

PROBLEM 5

Using a conventional cost system, the cost formula for one of a company's products is as follows:

$$Y = \$37,000 + \$15X_1$$

where X_1 = units sold

Using an ABC system, the cost formula for the same product is as follows:

$$Y = \$20,000 + \$15X_1 + \$3,000X_2 + \$400X_3$$

where X_1 = units sold
X_2 = number of batches
X_3 = number of engineering change orders

The unit selling price is $40. The company plans to produce and sell 4,000 units. For up to 4,000 units, the company expects to produce 5 batches and use 5 engineering change orders.

Instructions:

1. Using the conventional cost system data, calculate the breakeven point in units.

2. Using the ABC system data, calculate the breakeven point in units.

3. Using the ABC system data, calculate profit if 4,000 units are produced and sold.

4. Based on revised estimates, the company now expects to sell 7,000 units, which would require the production of 7 batches and the use of 6 engineering change orders. Using the ABC system data, calculate profit if 7,000 units are sold.

ANSWERS

KEY TERMS TEST

1. variable cost ratio
2. margin of safety
3. contribution margin ratio
4. breakeven point
5. Degree of operating leverage
6. sales mix
7. Operating leverage
8. cost–volume–profit graph
9. Contribution margin
10. Operating income
11. relevant range
12. Sensitivity analysis

CHAPTER QUIZ

1. sales, profit
2. Contribution margin, Fixed costs
3. Fixed costs, Contribution margin per unit
4. Fixed costs, Contribution margin ratio
5. After-tax profit, (1 – Tax rate)
6. Expected sales, Sales at breakeven
7. Contribution margin, Profit
8. Degree of operating leverage (DOL), Percentage change in sales
9. d
10. c

11. a
12. c $100 – ($20 + $25) = $55
13. d $55/$100 = 55%
14. a   ($30 + $10) × 1,000 units = $40,000; $40,000/$55 = 727 units
15. c   ($40,000 + $70,000)/55% = $200,000
16. b   ($30 × 1,000) +($10 × 1,000) + $70,000 = $110,000
17. d   [$40,000 + ($60,000/(1 – .40))]/$55 = 2,546 units

PRACTICE TEST

PROBLEM 1

1. Breakeven in units = $\dfrac{\text{Fixed cost}}{\text{Contribution margin per unit}}$

$$= \frac{\$800,000*}{\$20**}$$

$$= 40,000 \text{ units}$$

*Total fixed costs:

Budgeted fixed manufacturing overhead	$500,000
Budgeted fixed selling, general, and administrative	300,000
Total fixed costs	$800,000

**Contribution margin per unit:

Selling price per unit		$50
Variable cost per unit:		
Direct materials	$15	
Direct labour	5	
Variable manufacturing overhead	4	
Variable selling costs	6	
Total variable cost per unit		30
Contribution margin per unit		$20

2. Unit sales necessary to earn $100,000 in before-tax profit:

$$\text{Units} = \frac{\text{Fixed cost} + \text{Desired profit}}{\text{Contribution margin per unit}}$$

$$= \frac{\$800,000 + \$100,000}{\$20}$$

$$= 45,000 \text{ units}$$

3. Sales dollars necessary to earn a before-tax profit of $300,000:

$$\text{Sales dollars} = \frac{\text{Fixed cost} + \text{Desired profit}}{\text{Contribution margin ratio}}$$

$$= \frac{\$800,000 + \$300,000}{0.4*} = \$2,750,000$$

*Contribution margin ratio = $20/$50 = 0.4

4. Sales dollars necessary to earn an after-tax profit of $300,000:

$$\text{Sales dollars} = \frac{\text{Fixed cost} + [\text{After - tax profit}/(1 - \text{Tax rate})]}{\text{Contribution margin ratio}}$$

$$= \frac{\$800,000 + (\$300,000/.60)}{0.4}$$

$$= \frac{\$800,000 + \$500,000}{0.4} = \$3,250,000$$

PROBLEM 2

1. Breakeven in units $= \dfrac{\text{Fixed cost}}{\text{Contribution margin per unit}}$

$$= \frac{\$105,000}{\$12*}$$

$$= 8,750 \text{ units}$$

*Contribution margin per unit:

Selling price per unit ($200,000/10,000)		$20
Variable cost per unit:		
Variable manufacturing costs ($60,000/10,000)........	$6	
Variable selling costs ($20,000/10,000)	2	
Total variable cost per unit		8
Contribution margin per unit...........................		$12

2. Margin of safety in dollars:

Margin of safety = Expected sales – Sales at breakeven
= $200,000 – (8,750 units × $20)
= $200,000 – $175,000
= $25,000

Sales could decrease by $25,000 from the expected sales level before the company would reach breakeven.

3. For this alternative to be profitable, the contribution margin from the additional sales of 1,000 units must at least cover the additional advertising expenditure.

Incremental contribution margin from 1,000 units ($12 × 1,000 units)..........	$12,000
Less: Incremental advertising expenditures	16,000
Decrease in income	$ (4,000)

A new income statement that considers the effect on sales and costs could be prepared to verify the effect on income.

Anton Company
Projected Income Statement
For the Year Ending December 31, 2004

Revenues (11,000 × $20)		$220,000
Less variable costs:		
Variable manufacturing (11,000 × $6)...	$66,000	
Variable selling (11,000 × $2)	22,000	
Total variable costs		88,000
Contribution margin..		$132,000
Less fixed costs:		
Fixed manufacturing...	$80,000	
Fixed selling, general, and administrative ($25,000 + $16,000)	41,000	
Total fixed costs		121,000
Net income...		$ 11,000

The Anton Company's income would decrease from $15,000 to $11,000 if the advertising expenditures were made.

4. The maximum amount the company could pay for additional advertising in order to sell 1,000 more units would be $12,000.

Additional contribution margin from 1,000 units	$12,000
Less: Additional advertising expenditures	12,000
Effect on income...	$ –0–

The company also might want to consider the reliability of the estimates and the effect the advertising might have on sales in later periods.

5. A projected income statement based upon a $17 selling price and sales of 12,000 units follows:

Anton Company
Projected Income Statement
For the Year Ending December 31, 2004

Revenues (12,000 × $17)...		$204,000
Less variable costs:		
Variable manufacturing (12,000 × $6)	$72,000	
Variable selling (12,000 × $2)...	24,000	
Total variable costs		96,000
Contribution margin		$108,000
Less fixed costs:		
Fixed manufacturing	$80,000	
Fixed selling, general, and administrative..................................	25,000	
Total fixed costs		105,000
Net income		$ 3,000

No, Anton Company should not lower the sales price because income drops from $15,000 to $3,000.

PROBLEM 3

1.

	Selling Price		Variable Cost		Contribution Margin		Mix		
Regular	$ 75	–	$50	=	$25	×	8	=	$200
Deluxe..	100	–	50	=	50	×	2	=	100
Contribution margin per package...........									$300

$$\text{Breakeven packages} = \frac{\text{Fixed cost}}{\text{Package contribution margin}}$$

$$= \frac{\$150,000}{\$300}$$

$$= 500 \text{ packages}$$

The 500 packages would be divided as follows:

Regular (500 packages × 8 units)	4,000 units
Deluxe (500 packages × 2 units)........................	1,000 units
Total...	5,000 units

2. Unit sales necessary to generate a before-tax profit of $90,000:

$$\text{Sales packages} = \frac{\text{Fixed cost} + \text{Desired profit}}{\text{Package contribution margin}}$$

$$= \frac{\$150,000 + \$90,000}{\$300}$$

$$= 800 \text{ packages}$$

The 800 packages would be divided as follows:

Regular (800 packages × 8 units)	6,400 units
Deluxe (800 packages × 2 units)........................	1,600 units
Total...	8,000 units

3. Unit sales necessary to generate an after-tax profit of $90,000:

$$\text{Sales packages} = \frac{\text{Fixed cost} + [\text{After - tax profit}/(1 - \text{Tax rate})]}{\text{Package contribution margin}}$$

$$= \frac{\$150,000 + (\$90,000/.60)}{\$300}$$

$$= 1,000 \text{ packages}$$

The 1,000 packages would be divided as follows:

Regular (1,000 packages × 8 units)..................	8,000 units
Deluxe (1,000 packages × 2 units)	2,000 units
Total..	10,000 units

PROBLEM 4

1. Contribution margin ratio = $180,000/$300,000 = 0.6
   Breakeven sales = $60,000/0.6 = $100,000

2. ($60,000 + $150,000)/0.6 = $350,000

3. [$60,000 + ($210,000/(1 − .30))]/0.6 = $600,000

PROBLEM 5

1. $X = F/(P - V)$
   $= \$37,000/(\$40 - \$15)$
   $= 1,480$ units

2. $X_1 = (F + V_2 X_2 + V_3 X_3)/(P - V_1)$
   $= [\$20,000 + (\$3,000 \times 5) + (\$400 \times 5)]/\$25$
   $= (\$20,000 + \$15,000 + \$2,000)/\$25$
   $= \$37,000/\$25$
   $= 1,480$ units

3.
Revenues (4,000 × $40)	$160,000
Variable costs (4,000 × $15).............................	60,000
Contribution margin	$100,000
Nonunit-based costs:	
($3,000 × 5 batches)......................................	(15,000)
($400 × 5 engineering change orders)	(2,000)
Fixed costs	(20,000)
Net income..	$ 63,000

4.
Revenues (7,000 × $40)	$280,000
Variable costs (7,000 × $15).............................	105,000
Contribution margin	$175,000
Nonunit-based costs:	
($3,000 × 7 batches)......................................	(21,000)
($400 × 6 engineering change orders)	(2,400)
Fixed costs	(20,000)
Net income..	$131,600

CHAPTER 10
Tactical Decision Making

CHAPTER REVIEW

TACTICAL DECISION MAKING

❑ **Tactical decision making** involves choosing among alternatives and tends to be short-run in nature with an immediate end in view.

❑ **Strategic decision making** involves selecting among alternative strategies so a long-term competitive advantage is achieved.

❑ Sound tactical decision making results in decisions that achieve an immediate objective *and* serve the overall strategic goals of the organization.

Model for Making Tactical Decisions

❑ The six steps in the decision-making process are as follows:
1. Define the problem.
2. Identify alternatives as possible solutions to the problem; eliminate alternatives that are not feasible.
3. Identify the relevant costs and benefits associated with each feasible alternative; eliminate irrelevant costs and benefits from consideration.
4. Total the relevant costs and benefits for each alternative.
5. Assess qualitative factors.
6. Select the alternative with the greatest overall benefit.

❑ **Relevant costs:**
   ▪ are future costs, and
   ▪ differ among the alternatives.

❑ An irrelevant cost can be:
   ▪ a past cost, or
   ▪ a future cost that does not differ among the alternatives being considered.

❑ A **sunk cost** is a cost for which the outlay has already been made. Sunk costs are the result of past decisions and cannot be changed by current or future action. After sunk costs are incurred, they are unavoidable.

❑ Since sunk costs are past costs that do not differ among the alternatives, sunk costs are irrelevant costs.

❑ The acquisition cost of equipment purchased in the past is a sunk cost.

❑ Amortization of equipment acquired in the past is an allocation of a past cost; therefore, amortization of equipment already purchased is irrelevant.

❑ Allocations of common fixed costs are irrelevant if *total* common fixed costs do not differ among the alternatives.

Ethics in Tactical Decision Making

❑ In tactical decision making, ethical concerns relate to the way in which decisions are implemented and the possible sacrifice of long-run objectives for short-run gain.

❑ Objectives should be attained within an ethical framework and be consistent with the company's missions and goals.

RELEVANCY, COST BEHAVIOUR, AND THE ACTIVITY RESOURCE USAGE MODEL

❑ The activity resource usage model includes:
- flexible resources (resources acquired as used and needed)
- committed resources (resources acquired in advance of usage)

Flexible Resources

❑ Flexible resources can be easily purchased in the amount needed and at the time of use. For example, electricity to operate production equipment is acquired as needed at the time of use.

❑ Flexible resource costs are typically referred to as variable costs.

❑ If the demand for an activity changes across alternatives, then resource spending will change and the cost of the activity is relevant to the decision.

❑ The amount of resource demanded by the firm equals the amount of resource supplied.

Committed Resources

❑ Committed resources are purchased before they are used; therefore, there may be unused capacity.

❑ Two types of committed resources are:
1. those that can be altered in the short run, and
2. those that provide capacity for multiple periods.

Committed Resources for the Short Run

❑ Some committed resources are acquired in advance of usage through implicit contracting, such as with salaried and hourly employees. These resources are usually acquired in lumpy amounts, such as step-variable or step-fixed costs.

❑ If there is unused capacity available, an increase in demand for an activity across alternatives may not mean that the activity cost will increase.

❑ A change in resource spending can occur in one of two ways:
1. The demand for the resource exceeds the supply (increasing resource spending).
2. The demand for the resource drops permanently and supply exceeds demand enough so that activity capacity can be reduced (decreasing resource spending).

Committed Resources for Multiple Periods

❑ Often resources are acquired in advance for multiple periods before the resource demands are known. Leasing or buying a building is an example.

❑ Decisions involving multiperiod capabilities are called *capital investment decisions* and are discussed in Chapter 11.

❏ Changes in activity demands across alternatives rarely affect resource spending and are therefore not usually relevant for tactical decision making.

ILLUSTRATIVE EXAMPLES OF RELEVANT COST APPLICATIONS

Make-or-Buy Decisions

❏ A **make-or-buy decision** involves deciding whether to manufacture a product or component or buy it from another firm.

❏ The relevant costs of a make-or-buy analysis consist of the following avoidable costs:

- variable costs associated with producing the product: direct materials, direct labour, and variable overhead
- avoidable fixed overhead

❏ The relevant (avoidable) costs of manufacturing the product are then compared to the outside supplier's price. The firm cannot afford to pay more to an outside supplier than it saves (avoids) by not manufacturing the component.

❏ If the firm buys the component from an outside supplier, other uses of the manufacturing facilities may be possible, such as producing a different product.

❏ If the firm continues to produce the original component instead of buying it from an outside supplier, there is an opportunity cost associated with this choice: the firm foregoes the opportunity to produce a new product. The cost of foregoing this opportunity is the contribution margin lost by not producing the new product.

❏ If the firm can eliminate machinery and equipment as a result of buying a component from a supplier, there is an opportunity cost involved. If the firm continues to manufacture the component, the firm forgoes the opportunity to sell the machinery and equipment, invest the proceeds, and earn a return.

❏ If the alternative of making a component requires the acquisition of machinery and equipment, then it is a long-run investment decision rather than a short-run decision.

Qualitative Factors

❏ Qualitative factors are factors that cannot be quantified.

❏ Qualitative factors that should be considered are:

- How does the quality of the supplier's component compare to the quality of the component manufactured by the firm?
- Is the supplier reliable in terms of providing the needed quantities of the component on a timely basis?

Keep-or-Drop Decisions

❏ **Keep-or-drop decisions** concern whether to discontinue segments of an organization, such as the shoe department in a clothing store. Segments can be a product line or a territory.

❏ The analysis of dropping a segment relies upon the concept of relevant or avoidable costs.

❏ Based solely on quantitative factors, the segment should be kept if it contributes incremental profit.

❏ Incremental profit is determined by comparing the segment's revenues with avoidable costs associated with the segment.

❑ The loss in sales of other segments as a result of closing down a complementary segment should also be considered.

Keep-or-Drop Decisions with Alternative Use of Facilities

❑ If the space and resources used by the current segment could be used by another segment, an opportunity cost is involved.

❑ If the firm keeps the current segment, it foregoes the incremental profit generated by the other segment.

❑ If the incremental profit generated by the other segment exceeds the incremental profit generated by the current segment, then the current segment should be dropped (assuming all other factors are equal).

Special-Order Decisions

❑ A **special-order decision** focuses on whether a specially priced order should be accepted. Generally, the product is the same or similar to the firm's regular products.

❑ If there is excess capacity, the minimum acceptable price must cover the incremental costs associated with the special order:
  - variable costs
    - direct materials
    - direct labour
    - variable overhead
  - incremental fixed costs (out-of-pocket costs)

❑ If the firm is operating at full capacity, no additional production can occur without eliminating something that is currently being produced. Thus, if the firm accepts the special order, it forgoes the opportunity to produce and sell some of its regular products.

❑ When the firm is at full capacity, the minimum acceptable special order price must cover the following:
  - variable costs
  - incremental fixed costs
  - contribution margin forgone on the regular units not produced

❑ A firm may not want to produce a special order that is in direct competition with its regular products.

Decisions to Sell or Process Further

❑ **Joint products** have common processes and costs of production up to a split-off point. The **split-off point** is the point of separation where the products become distinguishable.

❑ Joint product decisions concern whether the product should be sold at split-off or processed further.

❑ Any joint costs that have been allocated to a joint product are sunk and irrelevant for decision making.

❑ In general, the product should be processed further if incremental revenues from further processing exceed the incremental costs of further processing.

❑ The relevant costs to be compared are:
  - the market value of the product at split-off, and

- the revenues resulting from further processing minus the incremental costs of further processing.

PRODUCT MIX DECISIONS

❑ In some cases product resources, such as materials, labour, or equipment, may be limited.

❑ **Constraints** are limitations due to limited resources or limited product demand. A manager must choose the optimal mix given the firm's constraints.

One Constrained Resource

❑ When there is one scarce resource, determine which product results in the *highest contribution margin per unit of the scarce resource*.

❑ For example, if the scarce resource is machine hours, for each product calculate the contribution margin per machine hour as follows:

$$\text{Contribution margin per machine hour} = \frac{\text{Contribution margin per unit of product}}{\text{Machine time required per unit}}$$

❑ The quantity needed of the product with the highest contribution margin per machine hour should be produced before producing the other products.

Multiple Constrained Resources

❑ When more than one resource is limited, *linear programming* can be used to determine the optimal solution.

PRICING

❑ Cost-based pricing uses a **markup**, or percentage applied to the base price, to determine the selling price.

❑ **Target costing** determines the cost of a product or service based on the price (target price) that customers are willing to pay. The marketing department determines what characteristics and price for the product are acceptable to customers, then engineers design and develop the product so that cost and profit can be covered by that price.

❑ **Predatory pricing** is the practice of setting prices below cost, attempting to injure competitors and eliminate competition. **Dumping** is predatory pricing on the international market.

❑ **Price discrimination** refers to charging different prices to different customers for essentially the same product. The 1986 Competition Act regulates price discrimination for manufacturers and wholesalers.

❑ **Price gouging** refers to the practice of setting an "excessively high price" by firms with market power.

APPENDIX: LINEAR PROGRAMMING

❑ **Linear programming** is a method that searches among possible solutions until it finds the optimal solution.

❑ In linear programming, the relationship between the variables must be linear; that is, the relationship can be represented by a straight line.

❑ Linear programming problems can be solved using:
  ▪ the graphical approach
  ▪ the simplex method

❑ There are four basic steps in the solution of a linear programming problem:
  1. Determine the **objective function**.
  2. Identify and express the constraints in equation form.
  3. Determine the feasible alternatives considering the constraints.
  4. Determine which alternative results in the optimal solution to the objective function. The **optimal solution** is the one that maximizes total contribution margin.

❑ The graphical approach can be used as long as only two products are involved.

❑ The four steps in the graphical approach are:
  1. Graph each constraint.
  2. Identify the **feasible set of solutions**.
  3. Identify all corner-point values in the feasible set.
  4. Select the corner point that yields the largest value for the objective function.

❑ The **simplex method** is a mathematical technique that is useful when a large number of variables and constraints are present in a linear programming problem. Computer programs are available to solve such linear programming problems.

KEY TERMS TEST

Test your recall of the key terms as follows. Try to recall as many key terms as possible without assistance. If you need assistance, refer to the list of key terms at the end of this section.

1. Relevant costing analysis that focuses on whether a component should be made internally or purchased externally is a(n) _____-_____-_____ _____.

2. Relevant costing analysis that focuses on whether a product should be processed beyond the split-off point is a decision to _____, _____ _____ _____.

3. The _____-_____ _____ is the point where products become distinguishable after passing through a common process.

4. A relevant costing analysis that focuses on keeping or dropping a segment of a business is a(n) _____-_____-_____ _____.

5. _____ _____ are future costs that differ among alternatives.

6. A(n) _____ _____ is a cost for which the outlay has already been made and that cannot be affected by a future decision.

7. Relevant costing analysis that focuses on whether a specially priced order should be accepted or rejected is a(n) _____-_____ _____.

8. _____ _____ _____ involves choosing among alternatives with an immediate or limited end in view.

9. _____ _____ _____ involves selecting strategies that yield a long-term competitive advantage.

10. _____ _____ is a method of determining the cost of a product or service based on the price (target price) that customers are willing to pay.

11. _____ is the percentage applied to a base cost and includes desired profit and any costs not included in the base cost.

12. _____ _____ is the practice of setting prices below cost for the purpose of injuring competitors and eliminating competition.

13. _____ is predatory pricing in the international market.

14. _____ _____ refers to the practice of setting an "excessively" high price.

15. _____ _____ is charging different prices to different customers for essentially the same product.

KEY TERMS

dumping

keep-or-drop decision

make-or-buy decision

markup

predatory pricing

price discrimination

price gouging

relevant costs

sell or process further

special-order decision

split-off point

strategic decision making

sunk cost

tactical decision making

target costing

ↁ **Compare your answers with those at the end of the chapter. Review any key terms missed.**

CHAPTER QUIZ

Write your answers in the spaces provided.

1. _____ _____ are the result of past decisions and cannot be changed by current or future actions.

2. _____ _____ is the sacrifice that results from pursuing one alternative and forgoing another alternative.

3. For a cost or revenue to be relevant to a particular decision, it must

    1. _____, and

    2. _____.

4. Avoidable costs in a make-or-buy decision consist of two types of costs:

    1. _____

    2. _____

5. List two qualitative factors that should be considered when evaluating a make-or-buy decision:

    1. _____

        _____

    2. _____

        _____

6. When deciding whether to keep or drop a segment, if the decision is based solely on quantitative factors, the segment should be kept if it contributes _____ _____.

7. When there is a scarce resource, the product with the highest contribution margin per _____ _____ should be produced first.

8. List two sunk costs:

    1. _____

    2. _____

9. If there is excess capacity, the minimum acceptable price for a special order must cover:

    1. _____

    2. _____

10. If the firm is at full capacity, the minimum acceptable price for a special order must cover:

    1. _____

    2. _____

    3. _____

11. In general when considering a sell-or-process-further decision, the product should be processed further if

    _____

    _____.

12. Linear programming problems can be solved using:

    1. _____, and

    2. _____.

Circle the single best answer.

Use the following information to answer Questions 13 through 15:

Liza Company produces a product with the following unit cost:

Direct materials	$2.75
Direct labour..	1.25
Variable overhead	4.00
Fixed overhead	2.50
Unit cost...	$10.50

Fixed selling costs are $600,000 per year, and variable selling costs are $1.50 per unit sold.

Production capacity is 500,000 units per year. However, the company expects to produce only 300,000 units next year. The product normally sells for $15 each. A customer has offered to buy 150,000 units for $10 each. The units would be sold in an area outside the market area currently served.

13. The incremental cost per unit associated with the special order is: (a) $8.00; (b) $9.25; (c) $9.50; (d) $10.00

14. Total incremental cost associated with the special order is: (a) $1,237,500; (b) $1,342,000; (c) $1,387,500; (d) $1,425,000

15. If the firm produces the special order, the effect on income would be a: (a) $75,000 increase; (b) $90,000 increase; (c) $2,500 decrease; (d) $12,500 decrease

 Compare your answers with those at the end of the chapter. Review any questions missed.

PRACTICE TEST

PROBLEM 1

The management of Garvin Industries is evaluating whether the company should continue manufacturing a component or buy it from an outside supplier. Based upon its accounting records, it appears that it costs the company $80 per unit to make the component. The $80 cost per component was determined as follows:

Direct materials	$16
Direct labour	30
Variable manufacturing overhead	12
Fixed manufacturing overhead	22
Unit cost	$80

Garvin Industries uses 10,000 components per year. After Stinson, Inc., submitted a bid of $70 per component, some members of management felt they could reduce costs by buying from outside and discontinuing production of the component.

If the component is obtained from Stinson, Inc., $5 of fixed manufacturing overhead per unit would be avoided and Garvin's unused production facilities could be leased to another company for $30,000 per year.

PROBLEM 1 *(Continued)*

Instructions:

1. Based upon relevant cost differences, should Garvin Industries make or buy the component? Include your supporting calculations.

   Supporting calculations:

2. Prepare a memorandum to Garvin management with your recommendation.

```
┌──────────────────────────────────────────────────────────────────┐
│                          MEMORANDUM                                │
│       DATE:                                                        │
│          TO:  Garvin Industries Management                         │
│       FROM:                                                        │
│     SUBJECT:                                                       │
│     ────────────────────────────────────────────────────────      │
│                                                                    │
│                                                                    │
│                                                                    │
│                                                                    │
│                                                                    │
│                                                                    │
│                                                                    │
│                                                                    │
└──────────────────────────────────────────────────────────────────┘
```

PROBLEM 2

The Critchfield Company has annual productive capacity of 60,000 units per year. Budgeted operating results for 2004 are as follows:

Revenues (50,000 units @ $10)		$500,000
Variable costs:		
Manufacturing (50,000 @ $3.20)	$160,000	
Selling (50,000 @ $0.80)	40,000	200,000
Contribution margin		$300,000
Fixed costs:		
Manufacturing	$100,000	
Selling and administrative	80,000	180,000
Operating income		$120,000

A wholesaler from another country wants to buy 5,000 units at a price of $8 per unit. All fixed costs would remain within the relevant range. Variable manufacturing costs would be the same per unit, but variable selling costs would increase by $2 per unit on the special order only.

Instructions:

1. Determine whether the company should produce the special order.

2. Assuming Critchfield's objective is to maximize profit, if the customer wants a special order of 20,000 units, should Critchfield accept or reject the special order?

PROBLEM 3

The Ahler Company manufactures three joint products: X, Y, and Z.

The cost of the joint process is $100,000.

Information about the three products follows:

Product	Anticipated Production	Selling Price per Pound at Split-Off	Additional Processing Costs per Pound after Split-Off (All Variable)	Selling Price per Pound after Further Processing	Allocated Joint Costs
X	10,000 lbs.	$10	$2	$20	$24,000
Y	30,000 lbs.	5	6	10	36,000
Z	20,000 lbs.	8	4	16	40,000

Instructions:

Determine whether each product should be sold at split-off or processed further.

PROBLEM 4

The operations of the Schmollinger Corporation are divided into the Perry Division and the Nicholas Division.

Projections for the next year are as follows:

	Perry Division	Nicholas Division	Total
Sales	$250,000	$100,000	$350,000
Variable costs	80,000	40,000	120,000
Contribution margin	$170,000	$ 60,000	$230,000
Direct fixed costs	60,000	40,000	100,000
Segment margin	$110,000	$ 20,000	$130,000
Allocated common costs	70,000	30,000	100,000
Operating income (loss)	$ 40,000	$(10,000)	$ 30,000

Instructions:

1. Determine operating income for the Schmollinger Corporation as a whole if the Nicholas Division were dropped.

2. Should the Nicholas Division be eliminated?

PROBLEM 5

The Royer Company manufactures two products, 12-07 and 19-01. Contribution margin per unit is determined as follows:

	12-07	19-01
Revenue.....................................	$25	$20
Variable costs	15	12
Contribution margin..................	$10	$ 8

Total demand for Product 12-07 is 5,000 units, and for Product 19-01 it is 10,000 units.

Direct labour is a scarce resource. During the year, 40,000 direct labour hours are available. Product 12-07 requires 5 direct labour hours per unit, while Product 19-01 requires 2 direct labour hours per unit.

Instructions:

How many units of Product 12-07 and Product 19-01 should the Royer Company produce?

PROBLEM 6

Nance Manufacturing has idle capacity. A customer has offered to purchase 1,000 units of one of Nance's products for $5 each. The product normally sells for $7.50. The customer is located in a state not previously serviced by Nance Manufacturing. The activity-based accounting system provided the following information:

	Cost Driver	Unused Capacity	Quantity Demanded*	Activity Rate Fixed	Activity Rate Variable
Direct materials.........	Units	0	1,000		$1.50
Direct labour	Direct labour hours	0	200		3.50
Setups	Setup hours	10	20	$25.00	4.00
Machining	Machining hours	3,000	2,000	2.00	0.50

*This only represents the amount of resources demanded by the special order being considered.

Any expansion of the setup resource must be acquired in lumpy amounts. Each "lumpy" amount provides an additional 50 hours of setup servicing and is priced at the fixed activity rate.

Instructions:

1. Compute the change in income for Nance Manufacturing if the order is accepted.

2. If the setup activity had 30 hours of unused capacity, how would this affect the analysis?

PROBLEM 6 *(Continued)*

3. Prepare a memorandum to management stating your recommendation regarding whether the order should be accepted or rejected. Include a discussion of the strategic issues affecting the decision.

MEMORANDUM

DATE:

TO:

FROM:

SUBJECT:

PROBLEM 7 (Appendix)

Hediger, Inc., manufactures two products, X and Y. Information for the two products is as follows:

	Product X	Product Y
Selling price per unit	$50	$30
Variable cost per unit...........................	$30	$15
Direct labour hours per unit..................	2	4
Machine hours per unit	10	5

During each month, 1,000 direct labour hours and 2,000 machine hours are available.

Instructions:

1. Formulate the linear programming objective function and constraint equations.

2. Using the graphical approach, determine the optimal solution.

ANSWERS

KEY TERMS TEST

1. make-or-buy decision
2. sell or process further
3. split-off point
4. keep-or-drop decision
5. Relevant costs
6. sunk cost
7. special-order decision
8. Tactical decision making
9. Strategic decision making
10. Target costing
11. Markup
12. Predatory pricing
13. Dumping
14. Price gouging
15. Price discrimination

CHAPTER QUIZ

1. Sunk costs
2. Opportunity cost
3. 1. differ between the alternatives being considered
   2. be a future cost
4. 1. the variable costs associated with producing the product: direct materials, direct labour, and variable overhead
   2. avoidable fixed overhead
5. 1. How does the quality of the supplier's component compare to the quality of the component manufactured by the firm?
   2. Is the supplier reliable in terms of providing the needed quantities of the component on a timely basis?
6. incremental profit
7. unit of scarce resource
8. 1. acquisition cost of equipment purchased in the past
   2. depreciation of equipment purchased in the past
9. 1. variable costs
   2. incremental fixed costs
10. 1. variable costs
    2. incremental fixed costs
    3. contribution margin foregone on the regular units not produced
11. the incremental revenues from further processing exceed the incremental costs of further processing
12. 1. the graphical approach
    2. the simplex method
13. c ($2.75 + $1.25 + $4.00 + $1.50) = $9.50
14. d ($9.50 × 150,000) = $1,425,000
15. a ($10.00 − $9.50) × 150,000 = $75,000 increase

PRACTICE TEST

PROBLEM 1

1.

	Buy	Make
Outside supplier's price (10,000 × $70)	$(700,000)	
Direct materials (10,000 × $16)		$(160,000)
Direct labour (10,000 × $30)		(300,000)
Variable manufacturing overhead (10,000 × $12)		(120,000)
Fixed manufacturing overhead:		
(10,000 × $22)		(220,000)
(10,000 × $17)	(170,000)	
Rental revenue	30,000	
Totals	$(840,000)	$(800,000)

There is a $40,000 difference in favour of manufacturing the component rather than buying it from the outside supplier.

The make-or-buy alternatives could also be analyzed as follows:

	Buy	Make
Outside supplier's price	$(700,000)	
Direct materials		$(160,000)
Direct labour		(300,000)
Variable manufacturing overhead		(120,000)
Avoidable fixed manufacturing overhead (10,000 × $5)		(50,000)
Rental revenue	30,000	
Totals	$(670,000)	$(630,000)

Notice that instead of including total fixed manufacturing overhead under each alternative, only the avoidable manufacturing overhead is included under the alternative of making the component. The difference in income is still $40,000 in favour of manufacturing the component.

2.

MEMORANDUM

DATE: *(insert current date here)*

TO: Garvin Industries Management

FROM: Management Consulting, Inc.

SUBJECT: Make-or-Buy Decision

This memo regards whether Garvin Industries should continue manufacturing one of its components or buy the component from an outside supplier.

Based on the attached calculations, I recommend that Garvin Industries continue manufacturing the component. There is a $40,000 difference in favour of manufacturing the component rather than buying it from an outside supplier. The net total cost of buying the component is $840,000. Fixed manufacturing overhead of $170,000 will be incurred even if the component is purchased. The net total cost of manufacturing the component is $800,000. Therefore, there is a cost difference of $40,000 in favour of manufacturing the component.

In addition, if we manufacture the component, we have control over the production scheduling and availability of the component. Another qualitative factor to consider is quality. Again, if the component is manufactured, we have control over the quality of the component produced.

If you have any questions concerning the analysis, please contact me at Extension 2531.

PROBLEM 2

1.

Incremental revenue (5,000 × $8)..............................	$40,000
Incremental costs:	
Variable manufacturing (5,000 × $3.20).................	(16,000)
Variable selling [5,000 × ($0.80 + $2.00)]	(14,000)
Incremental contribution margin..................................	$10,000

Since the company would still be operating within the relevant range, fixed costs would remain the same.

If the company produces the special order, contribution margin and operating income would increase by $10,000.

2.

	Without Special Order	With Special Order
Revenues:		
(50,000 × $10)..	$500,000	
(40,000 × $10)..		$400,000
(20,000 × $8)...		160,000
Less variable costs:		
Manufacturing:		
(50,000 × $3.20)...	(160,000)	
(60,000 × $3.20)...		(192,000)
Selling:		
(50,000 × $0.80)...	(40,000)	
(40,000 × $0.80)...		(32,000)
(20,000 × $2.80)...		(56,000)
Contribution margin...	$300,000	$280,000
Less fixed costs:		
Manufacturing	(100,000)	(100,000)
Selling and administrative	(80,000)	(80,000)
Operating income..	$120,000	$100,000

If Critchfield accepts the 20,000 unit special order, it would have to forgo 10,000 units in regular sales because of capacity constraints. This would result in a $20,000 decrease in contribution margin and operating income. Critchfield should reject the special order.

PROBLEM 3

Product	Sell at Split-Off	Process Further, Then Sell	Decision
X	$100,000	$200,000	
		(20,000)	Process Further
		$180,000	
Y	$150,000	$300,000	
		(180,000)	Sell at Split-Off
		$120,000	
Z	$160,000	$320,000	
		(80,000)	Process Further
		$240,000	

Notice that since the joint costs are incurred regardless of which action is taken, the joint costs are not relevant to the decision.

PROBLEM 4

1. If the Nicholas Division were dropped, the company's operating income would drop from $30,000 to $10,000.

Sales	$250,000
Less: Variable costs	80,000
Contribution margin	$170,000
Less: Direct fixed costs	60,000
Segment margin	$110,000
Less: Allocated common costs ($70,000 + $30,000)	100,000
Operating income (loss)	$ 10,000

The $30,000 of common costs allocated to the Nicholas Division will be incurred even if the Nicholas Division is dropped.

2. The Nicholas Division should not be dropped since it contributes $20,000 toward covering common corporate costs.

PROBLEM 5

Since direct labour hours are limited, the company should first produce the product that has the highest contribution margin per direct labour hour.

	12-07	19-01
Contribution margin per unit	$10	$8
Divided by:		
Direct labour hours required per unit	5	2
Contribution margin per direct labour hour	$ 2	$4

To maximize contribution margin, the Royer Company should produce 10,000 units of 19-01 and 4,000 units of 12-07.

Product	Units	DLH per Unit	DLH
19-01	10,000	2	20,000
12-07	4,000	5	20,000
Totals	14,000		40,000

PROBLEM 6

1. The relevant costs are those that change if the order is accepted. These costs would consist of the variable activity costs (resources acquired as needed) plus any cost of acquiring additional activity capacity (resources acquired in advance of usage). Income will change by the following amount:

Revenue ($5 × 1,000 units)	$5,000
Less increase in resource spending:	
Direct materials ($1.50 × 1,000 units)	(1,500)
Direct labour ($3.50 × 200 direct labour hours)	(700)
Setups [($25 × 50 hours) + ($4 × 20 hours)]	(1,330)
Machining ($0.50 × 2,000 machine hours)	(1,000)
Increase in income	$ 470

2. If 30 additional hours of excess setup capacity exists, then no additional resource spending for additional capacity would be required. Thus, the profitability of the special order would be increased by $1,250 ($25 × 50 hours—the increase in resource spending that would have been required). Total income would increase by $1,720 instead of only $470 if the order is accepted.

3. Your memorandum should contain discussion similar to the following:

The special order would increase income by $470, but it requires expansion of the setup activity capacity. If a long-term expansion is required, the special order should be rejected. Even if the expansion is short-run in nature, it is questionable whether the firm should undertake the special order.

If the expansion is a long-term commitment, the company would be exchanging a one-year benefit of $470 for an annual commitment of $1,250 (the cost of the expansion of setup activity capacity). Thus, the special order should be rejected if the expansion is a long-term commitment.

Even if the expansion is short-run in nature, is it worth $470 in additional profits? Strategic factors that affect this decision include:

- Will the special order affect any regular sales?
- Is there the possibility the customer might resell the merchandise to regular customers at the regular sales price, thus reducing Nance's regular sales?
- Will any regular customers learn of the price reduction and expect the same special price?
- Is this an opportunity for Nance "to get its foot in the door" in a new sales territory? Can Nance build on this business in the future?
- Is Nance searching for a permanent solution to its idle capacity?
- Is it attempting to reduce unused capacity or find additional regular sales to make use of the unused capacity?

PROBLEM 7 (APPENDIX)

1. Contribution margin per unit:

	X	Y
Selling price	$50	$30
Less: Variable costs	30	15
Contribution margin per unit	$20	$15

Objective function: Maximize contribution margin: $20X + $15Y
Constraints:
Labour hour constraint: $2X + 4Y \leq 1,000$ hours
Machine hour constraint: $10X + 5Y \leq 2,000$ hours
Nonnegativity constraints: $X \geq 0$
                             $Y \geq 0$

2. **a.** Graph the labour hour constraint as follows:

Determine the value of Product Y if none of Product X is produced:
$$(2)(0) + 4Y = 1,000$$
$$4Y = 1,000$$
$$Y = 250$$
$$(X = 0, Y = 250)$$

Determine the value of Product X if none of Product Y is produced:
$$2X + (4)(0) = 1,000$$
$$2X = 1,000$$
$$X = 500$$
$$(X = 500, Y = 0)$$

Locate these two points on the graph: $(X = 0, Y = 250)$
                                         $(X = 500, Y = 0)$

Draw a line on the graph connecting these two points.

b. Graph the machine hour constraint as follows:

Determine the value of Product Y if none of Product X is produced:
$$(10)(0) + 5Y = 2,000$$
$$5Y = 2,000$$
$$Y = 400$$

$(X = 0, Y = 400)$

Determine the value of Product X if none of Product Y is produced:

$$10X + (5)(0) = 2,000$$
$$10X = 2,000$$
$$X = 200$$
$$(X = 200, Y = 0)$$

Locate these two points on the graph: $(X = 0, Y = 400)$
$(X = 200, Y = 0)$

Draw a line on the graph connecting these two points.

Graph:

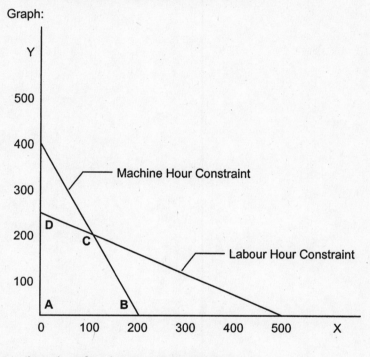

c. Compute the value of each corner point as follows:

Corner Point	X-Value	Y-Value	Z = $20X + $15Y
A	0	0	0
B	200	0	4,000
C	100	200	5,000*
D	0	250	3,750

*The optimal solution calls for producing and selling 100 units of Product X and 200 units of Product Y, resulting in a contribution margin of $5,000.

CHAPTER 11
Capital Investment Decisions

CHAPTER REVIEW

TYPES OF CAPITAL INVESTMENT DECISIONS

❑ **Capital investment decisions** involve planning, setting goals and priorities, arranging financing, and identifying criteria for making long-term investments.

❑ **Capital budgeting** is the process of determining which long-term capital assets to acquire.

❑ There are two types of capital investment projects:

- **independent projects** that do not affect the cash flows of other projects
- **mutually exclusive projects** that, if accepted, preclude the acceptance of all other competing projects

NONDISCOUNTING MODELS

❑ Capital budgeting decision models can be classified as:

- nondiscounting models, or
- discounting models.

❑ **Nondiscounting models** do *not* consider the time value of money. Two nondiscounting cash flow models are:

- payback period
- accounting rate of return (ARR)

❑ **Discounting models** consider the time value of money. Two discounting cash flow models are:

- net present value (NPV)
- internal rate of return (IRR)

Payback Period

❑ The **payback period** is the time required for a firm to recover its original investment.

❑ When the cash flows of a project are the same amount each period, payback is calculated as follows:

Payback period = Original investment/Annual cash flow

❑ If the cash flows are not the same amount each period, payback is calculated by adding the annual cash flows until the original investment is recovered.

❑ Firms may set a maximum payback period for all projects and reject projects that exceed the maximum payback period allowed.

❑ Reasons why the payback period may be used to screen projects are as follows:

- The payback period may be used as a rough measure of risk. (The longer the payback period, the riskier the project may be.)

- Firms with liquidity problems may want to select projects with quick paybacks.
- Firms in industries where the risk of obsolescence is high may want to recover invested funds rapidly.
- If a division manager's performance is based on short-run measures, such as net income, the manager may select projects with short paybacks in order to affect net income as quickly as possible.

❏ Two weaknesses of the payback period method are as follows:
- Payback ignores the time value of money.
- Payback ignores the profitability of investments beyond the payback period.

❏ Although payback should not be used as the sole evaluator for project selection, it may be used in conjunction with discounted cash flow methods that consider the time value of money.

Accounting Rate of Return

❏ The **accounting rate of return** measures a project's return in terms of accounting *income* instead of cash flows. Income differs from cash flows because of accruals and deferrals.

❏ The accounting rate of return is calculated as follows:

$$\text{Accounting rate of return} = \frac{\text{Average income}}{\text{Investment}}$$

$$\text{Accounting rate of return} = \frac{\text{Average annual net cash inflows} - \text{Average annual depreciation}}{\text{Investment *}}$$

*Either original investment or average investment can be used. Average investment is calculated as follows:

$$\text{Average investment} = \frac{(\text{Original investment} + \text{Salvage value})}{2}$$

❏ The accounting rate of return may be used:
1. as a screening measure to ensure that a new investment will not adversely affect accounting income, and
2. because bonuses of managers are often based on accounting income and managers may want to ensure that a new investment has a favourable effect on net income (and the manager's bonus).

❏ The disadvantage of the accounting rate of return is that it does not consider the time value of money.

DISCOUNTING MODELS: THE NET PRESENT VALUE METHOD

❏ Discounting models consider the time value of money.

❏ Two discounting models are:
- net present value (NPV)
- internal rate of return (IRR)

❏ When using the net present value method:
- the cash flows for each year are identified
- all cash flows are stated in terms of their present value (discounted), and
- the present values are added together to find the **net present value**.

❏ The present values are determined using the required rate of return as the discount rate.

❏ The **required rate of return** is the minimum return that a project must earn in order to be acceptable.

❏ The cost of capital is often used as the minimum required rate of return. The **cost of capital** is the cost of investment funds, usually viewed as a weighted average of the costs of funds from all sources.

❏ If net present value is positive, the project's return is greater than the required rate of return or discount rate.

DISCOUNTING MODELS: THE INTERNAL RATE OF RETURN METHOD

❏ The **internal rate of return** is the interest rate (discount rate) that results in a net present value of zero.

❏ When net present value equals zero, the present value of the project's cash inflows exactly equals the investment outlay. Therefore, the internal rate of return is the interest rate that equates the present value of the *future* cash flows to the investment.

❏ If the cash flows are an annuity, the internal rate of return can be determined as follows:
   1. Use the following equation to solve for the discount factor:

   Investment = Annual cash flow × Annuity discount factor
   Annuity discount factor = Investment/Annual cash flow

   2. Given the length of the investment, you can then use a financial calculator to determine the interest rate that corresponds with the discount factor. This is the internal rate of return. Refer to your financial calculator manual to learn how to enter the appropriate information to calculate the internal rate of return.

❏ If the cash flows are uneven, the internal rate of return can be determined using trial and error to find the net present value that equals zero or by using a computer program or financial calculator. Again refer to your financial calculator manual to learn how to calculate the internal rate of return with uneven cash flows.

❏ The internal rate of return method assumes that the cash inflows from the project are reinvested to earn a return equal to the internal rate of return for the remaining life of the project.

❏ The investment should be rejected if the internal rate of return is less than the required rate of return.

MUTUALLY EXCLUSIVE PROJECTS

NPV Compared with IRR

❏ When NPV and IRR produce different rankings for mutually exclusive projects, the NPV method correctly identifies the best investment alternative.

❏ Two major differences between NPV and IRR are as follows:
   1. The NPV method assumes that cash flows from the project are reinvested at the *discount rate*. The IRR method assumes that cash flows are reinvested at the *internal rate of return* of the project.
   2. The NPV method measures the profitability of a project in absolute terms (in dollars), whereas the IRR method measures the profitability of a project in relative terms (as a percentage).

❏ Since the wealth of firm owners is maximized by total dollars of profit earned, not relative profits, NPV should be used when choosing among competing, mutually exclusive projects.

❏ When evaluating independent projects, a project is acceptable if the NPV is positive.

❑ When evaluating mutually exclusive projects, the project with the largest NPV is selected.

❑ The three steps in selecting the best project are as follows:
1. Determine the cash-flow pattern for each project.
2. Calculate the NPV of each project.
3. Identify the project with the greatest NPV.

POSTAUDIT OF CAPITAL PROJECTS

❑ A **postaudit** of a capital project compares the actual performance of the project with its expected performance.

❑ The postaudit might indicate:
1. corrective action is needed to improve the performance of the project, or
2. the project should be abandoned.

❑ Benefits of postaudits include the following:
1. Postaudits ensure that resources are used wisely.
2. If managers are held accountable for capital investment decisions, they are more likely to make such decisions in the best interests of the firm.
3. Postaudits supply feedback to managers that should help improve future decision making.

❑ Limitations of postaudits include the following:
1. They are costly to perform.
2. The original analysis might have been based on assumptions that have been invalidated by changes in the actual operating environment.

COMPUTATION AND ADJUSTMENT OF CASH FLOWS

❑ Two steps in computing the cash flows for capital budgeting are:
1. forecasting revenues, expenses, and capital outlays, and
2. converting the pre-tax cash flows to after-tax cash flows.

Adjusting Forecasts for Inflation

❑ The effects of inflation are considered in NPV analysis by:
- using a cost of capital that consists of the real rate plus an inflation premium to compensate for the loss in general purchasing power of the dollar.
- adjusting the operating cash flows for the effects of inflation. For example, revenues might be expected to increase by 8 percent, while costs are expected to increase by 5 percent. Since amortization is based on actual (historical) costs, it is not affected by inflation.

Conversion of Gross Cash Flows to After-Tax Cash Flows

❑ After gross cash flows are estimated, they are adjusted for tax effects to determine after-tax cash flows.

After-Tax Cash Flows: Year 0

❑ The net cash outflow in Year 0 is the difference between the initial cost of the project and any cash inflows associated with the project in Year 0.

❑ The cost of the project includes:
- the cost of land

- the cost of equipment (including transportation and installation)
- taxes on gains from the sale of old assets
- increases in working capital

❑ Cash inflows occurring at the time of acquisition include:
- tax savings from the sale of old assets
- cash from the sale of old assets
- tax benefits, such as investment tax credits

❑ The net investment can be computed as follows:

> **Total cost of new machine**
> **– Net proceeds from old machine (net of tax effects)**
> **= Net investment (cash outflow)**

After-Tax Cash Flows from Operations: Life of the Project

❑ After-tax cash flow from operations can be calculated as follows:

> **After-tax cash flows = After-tax net income + Noncash expenses**

Noncash expenses include amortization, gains and losses.

❑ The incremental cash flow from operations can be calculated as follows:

> **Incremental cash inflow from sales**
> **– Incremental cash operating expenses**
> **= Cash flow from operations before taxes**
> **– Income taxes**
> **= Net cash flow from operations after taxes**

❑ After-tax cash flows from operations also can be calculated as follows:

> **After-tax cash flows = (Pre-tax cash flows)(1 – Tax rate)**

Cash Flow Consequences of Capital Cost Allowance (CCA)

❑ Amortization is not allowed as a deduction in determining taxable income, but CCA is. CCA is essentially Revenue Canada's version of amortization. CCA is *not* a cash outflow; however, since CCA is deductible for tax purposes, it reduces the amount of income taxes a company must pay. For example, assume a company had cash inflows from operations of $100,000 and no deduction for CCA. The company would pay $34,000 in taxes ($100,000 × 34%). If the company could deduct $10,000 of CCA on their tax return, the company would pay only $30,600 in taxes.

	Without CCA Deduction	With CCA Deduction
Cash inflow from operations excluding amortization	$100,000	$100,000
CCA	–0–	10,000
Taxable income	$100,000	$ 90,000
Income taxes (34%)	$ 34,000	$30,600

$3,400 tax savings

❏ Another way to calculate the tax savings from CCA is to multiply the CCA deduction by the tax rate.

Tax savings from CCA	**= CCA deduction × Tax rate**
	= $10,000 × 34%
	= $3,400

❏ The amount of CCA allowed for tax purposes is determined by the tax laws.

❏ The Tax Act classifies capital property into different classes. Each class has a CCA rate that is used to calculate the maximum allowable CCA for a tax year. Some examples are:

Class	Rate	Types of Assets
12	100%	Most small tools
10	30%	Trucks and computer equipment
8	20%	Most equipment, machinery, and office equipment

❏ The CCA that is allowed for a particular class in a tax year is calculated by multiplying the balance of the cost in the class, after adding new purchases of assets and deducting disposals of assets during the tax year, by the appropriate CCA rate. This process is similar to how the double declining balance method of amortization for accounting purposes works.

❏ The balance in the CCA class is determined by taking the original cost of all assets in the class and subtracting the total amount of CCA taken over the life of the class. This procedure is similar to calculating an asset's net book value (original cost less accumulated amortization).

❏ Two features of the CCA system are important for determining the appropriate after-tax or net cash flows for capital investment purposes.
- First, the CCA system is generally a declining-balance system
- Second, the capital costs of assets are combined in cost pools.

❏ An alternative way to determine the CCA tax shield is by using the following formula:

$$\text{PV of CCA tax shield} = \frac{(R \times C \times T)}{(R + i)}$$

Where **R = the CCA rate**

C = the original capital cost of the project

T = the tax rate

i = required rate of return

- When using this formula, you would not include the CCA in after-tax cash flow analysis.

❏ There are two other considerations in relation to the CCA system. They are the "one half rule" and a non-zero salvage value.
- The one half rule restricts the amount of CCA that can be claimed in the year of acquisition to one-half the CCA rate for the class.
- A non-zero salvage value generates a cash flow at the time of disposal that will have to be included in the NPV analysis. There are three potential effects of a non-zero salvage value: 1) When the asset is sold, the balance in the capital cost pool is reduced by the lesser of the salvage value or the original cost of the asset. The effect is to reduce the amount of tax shield produced from the cost pool, due to the reduction in the cost pool from selling an asset. 2) The deduction of salvage value may cause the balance in the pool to be negative and trigger a recapture of CCA, which would be treated like a taxable gain, thus increasing

taxes payable. 3) If the salvage value is greater than the original cost of the asset, a capital gain results, which increases taxes payable.

- If recapture (2 above) or a capital gain (3 above) results from a non-zero salvage value disposal of the project, we need to modify the above CCA tax shield formula by adding to it the following equation:

$$\text{CCA Adjustment for Salvage Value} = \left[\frac{(R \times S \times T)}{(R + i)} \right] \times \left[\frac{1}{(1 + i)^n} \right]$$

Where R = the CCA rate

S = the salvage value of the project

T = the tax rate

n = the period of sale on retirement

i = required rate of return

CAPITAL INVESTMENT: THE ADVANCED MANUFACTURING ENVIRONMENT

❑ Companies can realize benefits by:
- redesigning and simplifying the current manufacturing process
- automating by adding robotics
- automating by using flexible manufacturing systems
- automating by using completely integrated manufacturing systems
- automating by building *greenfield factories* (new factories designed and built from scratch with a commitment to automation)

❑ Capital budgeting in the advanced manufacturing environment differs from the traditional approach in the following ways:
- *Investment.* For standard manufacturing equipment, the direct costs of acquisition represent virtually the entire investment. For automated manufacturing, the direct costs can be as low as 50 percent to 60 percent of the total investment. In addition, software, engineering, training, and implementation costs must be considered as part of the total investment cost.
- *Estimates of Operating Cash Flows.* Typically, estimates of operating cash flows from investments in standard equipment were based on tangible benefits, such as direct savings from labour, power, and scrap. In the advanced manufacturing environment, it is important to consider intangible and indirect benefits, such as improved quality, greater reliability, improved customer satisfaction, and the ability to maintain or increase market share.
- *Salvage Value.* Because of the uncertainty involved in estimating salvage value, it has often been ignored or heavily discounted. However, salvage value could make the difference between investing and not investing; therefore, a better approach is to use **sensitivity analysis** (calculate the NPV using different salvage values). Being overly conservative with salvage values may result in the rejection of desirable projects.
- *Discount Rates.* In practice, future cash flows are uncertain and managers often compensate for this uncertainty by using a discount rate that is greater than the cost of capital. If the rate selected is excessively high, it biases the selection process toward short-term investments. Because the cash returns of an automated manufacturing system are received over a longer period of time, it is more difficult for automated manufacturing systems to appear acceptable. Being overly conservative with discount rates may result in the rejection of automated manufacturing systems.

KEY TERMS TEST

Test your recall of the key terms as follows. Try to recall as many key terms as possible without assistance. If you need assistance, refer to the list of key terms at the end of this section.

1. The process of determining which long-term capital assets to acquire is referred to as making _____ _____ _____.

2. There are two types of interest. Simple interest is paid each interest period. _____ _____ _____ is interest earned on interest.

3. Future cash flows expressed in present value terms are _____ _____ _____.

4. The factor used to convert a future cash flow to its present value is a(n) _____ _____.

5. _____ _____ is the value that will accumulate by the end of an investment's life if the investment earns a specified compounded return.

6. Projects that, if accepted or rejected, will not affect the cash flows of another project are _____ _____.

7. _____ _____ _____ is the difference between the present value of a project's cash inflows and the present value of its cash outflows.

8. _____ _____ are capital expenditure models that identify criteria for accepting or rejecting projects without considering the time value of money.

9. _____ _____ _____ _____ is the minimum rate of return that a project must earn in order to be acceptable.

10. The _____ _____ _____ _____ is calculated as income divided by the original or average investment.

11. A series of cash flows is a(n) _____.

12. The _____ _____ _____ is the cost of investment funds, usually viewed as a weighted cost of funds from all sources.

13. _____ is the act of finding the present value of future cash flows.

14. A(n) _____ _____ is any capital budgeting model that explicitly considers the time value of money in identifying criteria for accepting or rejecting proposed projects.

15. The _____ _____ is the rate of return used to compute the present value of future cash flows.

16. _____ _____ _____ _____ is the rate of return that equates the present value of a project's cash inflows with the present value of its cash outflows (the NPV equals zero).

17. Projects that, if accepted, preclude the acceptance of competing projects are _____ _____ _____.

18. The time required for a project to return its investment is called _____ _____.

19. _____ _____ is the current value of a future cash flow.

20. _____ _____ _____ is a method of accelerated amortization permitted by tax law. The amortization allowed is computed using a modified double-declining-balance method.

21. The _____-_____ _____ is a tax rule that assumes a newly acquired asset is in service for one-half of the taxable year regardless of when it is actually placed in service.

22. A follow-up analysis of an investment decision is called a(n) _____.

23. _____ _____ is the process of altering certain key variables to assess the effect on the original outcome.

KEY TERMS

accounting rate of return
annuity
capital cost allowance (CCA)
capital investment decisions
compounding of interest
cost of capital
discount factor
discount rate
discounted cash flows
discounting
discounting model
future value

independent projects
internal rate of return
mutually exclusive projects
net present value
nondiscounting models
one-half rule
payback period
postaudit
present value
required rate of return
sensitivity analysis

↻ **Compare your answers with those at the end of the chapter. Review any key terms missed.**

CHAPTER QUIZ

Write your answers in the spaces provided.

1. Capital expenditure decision models can be classified as nondiscounting models or discounting models. _____ models consider the time value of money. _____ models do not consider the time value of money.

2. Two nondiscounting cash flow models are:

    1. _____

    2. _____

3. Two discounting cash flow models are:

    1. _____

    2. _____

4. When the cash flows of a project are the same amount each period, payback is calculated as follows:

    Payback period = _____ /_____

5. Accounting rate of return is calculated as follows:

    ARR = (_____ – _____)

    / _____

6. Present values can be calculated using discount factors and the following formula:

    Present value = _____ × _____

7. The present value of an annuity can be calculated using an annuity discount factor and the following formula:

    Present value of an annuity = _____ × _____

8. When NPV and IRR produce different rankings for mutually exclusive projects, the _____ method correctly identifies the best investment alternative.

9. The NPV method assumes that cash flows from a project are reinvested at the _____.

10. The IRR method assumes that cash flows from a project are reinvested at the _____.

11. The tax savings from CCA can be calculated as follows:

    Tax savings from CCA = _____ × _____

12. CCA is generally calculated using a modified declining balance method. The CCA deduction is calculated as follows:

    CCA deduction = _____ × _____

Circle the single best answer.

13. Which of the following methods is used as a screening measure to ensure that a new investment will not adversely affect income? (a) payback period; (b) accounting rate of return; (c) internal rate of return; (d) net present value

14. Which of the following methods determines the interest rate that equates the present value of the future cash flows with the investment outlay? (a) payback period; (b) accounting rate of return; (c) internal rate of return; (d) net present value

15. Which of the following methods considers the time value of money? (Circle two answers.) (a) payback period; (b) accounting rate of return; (c) internal rate of return; (d) net present value

16. The discount rate is: (a) the rate used to compute payback; (b) the rate used to compute the accounting rate of return; (c) the rate used to compute the internal rate of return; (d) the rate used to compute NPV

17. Discounting: (a) is the process of determining value at a future time; (b) is the process of converting future cash flows to their present value; (c) is a process that does not consider the time value of money; (d) is a process that can only be used for a single amount (not annuities); (e) all of the above

18. The present value of $10,000 to be received 5 years from now and earning an annual return of 8% is: (a) $6,210; (b) $6,806; (c) $4,000; (d) $4,693

19. The present value of a 5-year annuity of $10,000, earning an annual return of 8% is: (a) $31,700; (b) $34,700; (c) $37,910; (d) $39,927

Use the following information to answer Questions 20 through 24:

Duane Flowers is considering the purchase of a small business that costs $500,000. The business is expected to generate annual cash inflows of $80,000. Duane plans to operate the business for 15 years and then turn it over to his son. The required rate of return is 10%. Ignore income taxes.

20. Payback for the project is: (a) 6.11 years; (b) 6.25 years; (c) 7.96 years; (d) 8.33 years

21. If amortization is $25,000 per year, the accounting rate of return based on the initial investment is: (a) 11%; (b) 12%; (c) 16%; (d) 17.2%

22. Using the cost of capital as the discount rate, the net present value of the project is: (a) $89,360; (b) $108,486; (c) $114,680; (d) $228,180

23. The approximate internal rate of return of the project is: (a) 8%; (b) 12%; (c) 12.5%; (d) 14%

24. Based on quantitative factors, should the project be accepted or rejected? (a) accept; (b) reject

25. Amortization is a cash outflow that should be considered when evaluating capital investments: (a) true; (b) false

26. If an asset is sold for less than its tax basis, a terminal loss results and the company will incur additional taxes: (a) true; (b) false

27. If a company purchases a class 8 asset for $210,000 and has no other class 8 assets, the CCA deduction would be $42,000 in the first year: (a) true; (b) false

28. If a company had a CCA deduction of $20,000 and a tax rate of 40%, the company would save $8,000 in taxes: (a) true; (b) false

29. If a company had pre-tax cash inflows from operations of $50,000 and a tax rate of 40%, after-tax cash inflows from operations would be $20,000: (a) true; (b) false

30. Under the Tax Act, trucks and computer equipment are classified as class 5 property: (a) true; (b) false

31. Most manufacturing equipment is considered class 8 property under the Tax Act: (a) true; (b) false

32. If a company disposes of property, the proceeds from the disposition do not affect the CCA calculation: (a) true; (b) false

33. If an asset is sold for more than its tax basis, a gain results and the company will incur additional taxes: (a) true; (b) false

34. For tax purposes, class 8 property is fully amortized after 5 years: (a) true; (b) false

35. Assuming a tax rate of 34%, if a company sells an asset with a tax basis of $30,000 for $20,000, the net cash flow at disposal would be $10,000: (a) true; (b) false

Use the following information to answer Questions 36 through 40:

The Reelitz Company is considering the purchase of the following production equipment:

Acquisition cost	$400,000
Annual cash inflow from operations	$90,000
Annual operating costs	$30,000
Expected salvage value	$50,000
Cost of capital	14%
Tax rate	34%
CCA class 8 – this is the only class 8 equipment the company has	20%

The company plans to keep the production equipment for 10 years and then sell it for its salvage value. (Round amounts to dollars.)

36. The CCA deduction in Year 1 would be: (a) $40,000; (b) $80,000; (c) $27,200; (d) $13,600

37. The tax savings from CCA in Year 1 would be: (a) $27,200; (b) $13,600; (c) $30,600; (d) $57,160

38. The annual after-tax cash flow from operations would be: (a) $20,400; (b) $30,600; (c) $33,000; (d) $39,600

39. The present value of equipment salvage value at the end of 10 years would be: (a) $50,000; (b) $20,003; (c) $13,487; (d) $13,150

40. The net present value of the project would be: (a) $292,444; (b) ($104,859); (c) ($107,565); (d) ($400,000)

◑ **Compare your answers with those at the end of the chapter. Review any questions missed.**

PRACTICE TEST

PROBLEM 1

A capital investment project requires an investment of $200,000. It has an expected life of five years with annual cash flows of $50,000 received at the end of each year. Ignore income taxes.

Instructions:

1. Compute the payback period for the project.

PROBLEM 1 *(Continued)*

2. Determine the accounting rate of return for the project based on the initial capital investment.

3. Compute the internal rate of return for the project.

4. Compute the net present value of the project using a 6% discount rate.

PROBLEM 2

A capital investment project requires an investment of $50,000 and has an expected life of four years. Ignore income taxes. Annual cash flows at the end of each year are expected to be as follows:

Year	Amount
1	$15,000
2	20,000
3	25,000
4	15,000

Instructions:

1. Compute the payback period assuming that the cash flows occur evenly throughout the year.

2. Determine the accounting rate of return for the project based on the initial investment.

3. Compute the net present value of the project using a 10% discount rate. (Round amounts to dollars.)

PROBLEM 2 *(Continued)*

4. Compute the internal rate of return for the project.

PROBLEM 3

The McEvers Company is considering a capital investment project that requires an investment of $37,910. The project is expected to have annual cash inflows of $10,000 occurring at the end of each of the next five years. Ignore income taxes.

Instructions:

1. Determine the internal rate of return for the project.

PROBLEM 3 *(Continued)*

2. Determine the net present value of the project using discount rates of:

   a. 8%

   b. 10%

   c. 12%

3. What are your observations about the effect the discount rate has upon the project's net present value?

PROBLEM 4

The Martin Company is evaluating two mutually exclusive projects with three-year lives. Each project requires an investment of $10,000. The projects have the following cash inflows received at the end of each year. Ignore income taxes.

Year	Project 1	Project 2
1	$ 2,000	$ 6,000
2	4,000	4,000
3	6,000	2,000
Total................	$12,000	$12,000

Instructions:

1. Determine the net present value of each project using an 8% discount rate.

2. What can you conclude about the effect the timing of the cash flows has upon a project's net present value?

PROBLEM 5

Bingham, Inc., is considering two mutually exclusive projects.

Project 1 requires an investment of $100,000, while Project 2 requires an investment of $110,000.

Revenues and costs for each project are shown below:

| Year | Project 1 | | | |
	1	2	3	4
Revenues............................	$40,000	$60,000	$70,000	$80,000
Variable costs.........................	10,000	15,000	20,000	20,000
Fixed costs.............................	5,000	5,000	6,000	8,000

| Year | Project 2 | | | |
	1	2	3	4
Revenues...............................	$60,000	$75,000	$51,000	$45,000
Variable costs.........................	20,000	25,000	17,000	15,000
Fixed costs.............................	7,000	7,000	7,000	8,000

The company estimates that at the end of the fourth year Project 1 would have a salvage value of $20,000 and Project 2 would have a salvage value of $10,000. Ignore income taxes.

Instructions:

Determine the net present value of each project using a 14% discount rate.

PROBLEM 5 *(Continued)*

Use this page to continue your answer.

PROBLEM 6

King Co. is evaluating a project that requires an investment of $400,000. The company plans to dispose of the property at the end of the fourth year for $121,620. Information about cash flows associated with the project is as follows:

Annual revenues	$250,000
Annual operating costs	$100,000

All cash flows occur at the end of the year. The required rate of return is 12% and the tax rate is 40%. The CCA rate is 30%.

Instructions:

Determine the net present value of the asset. (Round amounts to dollars.)

PROBLEM 7

Invincible Company is introducing a new product that will have a 3-year life. The project will require an initial investment in equipment of $24,000.

The asset is subject to capital cost allowance at the rate of 30%. The company plans to dispose of the equipment at the end of the third year for $11,832. The project will generate net after-tax cash flows from operations of $5,000 per year.

The above cash flows have not been adjusted for inflation, which is expected to average 6% per year. The company's cost of capital is 10%, which includes an adjustment for inflation. The tax rate is 40%.

Instructions:

1.   Compute the NPV using unadjusted cash flows. (Round amounts to dollars.)

PROBLEM 7 *(Continued)*

2. Compute the NPV using cash flows, which are adjusted for inflation. (Round amounts to dollars)

ANSWERS

KEY TERMS TEST

1. capital investment decisions
2. Compounding of interest
3. discounted cash flows
4. discount factor
5. Future value
6. independent projects
7. Net present value
8. Nondiscounting models
9. Required rate of return
10. accounting rate of return
11. annuity
12. cost of capital

13. Discounting
14. discounting model
15. discount rate
16. Internal rate of return
17. mutually exclusive projects
18. payback period
19. Present value
20. capital cost allowance
21. one-half rule
22. postaudit
23. Sensitivity analysis

CHAPTER QUIZ

1. Discounting, Nondiscounting
2. 1. payback period
   2. accounting rate of return
3. 1. net present value
   2. internal rate of return
4. Original investment/Annual cash flow
5. (Average annual net cash inflows − Average annual amortization)/Investment
6. Future value × Discount factor
7. Future value annuity × Annuity discount factor
8. NPV
9. discount rate
10. internal rate of return
11. CCA deduction × Tax rate
12. Capital cost pool balance × CCA rate (%)
13. b
14. c
15. c and d
16. d
17. b
18. b   FV=$10,000, I=8%, n=5, cpt PV = $6,806
19. d   PMT=$10,000, I=8%, n=5, cpt PV = $39,927
20. b   ($500,000/$80,000) = 6.25 years
21. a   ($80,000 − $25,000)/$500,000 = 11%
22. b   PMT=$80,000, I=10%, n=15, cpt PV =$608,486; $608,486 − $500,000 = $108,486
23. d $500,000/$80,000 = 6.25; The present value annuity factor for 15 years and 14% is 6.142; therefore, the internal rate of return is approximately 14%.
24. a
25. b   False. Amortization is *not* a cash flow. Amortization can be deducted for tax purposes resulting in a tax savings and reducing the cash outflow for taxes.
26. b   False. A loss produces a tax savings, which is viewed the same as a cash inflow.
27. b   False. Because of the one-half rule, the CCA deduction would be $21,000 for the first year.
28. a   True

29. b   False. After-tax cash inflows from operations would be $30,000 [$50,000 × (1 − .40)].
30. b   False. Trucks and computer equipment are classified as class 10 property.
31. a   True
32. b   False. The proceeds from disposal must be deducted from the asset class in calculating the current year's CCA.
33. a   True
34. b   False. Class 8 property's rate is 20%, this is perpetual until the assets in the class are sold.
35. b   False. The net cash flow at disposal would be $23,400, calculated as follows:

	Calculations	Cash Flows
Selling price..............	$ 20,000	$20,000
Tax basis	30,000	
Loss on sale	$(10,000)	
Tax savings (34% × loss)		3,400
Net cash flow from disposal		$23,400

36. a   ($400,000 × 20% x 0.5) = $40,000
37. b   ($400,000 × 20% × 0.5 x 34%) = $13,600
38. d   ($90,000 − $30,000) × 66% = $39,600
39. c   FV=$50,000, n=10, I=14%, cpt PV = $13,487
40. c   acquisition, cash outflow   (400,000)

After tax operating cash inflow

(90,000−30,000)(.66) = 36,900

Present value of net operating cash flow; pmt=39,600, I=14%, n=10, cpt PV=   206,558

Present value of salvage value (see answer 39)   13,487

CCA tax shield [(0.2 x 400,000 x 0.34)/ (0.2+0.14)] x [(1+0.5 x 0.14)/1.14]   75,087

CCA of Salvage value [(0.2x50,000x0.34)/ (0.2 + 0.14)] x 1/1.14^{10} (2,697)

NPV   (107,565)

PRACTICE TEST
PROBLEM 1

1. Payback period $= \dfrac{\text{Capital investment}}{\text{Annual cash flow}}$

    $= \dfrac{\$200,000}{\$50,000}$

    $= 4$ years

2. Accounting rate of return $= \dfrac{\text{Average annual incremental income}}{\text{Initial capital investment}}$

    $= \dfrac{\text{Average annual net cash inflows} - \text{Average annual amortization}}{\text{Initial capital investment}}$

    $= \dfrac{\$50,000 - \$40,000*}{\$200,000}$

    $= 5\%$

    *Amortization $= \$200,000/5$ years $= \$40,000$

3. Internal rate of return:

    Use the following equation to solve for the present value factor:

    Investment = Annual cash flows × Annuity discount factor
    $200,000 = $50,000 × Annuity discount factor

    Annuity discount factor = 4

    Using trial and error, the annuity discount factor of 4 falls between 6% and 8%. The exact IRR can be determined using interpolation:

Discount factor, 6%...........................	4.212	4.212
Discount factor—IRR	4.000	
Discount factor, 8%...........................		3.993
	.212	.219

    $\text{IRR} = 6\% + \left[2\% \times \dfrac{.212}{.219} \right]$

    $= 7.94\%$

4. Net present value using a 6% discount rate:

Year	Cash Flow Description	Cash Flow Amount	Discount Factor	Present Value
0	Investment	$(200,000)	1.000	$(200,000)
1–5	Cash inflows (annuity)	Pmt=50,000	N=5, I=6%	210,618
Net present value				$ 10,618

PROBLEM 2

1. If the cash flows occurred evenly throughout the year, payback would occur in 2.6 years:

Year	Projected Net Cash Inflows
1	$15,000
2	20,000
3	15,000 (.6 × $25,000)
	$50,000

2. Average annual net cash inflows = $\dfrac{\$15,000 + \$20,000 + \$25,000 + \$15,000}{4}$ = $18,750

   Average annual amortization = $\dfrac{\$50,000}{4\ \text{years}}$ = $12,500

   ARR = $\dfrac{\$18,750 - \$12,500}{\$50,000}$ = 12.5%

3. Net present value:

Year	Cash Flow Description	Cash Flow Amount	Discount Factor	Present Value
0	Investment	$(50,000)	1.000	$(50,000)
1	Operations	FV=15,000	N=1, I=10%	13,636
2	Operations	FV=20,000	N=2, I=10%	16,529
3	Operations	FV=25,000	N=3, I=10%	18,783
4	Operations	FV=15,000	N=4, I=10%	10,245
Net present value				$ 9,193

4. Because the cash flows are uneven, the IRR method must be determined using trial and error.
   The IRR is the discount rate that results in a NPV of zero.
   Since a positive NPV resulted when using 10% discount rate, the IRR must be greater than 10%.

   Net present value using 18% discount rate:

Year	Cash Flow Description	Cash Flow Amount	Discount Factor	Present Value
0	Investment	$(50,000)	1.000	$(50,000)
1	Operations	FV=15,000	N=1, I=18%	12,712
2	Operations	FV=20,000	N=2, I=18%	14,364
3	Operations	FV=25,000	N=3, I=18%	15,216
4	Operations	FV=15,000	N=4, I=18%	7,737
Net present value				$ 29

   Net present value using 20% discount rate:

Year	Cash Flow Description	Cash Flow Amount	Discount Factor	Present Value
0	Investment	$(50,000)	1.000	$(50,000)
1	Operations	FV=15,000	N=1, I=20%	12,500
2	Operations	FV=20,000	N=2, I=20%	13,889
3	Operations	FV=25,000	N=3, I=20%	14,468
4	Operations	FV=15,000	N=4, I=20%	7,234
Net present value				$ (1,909)

   Interpolation:

Present value, 18%	$50,029	
Investment	50,000	$50,000
Present value, 20%		48,091
	$ 29	$ 1,909

$$IRR = 18\% + \left[2\% \times \frac{\$29}{\$1,909} \right]$$

$$= 18.03\%$$

PROBLEM 3

1. Use the following equation to solve for the annuity discount factor:

Investment = Annual cash flows × Annuity discount factor
$37,910 = $10,000 × Annuity discount factor

Annuity discount factor = 3.791

Under 5 years, the annuity discount factor of 3.791 corresponds to approximately 10%.

2. **a.** Net present value using an 8% discount factor:

Year	Cash Flow Description	Cash Flow Amount	Discount Factor	Present Value
0	Investment	$(37,910)	1.000	$(37,910)
1–5	Cash inflows (annuity)	Pmt=10,000	N=5, I=8%	39,927
Net present value				$ 2,017

b. Net present value using a 10% discount factor:

Year	Cash Flow Description	Cash Flow Amount	Discount Factor	Present Value
0	Investment	$(37,910)	1.000	$(37,910)
1–5	Cash inflows (annuity)	Pmt=10,000	N=5,I=10%	37,908
Net present value				$ (2)

c. Net present value using a 12% discount factor:

Year	Cash Flow Description	Cash Flow Amount	Discount Factor	Present Value
0	Investment	$(37,910)	1.000	$(37,910)
1–5	Cash inflows (annuity)	Pmt=10,000	N=5,I=12%	36,048
Net present value				$ (1,862)

3. There is an inverse relationship between the discount rate and the NPV. When the discount rate increased, the NPV decreased. Also note that the discount rate of 10% that resulted in an NPV of almost zero was the IRR calculated in Requirement 2.

PROBLEM 4

1. Net present value of Project 1:

Year	Cash Flow Description	Cash Flow Amount	Discount Factor	Present Value
0	Investment	$(10,000)	1.000	$(10,000)
1	Operations	FV=2,000	N=1, I=8%	1,852
2	Operations	FV=4,000	N=2, I=8%	3,429
3	Operations	FV=6,000	N=3, I=8%	4,763
Net present value				$ 44

Net present value of Project 2:

Year	Cash Flow Description	Cash Flow Amount	Discount Factor	Present Value
0	Investment	$(10,000)	1.000	$(10,000)
1	Operations	FV=6,000	N=1, I=8%	5,556
2	Operations	FV=4,000	N=2, I=8%	3,429
3	Operations	FV=2,000	N=3, I=8%	1,588
Net present value				$ 573

2. Since money has a time value, the sooner the money will be received, the greater the present value will be.

PROBLEM 5

Schedule of cash flows for Project 1:

Year	Revenues	Variable Costs	Fixed Costs	Salvage Value	Total Cash Flow
1	$40,000	$(10,000)	$(5,000)		$25,000
2	60,000	(15,000)	(5,000)		40,000
3	70,000	(20,000)	(6,000)		44,000
4	80,000	(20,000)	(8,000)	$20,000	72,000

Net present value of Project 1:

Year	Cash Flow Description	Cash Flow Amount	Discount Factor	Present Value
0	Investment	$(100,000)	1.000	$(100,000)
1	Operations	25,000	I=14%, n=1	21,930
2	Operations	40,000	I=14%, n=2	30,779
3	Operations	44,000	I=14%, n=3	29,699
4	Operations and Salvage value	72,000	I=14%, n=4	42,630
Net present value				$ 25,038

Schedule of cash flows for Project 2:

Year	Revenues	Variable Costs	Fixed Costs	Salvage Value	Total Cash Flow
1	$60,000	$(20,000)	$(7,000)		$33,000
2	75,000	(25,000)	(7,000)		43,000
3	51,000	(17,000)	(7,000)		27,000
4	45,000	(15,000)	(8,000)	$10,000	32,000

Net present value of Project 2:

Year	Cash Flow Description	Cash Flow Amount	Discount Factor	Present Value
0	Investment	$(110,000)	1.000	$(110,000)
1	Operations	33,000	I=14%, n=1	28,947
2	Operations	43,000	I=14%, n=2	33,087
3	Operations	27,000	I=14%, n=3	18,224
4	Operations and Salvage value	32,000	I=14%, n=4	18,947
Net present value				$ (10,795)

PROBLEM 6

Calculation of tax savings from CCA:

	CCA	CCA x tax rate
Year 1	60,000	24,000
Year 2	102,000	40,800
Year 3	71,400	28,560
Year 4	49,980	19,992

We use the above tax savings in our calculations of the net present value as shown in the following table:

Calculation of Net present value:

	0	1	2	3	4
Investment cost	($400,000)				
Cash revenues		$250,000	$250,000	$250,000	$250,000
Operating costs		(100,000)	(100,000)	(100,000)	(100,000)
Net cash inflows		150,000	150,000	150,000	150,000
Net cash inflows after tax		90,000	90,000	90,000	90,000
Tax savings from CCA		24,000	40,800	28,560	19,992
Salvage value					121,620
Net cash flows (FV)		114,000	130,800	118,560	231,612
Present values (12%)	437,642	101,786	104,273	84,389	147,194
Net present value	$37,642				

PROBLEM 7

1. No adjustment for inflation

	0	1	2	3
Investment cost	($24,000)			
Net cash flows after tax		$5,000	$5,000	$5,000
Tax savings from CCA*		1,440	2,016	1,411
Salvage value				11,832
Net cash flows		6,440	7,016	18,243
Present values (10%)	$25,359	5,855	5,798	13,706
NPV	$1,359			

* Tax savings from CCA

	CCA	CCA x tax rate
Year 1	3,600	1,440
Year 2	5,040	2,016
Year 3	3,528	1,411

2. Adjusted for inflation

	0	1	2	3
Investment cost	($24,000)			
Net cash flows after tax				
(5,000 x 1.06)		$5,300		
(5,300 x 1.06)			5,618	
(5,618 x 1.06)				5,955
Tax savings from CCA*		1,440	2,016	1,411
Salvage value				11,832
Net cash flows		6,740	7,634	19,198
Present values (10%)	$26,860	6,127	6,309	14,424
NPV	$2,860			

CHAPTER 12
Inventory Management

CHAPTER REVIEW

TRADITIONAL INVENTORY MANAGEMENT

Inventory Costs

☐ If inventory consists of goods purchased from an outside supplier, the two inventory-related costs are:

- ordering costs, and
- carrying costs.

☐ If inventory consists of goods produced internally, the two inventory-related costs are:

- setup costs, and
- carrying costs.

☐ **Ordering costs** are the costs of placing and receiving an order. Examples include the clerical costs of processing an order, the cost of insurance for shipment, and unloading costs.

☐ **Setup costs** are the costs of preparing equipment and facilities for production. Examples include wages of idled production workers, lost income from idled production facilities, and the costs of test runs (labour, materials, and overhead).

☐ **Carrying costs** are the costs of carrying inventory, such as storage and handling costs, the opportunity cost of funds invested in inventory, and insurance and taxes on the inventory.

☐ Since both ordering costs and setup costs are costs of acquiring inventory, they are treated in the same manner.

☐ **Stockout costs** are the costs associated with having insufficient amounts of inventory. Stock-out costs include:

- lost sales (both current and future)
- costs of expediting (overtime or increased transportation costs)
- costs of interrupted production

Traditional Reasons for Holding Inventory

☐ Traditional reasons for holding inventories are:

- to satisfy customer demand (meet delivery dates)
- to avoid shutting down manufacturing facilities due to machine failure, defective or unavailable parts, and/or late delivery of parts
- to buffer against unreliable production processes
- to take advantage of discounts
- to hedge against future price increases

Economic Order Quantity: The Traditional Inventory Model

❏ An inventory policy addresses two questions:
  - How much inventory should be ordered (or produced)?
  - When should the order be placed (or the setup performed)?

Order Quantity and Total Ordering and Carrying Costs

❏ The order quantity used should minimize the total cost of ordering and carrying inventory.

Total cost = Ordering cost + Carrying cost
= PD/Q + CQ/2

where P = the cost of placing and receiving an order (or the setup cost for a production run)
  D = the known annual demand
  Q = quantity (the number of units ordered each time an order is placed or the lot size for a production run)
  C = the cost of carrying one unit of stock for one year

❏ The **economic order quantity** is the order quantity that minimizes the total cost.

Computing EOQ

❏ The economic order quantity is calculated as:

$$EOQ = \sqrt{2PD / C}$$

❏ The EOQ is the order size that results in ordering costs equalling carrying costs.

❏ The economic order quantity model can also be used to determine the most economical size of a production run. The only difference is that setup costs for starting a production run are substituted for ordering costs.

Reorder Point

❏ The **reorder point** is the point at which a new order should be placed (or a setup started).

❏ The reorder point equals the amount of inventory that will be used from the time the order is placed until it arrives.

❏ **Lead time** is the time required to receive an order once it is placed (or a setup is initiated). The reorder point (ROP) is calculated as follows:

ROP = Rate of usage × Lead time

❏ **Safety stock** is extra inventory that serves as a cushion for preventing stockouts. Safety stock is calculated as follows:

Safety stock = (Maximum usage – Average usage) × Lead time

❏ With safety stock, the reorder point becomes:

ROP = (Average rate of usage × Lead time) + Safety stock

EOQ and Inventory Management

❏ The traditional approach to inventory management is called a *just-in-case system*.

❏ The traditional manufacturing environment uses mass production of a few standardized products that typically have a very high setup cost. The high setup cost encourages a large batch size and long production runs. Diversity is viewed as being costly and is avoided.

JIT INVENTORY MANAGEMENT

❑ Competitive pressures have led many firms to abandon the EOQ model in favour of the JIT approach. JIT offers increased cost efficiency and simultaneously has the flexibility to respond to customer demands for better quality and more variety.

❑ Two strategic objectives of JIT are:
- to increase profits, and
- to improve a firm's competitive position.

❑ JIT pursues continuous improvement by eliminating waste and nonvalue-added activities. Nonvalue-added activities are either unnecessary, or necessary but inefficient and improvable. Necessary activities that are performed efficiently are essential to the business and/or are of value to customers.

❑ JIT challenges the traditional reasons for holding inventory and uses other solutions to the problems.

Setup and Carrying Costs: The JIT Approach

❑ The traditional approach takes setup costs as given and then tries to minimize total carrying costs and setup costs.

❑ JIT attempts to reduce setup costs (or ordering costs) by:
- reducing the time it takes to set up for production, and
- reducing the number of orders through long-term contracting.

❑ If setup and ordering costs are insignificant, the only remaining cost to minimize is carrying cost, which is minimized by reducing inventories to insignificant levels.

❑ **Continuous replenishment** is a system in which a manufacturer assumes the inventory management function for the retailer, telling the retailer when and how much stock to reorder.

❑ **Electronic data interchange (EDI)** allows suppliers access to a buyer's on-line database, permitting the supplier to deliver needed inventory just in time for use.

Due-Date Performance: The JIT Solution

❑ In the past, finished goods inventories have been used to ensure a firm's ability to meet a requested delivery date.

❑ JIT uses shorter lead times to meet requested delivery dates and to respond quickly to the demands of the market.

❑ JIT reduces lead time by:
- reducing setup times
- improving quality, and
- using manufacturing cells to reduce travel distance between machines and inventory.

Avoidance of Shutdown and Process Reliability: The JIT Approach

- ❏ Most shutdowns occur for one of three reasons:
  - machine failure
  - defective material or subassembly
  - unavailability of raw material or subassembly
- ❏ The traditional solution to the above problems is to hold inventory.
- ❏ JIT solves the problems by emphasizing:
  - **total preventive maintenance** to reduce machine failures. Cell workers perform preventive maintenance during idle manufacturing time, thereby reducing downtime for unexpected repairs.
  - total quality control to reduce defective materials or subassemblies. The goal is zero defects.
  - the right kind of a relationship with suppliers to ensure the availability of raw material or sub-assemblies.

The Kanban System

- ❏ The Kanban system is used to ensure that parts or materials are available when needed.
- ❏ The **Kanban system** is an information system that uses markers or cards to control production.
- ❏ The basic Kanban system uses three Kanban cards:
  - a **withdrawal Kanban**, which specifies the quantity that a subsequent process should withdraw from a preceding process
  - a **production Kanban**, which specifies the quantity that the preceding process should produce
  - a **vendor Kanban**, which indicates to the supplier the quantity of materials to deliver and the time of delivery
- ❏ The use of Kanbans ensures that the subsequent process withdraws the necessary quantity from the preceding process at the appropriate time. The Kanban system also controls the preceding process by allowing it to produce only the quantities withdrawn by the subsequent process. In this way, inventories are kept at a minimum, and the components arrive just in time to be used.

Discounts and Price Increases: JIT Purchasing versus Holding Inventories

- ❏ Traditionally, inventories are held so that a firm can take advantage of quantity discounts and hedge against future price increases.
- ❏ JIT uses long-term contracts with a few chosen suppliers who are selected based on price, quality, and reliability.
- ❏ Benefits of long-term contracts include:
  - they stipulate prices
  - they stipulate quality levels
  - they reduce the number of orders placed, thereby reducing ordering costs

JIT's Limitations

- ❏ Sharp reductions in inventory when implementing JIT may cause high levels of stress in workers.

❑ JIT may result in shortages and lost sales, as there is no inventory buffer.

THEORY OF CONSTRAINTS

❑ The theory of constraints (TOC) recognizes that the performance of any organization is limited by its **constraints** of limited resources and limited demand.

❑ TOC focuses on three objectives:

- *Increasing throughput.* **Throughput** is the rate at which an organization generates money through sales.
- *Minimizing inventory.* **Inventory** is the money spent in turning raw materials into throughput.
- *Decreasing operating expenses.* **Operating expenses** are defined as the money spent in turning inventories into throughput.

TOC Steps

❑ The organization wants to produce the optimal product mix given the firm's constraints. The TOC inventory system is often called the **Drum-Buffer-Rope (DBR) System**. There are five steps to improve performance by managing constraints:

1. Identify the organization's constraint(s).
   - **External constraints** are limiting factors from external sources (such as market demand).
   - **Internal constraints** are limiting factors found within the firm (such as machine-time availability).
   - **Loose constraints** are constraints whose limited resources are not fully used by a product mix.
   - **Binding constraints** are constraints where all the resources available are fully utilized.
   - Identify the one binding internal constraint. Determine the product mix to produce using the *contribution margin per unit of scarce resource* as the critical factor.
   - Consider any external binding constraints on the product mix.
2. Exploit the binding constraint(s).
   - The major binding constraint is called the *drummer* (setting the drumbeat for the entire plant). The drummer constraint's production rate sets the production rate for the entire plant.
   - A **time buffer** is the inventory needed to keep the constrained resource (drummer) busy for a specified period of time. In scheduling, the operation immediately preceding the drummer constraint should produce the parts needed by the drummer resource for a specified period of time (inventory or *time buffer*).
   - **Ropes** tie the rate at which raw materials are released into the plant's first operation to the production rate of the drummer constraint. The drummer rate controls the rate at which the first operation produces.
3. Subordinate everything else to the decisions made in Step 2.
4. Elevate the binding constraint(s). Use a program of continuous improvement to reduce the limitations that the binding constraint(s) have on the organization's performance. For example, add a shift to the drummer constraint to create more machine time.
5. Repeat the process. Improve the drummer constraint until the new drummer constraint is identified. Then repeat the TOC process.

KEY TERMS TEST

Test your recall of the key terms as follows. Try to recall as many key terms as possible without assistance. If you need assistance, refer to the list of key terms at the end of this section.

1. _____ _____ is the time to receive an order once placed or the time to produce a product from start to finish.

2. _____ _____ are the costs of placing and receiving an order.

3. _____ _____ is extra inventory that serves as a cushion for preventing stockouts.

4. _____ _____ are costs of preparing equipment and facilities so that they can be used for production.

5. The point in time at which a new order (or setup) should be initiated is the _____ _____.

6. _____ _____ are the costs of holding inventory.

7. _____ _____ _____ or _____ is the amount that should be ordered (or produced) to minimize the total ordering (or setup) and carrying costs.

8. _____ _____ are the costs of insufficient inventory.

9. An information system that controls production on a demand-pull basis through the use of cards or markers is a(n) _____ _____.

10. A card or marker that specifies the quantity that the preceding process should produce is a(n) _____ _____.

11. A card or marker that signals to a supplier the quantity of materials that need to be delivered and the time of delivery is a(n) _____ _____.

12. A marker or card that specifies the quantity that a subsequent process should withdraw from a preceding process is a(n) _____ _____.

13. _____ _____ _____ has a goal of zero machine failures.

14. _____ is the money an organization spends in turning raw materials into throughput.

15. _____ _____ are the money an organization spends in turning inventories into throughput.

16. _____ _____ _____ or _____ is an inventory management method that allows suppliers access to a buyer's on-line database.

17. A system in which a manufacturer assumes the inventory management function for the retailer is called _____ _____.

18. _____ is the rate at which an organization generates money through sales.

19. A mathematical expression that expresses a resource limitation is a(n) _____.

20. Constraints whose resources are fully utilized are _____ _____.

21. Constraints whose limited resources are not fully used by a product mix are _____ _____.

22. _____ _____ are limiting factors imposed on the firm from external sources (such as market demand).

23. _____ _____ are limiting factors found within the firm (such as machine time availability).

24. A(n) _____-_____-_____ _____ is the TOC inventory management system that relies on the drumbeat of the major constrained resource, time buffers, and ropes to determine inventory levels.

25. A(n) _____ _____ is the inventory needed to keep the constrained resource busy for a specified time interval.

26. _____ are actions taken to tie the rate at which raw material is released into the plant (at the first operation) to the production rate of the constrained resource.

KEY TERMS

binding constraints

carrying costs

constraints

continuous replenishment

Drum-Buffer-Rope System

economic order quantity (EOQ)

electronic data interchange (EDI)

external constraints

internal constraints

inventory

Kanban system

lead time

loose constraints

operating expenses

ordering costs

production Kanban

reorder point

ropes

safety stock

setup costs

stockout costs

throughput

time buffer

total preventive maintenance

vendor Kanban

withdrawal Kanban

↻ **Compare your answers with those at the end of the chapter. Review any key terms missed.**

CHAPTER QUIZ

Write your answers in the spaces provided.

1. If inventory consists of goods purchased from an outside supplier, the two inventory-related costs are:

    1. _____

    2. _____

2. If inventory consists of goods produced internally, the two inventory-related costs are:

    1. _____

    2. _____

3. Three examples of carrying costs are:

    1. _____

    2. _____

    3. _____

4. The economic order quantity is the order size that results in _____ equalling _____. It is the order quantity that minimizes total inventory costs.

5. The reorder point is the point at which a new order should be placed. The reorder point is calculated as:

    ROP = _____ × _____

6. Safety stock serves as a cushion for preventing _____.

7. If safety stock is carried, the reorder point is calculated as:

    ROP = (_____ × _____) + _____

8. List three reasons why companies have traditionally held inventory:

    1. _____

    2. _____

    3. _____

9. When JIT is used, cell workers perform _____ during idle time.

10. When JIT manufacturing is used, suppliers are selected based upon:

    1. _____

    2. _____

    3. _____

11. Benefits of using long-term contracts with suppliers include:

1. _____

2. _____

3. _____

↻ **Compare your answers with those at the end of the chapter. Review any questions missed.**

PRACTICE TEST

PROBLEM 1

Instructions:

Below are listed five reasons why companies have traditionally held inventory. Indicate the JIT solution for each of the reasons for holding inventory.

Traditional Approach	**JIT Approach**
1. Hold inventories to minimize total carrying costs and setup costs.	_____ _____ _____
2. Use inventories to ensure the firm meets delivery dates and avoids stockouts.	_____ _____ _____
3. Hold inventory in case there is a shutdown due to machine failure.	_____ _____ _____
4. Hold inventory to avoid shutdowns due to defective parts.	_____ _____ _____
5. Hold inventory to take advantage of quantity discounts and hedge against future price increases.	_____ _____

PROBLEM 2

The Till Company manufactures a special blend of tea. The company buys one of the spices used in the tea in 10-pound bags that cost $5 each. The company uses 50,000 of the bags per year, and usage occurs evenly throughout the year.

The average cost to carry a 10-pound bag in inventory per year is $1, and the cost to place an order is $12.

Instructions:

1. Determine the economic order quantity for the spice in terms of 10-pound bags.

2. If the company works 250 days per year, on the average how many bags of spice are used per working day?

3. If the lead time for an order is normally 5 working days, determine the reorder point.

4. If the company normally carries 50 bags as safety stock, determine the reorder point for the spice.

PROBLEM 3

Smith Manufacturing produces lawn mowers. In order to produce the frames for the mowers, special equipment must be set up. The setup cost per frame is $50. The cost of carrying frames in inventory is $4 per frame per year. The company produces 10,000 mowers per year.

Instructions:

1. Compute the number of frames that should be produced per setup in order to minimize total setup and carrying costs.

2. Compute the total setup and carrying costs associated with the economic order quantity.

PROBLEM 4

Craig Corporation produces two types of products, A and B. Product A has a unit contribution margin of $50, and Product B has a unit contribution margin of $100. Product A uses 1 hour of grinding time, and Product B uses 4 hours of grinding time. There are 200 hours of grinding time available per week. This is the only constrained resource.

Instructions:

1. a. Determine the optimal mix.

    b. What is the total contribution margin?

2. Assume that market conditions will allow the sale of only 100 units of each product.

    a. Determine the optimal mix.

    b. What is the total contribution margin?

ANSWERS

KEY TERMS TEST

1. Lead time
2. Ordering costs
3. Safety stock
4. Setup costs
5. reorder point
6. Carrying costs
7. Economic order quantity, EOQ
8. Stockout costs
9. Kanban system
10. production Kanban
11. vendor Kanban
12. withdrawal Kanban
13. Total preventive maintenance
14. Inventory
15. Operating expenses
16. Electronic data interchange, EDI
17. continuous replenishment
18. Throughput
19. constraint
20. binding constraints
21. loose constraints
22. External constraints
23. Internal constraints
24. Drum-Buffer-Rope System
25. time buffer
26. Ropes

CHAPTER QUIZ

1. 1. ordering costs
   2. carrying costs
2. 1. setup costs
   2. carrying costs
3. 1. storage and handling costs
   2. the opportunity cost of funds invested in inventory
   3. insurance and taxes on the inventory
4. ordering costs, carrying costs
5. Rate of usage × Lead time
6. stockouts
7. (Average rate of usage × Lead time) + Safety stock

8. 1. to balance ordering or setup costs and carrying costs
   2. to satisfy customer demand
   3. to avoid shutdowns
      (There are other possible correct answers.)
9. preventive maintenance
10. 1. price
    2. quality
    3. reliability
11. 1. They stipulate prices.
    2. They stipulate quality levels.
    3. They reduce the number of orders placed, thereby reducing ordering costs.

PRACTICE TEST

PROBLEM 1

1. Reduces setup costs and then minimizes inventory carrying costs.
2. Reduces lead time by reducing setup time and uses manufacturing cells to reduce distance between machines.
3. Uses total preventive maintenance to reduce downtime for unexpected repairs.
4. Uses total quality control and strives for zero defects.
5. Uses long-term contracts with a few suppliers to obtain price concessions and a reliable supply.

PROBLEM 2

1. $EOQ = \sqrt{2PD/C}$

   where EOQ = economic order quantity
   P = cost of placing and receiving an order
   D = annual demand in units
   C = annual cost of carrying one unit in stock for one year

   $EOQ = \sqrt{(2)(\$12)(50,000)/\$1}$
   = 1,095 bags

   The economic order quantity is 1,095 bags of spice.

2. Bags used per day = 50,000 bags used per year/250 working days
   = 200 bags per working day

   The Till Company would use an average of 200 bags of spice per working day.

3. Reorder point = Rate of usage × Lead time
                  = 200 bags × 5 working days
                  = 1,000 bags

4. Reorder point = (Average rate of usage × Lead time) + Safety stock
                  = (200 bags × 5 working days) + 50 bags
                  = 1,050 bags

PROBLEM 3

1. $EOQ = \sqrt{(2)(\$50)(10,000) / \$4}$

    $EOQ = 500$

    In order to minimize costs, 500 frames should be produced per setup.

2. Total setup costs = ($50)(10,000/500)
                       = $1,000

    Total carrying costs = ($4)(500/2)
                         = $1,000

    The EOQ results in total setup costs equalling total carrying costs.

PROBLEM 4

1. a. Contribution margin per scarce resource:
        Product A: $50/1 hour = $50 per hour of grinding time
        Product B: $100/4 hours = $25 per hour of grinding time
        Optimal mix: 200 units of Product A

    b. Total contribution margin:
        200 hours grinding time/1 hour per unit of Product A = 200 units of Product A
        200 units × $50 contribution margin per unit = $10,000

2. a. Optimal mix:
        Product A: 100 units
        Product B: 25 units
        200 hours – (100 units × 1 hour) = 100 hours available
        100 hours available/4 hours per unit = 25 units of Product B

    b. Total contribution margin:
        100 units of Product A × $50 = $5,000
        25 units of Product B × $25 = <u>625</u>
                                       <u>$5,625</u>

CHAPTER 13
Budgeting for Planning and Control

CHAPTER REVIEW

DESCRIPTION OF BUDGETING

Budgeting and Planning and Control

❑ **Planning** involves looking ahead and determining what actions should be taken to attain particular goals. Planning is also referred to as **feedforward control**.

❑ **Control** involves looking backwards and comparing actual result to plans. Control is referred to as **feedback control**.

❑ A **budget** is a plan of action expressed in financial terms.

❑ Budgeting is a planning and control tool used by managers.

Planning Tool	Control Tool
Identify objectives.	Compare actual results with budgeted (planned) amounts.
Identify actions needed to achieve objectives.	Corrective action can be taken, if needed.

❑ The steps involved in the planning and control process are as follows:
- Develop a strategic plan. A **strategic plan** identifies strategies for future activities and operations, generally covering at least five years.
- Translate the strategic plan into long-term and short-term objectives.
- From the objectives, develop short-term plans to achieve the objectives.
- Develop budgets based upon the short-term plans.
- Compare actual results with planned (budgeted) amounts.
- Take corrective action, if necessary.

Purposes of Budgeting

❑ Advantages of budgeting include the following:
- Budgets force managers to plan.
- Budgets provide information that can be used to improve decision making.
- Budgets provide standards used for performance evaluation and control.
- Budgets improve communication and coordination.

Dimensions of Budgeting

❑ Two dimensions of budgeting are:
1. how the budget is prepared (the mechanics of budget preparation), and

2. how the budget is used to implement the organization's plans (how individuals within an organization react to a budgetary system).

❏ The success or failure of budgeting depends upon how well management considers the second dimension—the behavioural implications.

BUDGET PREPARATION

❏ Most budgets are for a one-year period, further broken down into quarterly and/or monthly budgets.

❏ A **continuous budget** is a moving twelve-month budget. As a month expires in the budget, an additional month is added so that the company always has a twelve-month plan on hand.

Directing and Coordinating

❏ The **budget committee** provides policy guidelines and budgetary goals, reviews the budget, resolves budgeting disputes, approves the budget and monitors actual progress.

❏ The person responsible for directing and coordinating the budgeting process is the **budget director**. This person works under the direction of the budget committee.

Master Budget

❏ The **master budget** is a comprehensive financial plan consisting of various individual budgets.

	Master Budget	
	Operating Budgets	**Financial Budgets**
Definition:	budgets concerned with income-generating activities	budgets concerned with cash flows and financial position at end of period
Examples:	sales budget production budget direct materials purchases budget direct labour budget overhead budget selling and administrative expenses budget ending finished goods inventory budget cost of goods sold budget budgeted income statement	cash budget budgeted balance sheet budget for capital expenditures

Preparing the Operating Budget

❏ The sales forecast is the basis for the sales budget and is usually the responsibility of the marketing department.

❏ Sales may be forecast using:
- the *bottom-up approach* based on feedback from salespeople
- time-series analysis

- correlation analysis
- econometric modelling

Sales Budget

❏ The **sales budget** is the projection of expected sales in units and dollars.

Production Budget

❏ The **production budget** indicates the number of units of finished product to be produced in order to meet:

- sales needs
- inventory requirements

❏ The production budget is prepared after the sales budget has been finalized.

❏ If production is related to sales of the next period, production needs for a manufacturer can be calculated as follows:

> **Budgeted sales in units**
> **+ Desired ending inventory in units**
> **= Total units needed**
> **− Beginning inventory (units on hand)**
> **= Units to be produced**

❏ In a JIT environment budgeted sales units would equal the budgeted production.

Direct Materials Purchases Budget

❏ The **direct materials purchases budget** is a budget of the expected usage of materials in production and the purchase of the direct materials required.

❏ The steps involved in preparing a direct materials purchases budget are as follows:

1. Determine the amount of direct materials necessary to manufacture the number of units to be produced.
2. Determine the *quantity* of direct materials to be purchased as follows:

> **Quantity of direct materials needed for production**
> **+ Desired ending inventory of direct materials**
> **= Total quantity of direct materials needed**
> **− Beginning inventory of direct materials**
> **= Quantity of direct materials to be purchased**

3. Determine the cost of the direct materials to be purchased by multiplying the quantity of direct materials to be purchased by the expected cost per unit of direct material.

Direct Labour Budget

❏ The **direct labour budget** is a budget of planned expenditures for direct labour. The direct labour budget indicates the rate per hour and the number of hours necessary to meet production requirements.

Overhead Budget

❏ The **overhead budget** shows the expected cost of all manufacturing costs other than direct materials and direct labour.

❑ Budgeted variable overhead costs are based on a budgeted variable overhead rate multiplied by budgeted activity.

❑ Budgeted fixed overhead costs remain unchanged within the relevant activity range.

Selling and Administrative Expenses Budget

❑ The **selling and administrative expenses budget** is a budget of planned expenditures for nonmanufacturing activities, such as sales commissions and office salaries.

❑ Selling and administrative expenses have a variable component that varies with the level of production or sales and a fixed component that remains constant within the relevant range.

Ending Finished Goods Inventory Budget

❑ The **ending finished goods inventory budget** contains:
   1. calculations of the unit cost of the product, and
   2. the cost of the planned ending inventory.

Cost of Goods Sold Budget

❑ The **cost of goods sold budget** calculates the expected costs of the goods to be sold.

❑ Budgeted cost of goods sold is calculated as follows:

> **Direct materials used**
> + **Direct labour used**
> + **Overhead**
> = **Budgeted manufacturing costs**
> + **Beginning finished goods**
> = **Goods available for sale**
> − **Ending finished goods**
> = **Budgeted cost of goods sold**

Budgeted Income Statement

❑ The budgeted income statement calculates net income as follows:

> **Sales**
> − **Cost of goods sold**
> = **Gross margin**
> − **Selling and administrative expenses**
> = **Operating income**
> − **Interest expense**
> = **Income before taxes**
> − **Income taxes**
> = **Net income**

Preparing the Financial Budget

❑ The financial budgets are:
   1. the cash budget
   2. the budgeted balance sheet, and
   3. the budget for capital expenditures.

Cash Budget

☐ The **cash budget** is a summary of planned cash receipts and cash payments. A cash budget might include the following items:

> **Beginning cash balance**
> + **Cash receipts:**
>> Cash collections on accounts receivable
>> Cash sales
> = **Cash available**
> − **Cash payments:**
>> Cash payments on accounts payable (for material purchases)
>> Direct labour wages
>> Variable overhead
>> Fixed overhead[a]
>> Variable selling and administrative expenses[b]
>> Fixed selling and administrative expenses[a]
>> Income taxes
>> Dividends
>> Purchases of property or equipment requiring cash[c]
>>> Total cash payments
> − **Minimum cash balance**
> = **Excess cash (or deficiency)**
> **Investments:**
> − Investment of excess cash
> + Liquidation of investment
> **Financing:**
> + Borrowings to cover deficiency
> − Repayment of loan
> − Interest payments
> = **Ending cash balance**

[a]Amortization is considered a fixed cost; however, it is not a cash outflow. Therefore, amortization would not be included in the cash budget.

[b]Bad debt expense is included in the selling and administrative expenses budget; however, it is not included in the cash budget. Instead, bad debt expense is shown as a reduction in the amount the firm expects to collect on accounts receivable.

[c]Only purchases of property and equipment *requiring cash* would be shown on the cash budget. If the property or equipment purchase was financed by long-term debt, cash repayments of the debt would be shown as a cash payment in the cash budget.

☐ A firm may desire or be required to maintain a minimum cash balance.

☐ Excess cash should be invested to earn a return.

☐ If the firm has a cash deficiency, borrowing will be necessary to maintain the minimum cash balance.

Budgeted Balance Sheet

☐ The final statement to be prepared in the budgeting process is the pro forma balance sheet. Most of the amounts appearing in the pro forma balance sheet can be traced to one of the other budgets or schedules.

☐ See text Exhibit 13–5 for a diagram of the interrelationships of the budgets.

USING BUDGETS FOR PERFORMANCE EVALUATION

Static Budgets versus Flexible Budgets

❑ A **static budget** is a budget for a particular level of activity, such as a sales level of 1,000 units. Static budgets are not very useful for performance reports because the actual activity level may differ from the static budget activity level.

❑ **Flexible budgets** compute expected costs at different levels of activity. A flexible budget is used to compute what costs should have been for the actual activity level. Flexible budgets permit management to prepare performance reports that compare actual and budgeted costs for the actual level of activity. When preparing a flexible budget, variable costs and fixed costs are identified and calculated for the different activity levels.

❑ **Flexible budget variance** is the difference between the actual amount and the flexible budget amount for the actual activity level.

❑ **Flexible budgets** can also be used for revenues as well as costs, thereby creating an evaluation of profit performance.

The Behavioural Dimension of Budgeting

❑ Budgets are often used to judge the performance of managers.

❑ A manager's bonuses, salary increases, and promotions are affected by the manager's ability to achieve budgeted goals; therefore, budgets can have a significant effect on a manager's behaviour.

❑ Whether the effect is positive or negative depends upon how the budgets are administered.

❑ An ideal budgetary system:
  ▪ promotes **goal congruence** (the manager's personal goals are congruent or consistent with the organization's goals), and
  ▪ creates a drive in managers to achieve the goals.

❑ **Dysfunctional behaviour** is behaviour that is in conflict with the organization's goals. If the budget is improperly administered, dysfunctional behaviour may result.

❑ Key features of a budgeting system that encourage positive behaviour are:
  ▪ frequent feedback on performance
  ▪ monetary and nonmonetary incentives
  ▪ participative budgeting
  ▪ realistic standards
  ▪ controllability of costs
  ▪ multiple measures of performance

Frequent Feedback on Performance

❑ Frequent feedback on performance lets managers know how they are doing as the year unfolds. This gives managers the opportunity to take corrective action and adapt to changing conditions.

❑ *Management by exception* uses performance reports that show variances (deviations from planned results). This allows managers to focus only on the areas that need attention.

Monetary and Nonmonetary Incentives

❑ **Incentives** are measures used to induce a manager to work toward achieving the organization's goals.

❑ Negative incentives use fear of punishment to motivate.

❑ Positive incentives use the expectation of a reward to motivate.

❑ **Monetary incentives** are economic rewards, such as salary increases, bonuses, and promotions.

❑ **Nonmonetary incentives** are psychological and social rewards to motivate managers, such as the satisfaction of a job well done, recognition, and increased responsibility.

❑ Monetary awards alone are not sufficient to highly motivate managers.

Participative Budgeting

❑ **Participative budgeting** allows managers to participate in creating the budget used to evaluate their performance.

❑ Participative budgeting can:
- increase goal congruence
- provide nonmonetary incentives (Individuals involved in setting their own standards work harder to achieve them.)
- use the knowledge of individuals who are aware of local conditions

❑ Three potential problems of participative budgeting are:
- standard-setting problems—If the goals are too low and too easily achieved, the manager's performance may drop because there is no challenge. If the goals are set too high, the manager may become frustrated and give up when he or she does not meet the goal. In participative budgeting, the goals should be high but achievable.
- **budgetary slack**—Participatory budgeting creates the opportunity for managers to build slack into the budget (pad the budget). Top management should conduct a careful review of budgets proposed by subordinate managers to eliminate slack.
- **pseudoparticipation**—Top management assumes total control and subordinate manager participation is limited to endorsing the budget.

Realistic Standards

❑ Realistic standards should include allowances for seasonal variations and general economic conditions.

Controllability of Costs

❑ **Controllable costs** are costs a manager can influence.

❑ Managers should not be held accountable for costs they cannot control.

❑ Many firms still include noncontrollable costs in a manager's budget to make the manager aware of these costs. However, if noncontrollable costs are included in a manager's budget, they should be labelled as noncontrollable and separated from controllable costs.

Multiple Measures of Performance

❑ Budgets should not be the only measure used to evaluate manager performance.

❑ If budget performance is overemphasized, **myopic behaviour** can occur where the manager takes actions that improve budgetary performance in the short run but cause long-run harm to the firm.

❏ Since managers of responsibility centres usually spend only three to five years before being promoted or moving to another position, their successors are the ones who must deal with the effects of myopic behaviour.

❏ The best way to prevent myopic behaviour is to measure manager performance based on several measures of performance, such as market share, productivity, quality, and personnel development.

ACTIVITY-BASED BUDGETING

❏ **Activity-based budgeting** identifies activities, demands for activity output, and the cost of resources needed to support the activity output demanded.

❏ Activities consume resources and thus are the causes of costs. Therefore, activity-based budgeting can be used to emphasize cost reduction through:
   ▪ elimination of wasteful activities, and
   ▪ improvement of efficiency of necessary activities.

❏ The principal difference between a traditional, functional-based budget approach and an activity-based approach is a detailed listing of activities and their expected costs within the overhead, selling, and administrative categories.

Activity Flexible Budgeting

❏ **Activity flexible budgeting** allows prediction of what activity costs will be as activity usage (output) changes.

❏ In a functional-based budget, budgeted costs are based on a single unit-based driver (usually direct labour hours). A cost formula is developed for each cost item as a function of direct labour hours. The formula is then used to predict what costs should be at any level of activity.

❏ An alternative is to develop flexible budget formulas using multiple drivers instead of a single driver. For example,
   ▪ Labour and supplies costs might be driven by direct labour hours.
   ▪ Maintenance costs might be driven by machine hours.
   ▪ Setup costs might be driven by the number of setups.

❏ Cost formulas are developed for each activity.

❏ The variable-cost component for each activity corresponds to resources acquired as needed (flexible resources). The fixed-cost component corresponds to resources acquired in advance of usage (committed resources).

❏ This multiple-formula approach permits managers to predict more accurately what costs should be at different levels.

❏ The flexible budget amounts based on multiple cost drivers can be compared to actual costs for control purposes. Variances are calculated as the differences between the flexible budget amount and the actual amount as shown below:

Activity	Actual Cost	Budgeted Cost	Variance (F or U)
Maintenance costs:			
Fixed......................	$15,000	$14,000	$1,000 U
Variable	42,000	45,000	3,000 F
Total...................	$57,000	$59,000	$2,000 F

❑ Breaking variances into fixed and variable components provides more insight into the source of the variation in planned and actual expenditures.

KEY TERMS TEST

Test your recall of the key terms as follows. Try to recall as many key terms as possible without assistance. If you need assistance, refer to the list of key terms at the end of this section.

1. A(n) _____ is a plan of action expressed in financial terms.

2. A(n) _____ _____ is the long-term plan for future activities and operations, usually involving at least five years.

3. The _____ _____ is responsible for setting budgetary policies and goals, reviewing and approving the budget, and resolving any differences that arise in the budgetary process.

4. A moving twelve-month budget where a future month is added as the current month expires is called a(n) _____ _____.

5. The _____ _____ is the portion of the master budget that includes the cash budget, the budgeted balance sheet, and the capital budget.

6. The collection of all area and activity budgets, representing a firm's comprehensive plan of action is the _____ _____.

7. Budgets associated with the income-producing activities of an organization are called _____ _____.

8. The _____ _____ shows the planned expenditures for all indirect manufacturing items.

9. The _____ _____ shows how many units must be produced to meet sales needs and satisfy ending inventory requirements.

10. The _____ _____ describes expected sales in units and dollars for the coming period.

11. The _____ _____ _____ _____ _____ outlines planned expenditures for nonmanufacturing activities.

12. A(n) _____ _____ is a detailed plan that outlines all sources and uses of cash.

13. The _____ _____ _____ shows total direct labour hours needed and the associated cost for the number of units in the production budget.

14. The _____ _____ _____ _____ outlines the expected usage of materials in production and the purchases of the direct materials required.

15. The process of padding the budget by overestimating costs and underestimating revenues is called _____ _____.

16. _____ involves receiving feedback on actual performance, and taking corrective action whenever actual performance deviates significantly from planned performance.

17. _____ _____ are costs that managers have the power to influence.

18. Individual behaviour that is in conflict with the goals of the organization is _____ _____.

19. Claiming that a participative budgetary system exists when, in reality, budgets are dictated from above is called _____.

20. _____ _____ is the alignment of a manager's personal goals with those of the organization.

21. Managerial actions that improve budgetary performance in the short-run at the expense of the long-run welfare of the organization are called _____ _____.

22. _____ are positive or negative measures taken by an organization to induce a manager to exert effort toward achieving the organization's goals.

23. _____ _____ are economic rewards to motivate managers.

24. _____ _____ are psychological and social rewards to motivate managers.

25. _____ _____ allows managers who will be held accountable for budgetary performance to participate in the budget's development.

26. A(n) _____-_____ _____ _____ estimates the demand for each activity's output and assesses the cost of resources required to produce this output.

27. A(n) _____ _____ is a budget for a particular level of activity.

28. A(n) _____ _____ computes budgeted costs for different levels of activity.

KEY TERMS

activity-based budgeting system
budget
budget committee
budgetary slack
cash budget
continuous budget
control
controllable costs
direct labour budget
direct materials purchases budget
dysfunctional behaviour
financial budget
flexible budget
goal congruence

incentives
master budget
monetary incentives
myopic behaviour
nonmonetary incentives
operating budgets
overhead budget
participative budgeting
production budget
pseudoparticipation
sales budget
selling and administrative expenses budget
static budget
strategic plan

↻ **Compare your answers with those at the end of the chapter. Review any key terms missed.**

CHAPTER QUIZ

Circle the single best answer.

1. Budgeting is a means of coordinating the activities of the organization and communicating the goals of the company: (a) true; (b) false

2. Budgeting is important only as a planning tool: (a) true; (b) false

3. The first step in the budgeting process is the preparation of the production budget: (a) true; (b) false

4. Bad debt expense is not included in the cash budget because it is shown as a reduction in the amount collected from accounts receivable: (a) true; (b) false

5. Amortization is included in the cash budget because it is a cash outflow for equipment: (a) true; (b) false

6. On an income statement prepared using a contribution margin approach, costs would be classified by function (production costs versus selling and administrative costs): (a) true; (b) false

7. When participative budgeting is used, the flow of information for budgeting purposes is from the upper to the lower levels of the company: (a) true; (b) false

8. Equipment purchased using long-term debt would be shown in the cash budget as a cash outflow at the time the equipment is purchased: (a) true; (b) false

9. Budgets can affect managers' behaviour because the managers' bonuses, salary increases, and promotions are often affected by the managers' ability to achieve budgeted goals: (a) true; (b) false

Write your answers in the spaces provided.

10. List the order in which the following budgets and schedules are prepared.

Cash budget	**1.**	_____
Direct labour budget	**2.**	_____
Manufacturing overhead budget	**3.**	_____
Production budget	**4.**	_____
Direct materials purchases budget	**5.**	_____
Sales budget	**6.**	_____
Sales forecast	**7.**	_____

11. The production needed for the period would be determined as follows:

       Budgeted sales in units

    + _____

    = Total units needed

    – _____

    = Units to be produced

12. The purchases budget for direct materials for a manufacturer is based upon the quantity of direct materials to be purchased. The quantity of direct materials to be purchased would be determined as follows:

      _____

    + _____

    = Total quantity of direct materials needed

    – _____

    = Quantity of direct materials to be purchased

13. List six key features of a budgetary system that encourage positive behaviour:

    1. _____

    2. _____

    3. _____

    4. _____

    5. _____

    6. _____

Circle the single best answer.

Use the following information to answer Questions 14 through 19:

Projected sales for Silver, Inc., for next year and beginning and ending inventory data are as follows:

Sales...	40,000 units
Unit price...	$20
Beginning inventory.................................	20,000 units
Targeted ending inventory.......................	10,000 units

Each unit requires 5 pounds of material which costs $3.00 per pound. The beginning inventory of raw materials is 5,000 pounds. The company wants to have 3,000 pounds of material in inventory at the end of the year. Each unit produced requires 2 hours of direct labour time, which is billed at $8 per hour.

14. Budgeted sales would be: (a) $580,000; (b) $600,000; (c) $800,000; (d) $840,000

15. According to the production budget, how many units should be produced? (a) 30,000; (b) 42,000; (c) 46,000; (d) 50,000

16. Pounds of material to be purchased would be: (a) 142,000; (b) 148,000; (c) 150,000; (d) 152,000

17. The budgeted total purchase cost of direct materials would be: (a) $456,000; (b) $450,000; (c) $444,000; (d) $426,000

18. The budgeted number of total direct labour hours needed would be: (a) 30,000; (b) 40,000; (c) 46,000; (d) 60,000

19. The budgeted total direct labour cost would be: (a) $320,000; (b) $442,000; (c) $480,000; (d) $496,000

♉ Compare your answers with those at the end of the chapter. Review any questions missed.

PRACTICE TEST

NOTE: The following problems are interrelated.

PROBLEM 1

The Baumberger Company manufactures oak bookcases that sell for $400 each. Budgeted sales for the first four months of the year are as follows:

Month	Budgeted Sales (Units)
January	1,000
February	1,500
March	2,500
April	2,000

Instructions:

Prepare a sales budget in dollars for each month and in total for the first quarter of the year.

	January	February	March	Total

PROBLEM 2

Each bookcase requires 20 square feet of oak at a cost of $10 per square foot. The company wants to maintain an inventory of bookcases equal to 10% of the following month's sales. Inventory on January 1 consisted of 80 bookcases.

Instructions:

1. Prepare a production budget in units for each month and in total for the first quarter.

	January	February	March	Total

2. The company wants to maintain an inventory of oak equal to 20% of the next month's requirements. Materials inventory on January 1 consisted of 11,000 square feet of oak. The company estimates an inventory of oak on hand at the end of March of approximately 8,000 square feet.

Prepare a purchases budget in dollars for direct materials for each month and in total for the first quarter.

	January	February	March	Total

PROBLEM 3

Each bookcase requires 5 hours of direct labour at a cost of $8.00 per hour. Variable manufacturing overhead is budgeted at $2 per direct labour hour.

Monthly fixed overhead consists of the following:

Supervisors' salaries...	$ 6,000
Insurance...	2,000
Amortization on production equipment.............	500
Amortization on production facility	10,000
Total..	$18,500

Instructions:

1. Prepare a direct labour budget for each month and in total for the first quarter.

	January	February	March	Total

2. Prepare a manufacturing overhead budget for each month and in total for the first quarter.

	January	February	March	Total

PROBLEM 4

The company expects 60% of the sales each month will be collected in that month, with 35% collected in the following month. Five percent of all sales are uncollectible and written off in the following month.

The accounts receivable balance at the beginning of the year is $200,000, which is 40% of last year's December sales of $500,000.

Instructions:

Prepare a schedule of cash collections on accounts receivable for each month and in total for the first quarter.

	January	February	March	Total

PROBLEM 5

The company normally pays for 70% of its purchases in the month of purchase. The remaining 30% is paid in the following month.

Accounts payable at the beginning of the year is $54,000, which is 30% of December purchases of $180,000.

Instructions:

Prepare a schedule of cash payments on accounts payable for each month and in total for the first quarter.

	January	February	March	Total

PROBLEM 6

Use the information from the previous problems. In addition, assume variable selling costs equal 5% of sales and are paid in the month following the sale.

Fixed selling, general, and administrative costs are $50,000 and, except for $10,000 of amortization, are paid in the month incurred. Estimated tax payments equal to 40% of estimated income for the quarter are made at the end of each quarter.

Instructions:

Prepare a pro forma income statement for each month and in total for the first quarter.

	January	February	March	Total

PROBLEM 7

Use the information from the previous problems and assume the company attempts to maintain a cash balance of $100,000 at all times. Any excess is invested in marketable securities of $10,000 denominations earning an 8% return.

Any deficiencies are covered by borrowing from a local bank at 10% interest.

The cash balance at the beginning of the year is $105,000.

Instructions:

Prepare a cash budget for each month and in total for the first quarter.

	January	February	March	Total

PROBLEM 8

Barth Company produces two types of herbal remedies: Formula X and Formula Z.

The product is sold in cases of 12 bottles. The company expects to produce and sell 100,000 cases of each product during the coming year. Formula X requires 1 direct labour hour per case, and Formula Z requires 1.2 direct labour hours per case.

The following variable and fixed cost estimates have been developed for four overhead items used in producing the products:

Overhead Item	Fixed Cost	Variable Rate per DLH
Maintenance..........................	$ 8,000	$0.20
Utilities		0.10
Indirect labour	25,000	1.00
Rent	12,000	

Instructions:

1. Calculate the expected activity level in direct labour hours if the expected activity level is 100,000 cases per product.

2. Prepare an overhead budget for the expected activity level of 100,000 cases for each product.

Barth Company
Overhead Budget
For the Year 2004

	Formula	Budgeted Costs at Activity Level of 100,000 Cases Each or _____ DLHs	
Variable costs:			
Maintenance...........................	$0.20	$_____	
Utilities..................................	_____	_____	
Indirect labour........................	_____	_____	
Total variable costs			$_____
Fixed costs:			
Maintenance...........................		$_____	
Utilities..................................		_____	
Rent		_____	
Total fixed costs		_____	
Total overhead costs.................			$_____

PROBLEM 8 *(Continued)*

3. Given the recent increase in demand for herbal remedies, the president of the company asks you to prepare an overhead budget for the production budget that is 20% higher than expected activity level of 100,000 cases per product.

Barth Company
Overhead Budget
For the Year 2004

	Formula	Budgeted Costs at Activity Level of _____ Cases Each or ____ DLHs	
Variable costs:			
Maintenance	$_____	$_____	
Utilities	_____	_____	
Indirect labour........................	_____	_____	
Total variable costs.................			$_____
Fixed costs:			
Maintenance		$_____	
Utilities		_____	
Rent...		_____	
Total fixed costs.......................			_____
Total overhead costs			$_____

PROBLEM 9

In order to improve the accuracy of budget estimates, Hampton Corporation has instituted the use of an activity-based budgeting system. The number of setups drives the cost of activities of inspections and setups. Cost estimates for inspections and setups are as follows:

	Fixed	Variable
Inspections	$40,000	$1,050
Setups	2,000	900

Instructions:

1. Calculate the budgeted cost of inspections and setups if the activity level is 50 setups.

	Fixed	Variable	Budgeted Cost (50 Setups)
Inspections cost	$40,000	$1,050	$_____
Setups cost	2,000	900	$_____

2. Calculate the budgeted cost of inspection and setups if the activity level is 60 setups.

	Fixed	Variable	Budgeted Cost (60 Setups)
Inspections cost	$40,000	$1,050	$_____
Setups cost	2,000	900	$_____

3. Calculate variable and fixed budget variances for inspection and setup costs if the activity level is 60 setups and actual costs are as follows:

	Actual Fixed Costs	Actual Variable Costs
Inspections cost	$41,000	$60,000
Setups cost	1,800	55,500

ANSWERS

KEY TERMS TEST

1. budget
2. strategic plan
3. budget committee
4. continuous budget
5. financial budget
6. master budget
7. operating budgets
8. overhead budget
9. production budget
10. sales budget
11. selling and administrative expenses budget
12. cash budget
13. direct labour budget
14. direct materials purchases budget

15. budgetary slack
16. Control
17. Controllable costs
18. dysfunctional behaviour
19. pseudoparticipation
20. Goal congruence
21. myopic behaviour
22. Incentives
23. Monetary incentives
24. Nonmonetary incentives
25. Participative budgeting
26. activity-based budgeting system
27. static budget
28. flexible budget

CHAPTER QUIZ

1. a True
2. b False. Budgeting is also an important means of controlling operations by comparing actual results with budgeted amounts.
3. b False. The first step in the budgeting process is preparation of the sales forecast.
4. a True
5. b False. Amortization is not a cash outflow; therefore, it is not included in the cash budget.
6. b False. On an income statement prepared using a contribution margin approach, costs would be classified by behaviour (fixed versus variable costs).
7. b False. When participatory budgeting is used, the flow of information is from the lower to the upper levels of the company.
8. b False. Equipment purchased using long-term debt would result in a cash outflow as the debt is repaid.
9. a True
10. 1. Sales forecast
    2. Sales budget
    3. Production budget

4. Direct materials purchases budget
5. Direct labour budget
6. Manufacturing overhead budget
7. Cash budget
11. Desired level of ending inventory
    Beginning inventory
12. Quantity of direct material needed for production
    Ending inventory of direct material
    Beginning inventory of direct material
13. 1. frequent feedback on performance
    2. monetary and nonmonetary incentives
    3. participative budgeting
    4. realistic standards
    5. controllability of costs
    6. multiple measures of performance
14. c $(40,000 \times \$20) = \$800,000$
15. a $40,000 + 10,000 - 20,000 = 30,000$ units
16. b $(30,000 \times 5 \text{ pounds}) + 3,000 \text{ pounds} - 5,000 \text{ pounds} = 148,000 \text{ pounds}$
17. c $148,000 \text{ pounds} \times \$3/\text{pound} = \$444,000$
18. d $30,000 \text{ units} \times 2 \text{ hours} = 60,000 \text{ hours}$
19. c $60,000 \text{ hours} \times \$8 = \$480,000$

PRACTICE TEST

PROBLEM 1

Sales Budget (in dollars)

	January	February	March	Total
Budgeted sales in units	1,000	1,500	2,500	5,000
Multiplied by: Selling price	× $400	× $400	× $400	× $400
Budgeted sales.......................................	$400,000	$600,000	$1,000,000	$2,000,000

PROBLEM 2

1.

Production Budget (in units)

	January	February	March	Total
Budgeted sales in units	1,000	1,500	2,500	5,000
Add: Desired ending inventory				
(10% of next month's sales)................	150	250	200*	200
Total units needed..	1,150	1,750	2,700	5,200
Less: Beginning inventory	80	150	250	80
Units to be produced	1,070	1,600	2,450	5,120

*2,000 units budgeted sales for April multiplied by 10%

2.

Purchases Budget (in dollars)

	January	February	March	Total
Units to be produced	1,070	1,600	2,450	5,120
Multiplied by: Sq. ft. of oak per unit	× 20	× 20	× 20	× 20
Sq. ft. of material needed for production	21,400	32,000	49,000	102,400
Add: Desired ending inventory				
(20% of next month's needs)	6,400	9,800	8,000	8,000
Total sq. ft. needed......................................	27,800	41,800	57,000	110,400
Less: Beginning inventory	11,000	6,400	9,800	11,000
Sq. ft. to be purchased	16,800	35,400	47,200	99,400
Multiplied by: Cost per sq. ft.	× $10	× $10	× $10	× $10
Cost of raw material purchases....................	$168,000	$354,000	$472,000	$994,000

PROBLEM 3

1.

Direct Labour Budget

	January	February	March	Total
Units to be produced	1,070	1,600	2,450	5,120
Multiplied by: Direct labour hours per unit	× 5	× 5	× 5	× 5
Direct labour hours needed	5,350	8,000	12,250	25,600
Multiplied by: Labour cost per hour	× $8	× $8	× $8	× $8
Total direct labour cost.................................	$42,800	$64,000	$98,000	$204,800

2.

Manufacturing Overhead Budget (in dollars)

	January	February	March	Total
Budgeted direct labour hours	5,350	8,000	12,250	25,600
Multiplied by: Variable overhead rate	× $2	× $2	× $2	× $2
Budgeted variable overhead	$10,700	$16,000	$24,500	$ 51,200
Budgeted fixed overhead:				
Supervisors' salaries	$ 6,000	$ 6,000	$ 6,000	$ 18,000
Insurance...	2,000	2,000	2,000	6,000
Amortization—equipment	500	500	500	1,500
Amortization—facility...............................	10,000	10,000	10,000	30,000
Total fixed overhead......................................	$18,500	$18,500	$18,500	$ 55,500
Total budgeted overhead	$29,200	$34,500	$43,000	$106,700

PROBLEM 4

Cash Collections on Accounts Receivable

	January	February	March	Total
Accounts receivable, beginning of month......	$ 200,000[a]	$ 160,000	$ 240,000	$ 200,000
Add: Sales	400,000	600,000	1,000,000	2,000,000
Total amount due from customers	$ 600,000	$ 760,000	$1,240,000	$ 2,200,000
Deduct cash collections:				
60% of sales for current month	$(240,000)	$(360,000)	$ (600,000)	$(1,200,000)
35% of sales for previous month...............	(175,000)[b]	(140,000)	(210,000)	(525,000)
Deduct writeoffs:				
5% of previous month's sales	(25,000)	(20,000)	(30,000)	(75,000)
Accounts receivable, end of month...............	$ 160,000	$ 240,000	$ 400,000	$ 400,000

[a]40% of December sales of $500,000
[b]35% of December sales of $500,000

PROBLEM 5

Cash Payments on Accounts Payable

	January	February	March	Total
Accounts payable, beginning of month..........	$ 54,000[a]	$ 50,400	$106,200	$ 54,000
Add: Purchases	168,000	354,000	472,000	994,000
Total amount owed	$222,000	$404,400	$578,200	$1,048,000
Deduct cash payments:				
70% of purchases for current month.........	$117,600	$247,800	$330,400	$ 695,800
30% of purchases for previous month	54,000	50,400	106,200	210,600
Total cash payments................................	$171,600	$298,200	$436,600	$ 906,400
Accounts payable, end of month	$ 50,400	$106,200	$141,600	$ 141,600

[a]30% of December purchases of $180,000

PROBLEM 6

Pro Forma Statements of Income

	January 1,000 Units	February 1,500 Units	March 2,500 Units	Total 5,000 Units
Sales revenue...	$400,000[a]	$600,000	$1,000,000	$2,000,000
Variable expenses:				
Production expenses[a]	$250,000	$375,000	$ 625,000	$1,250,000
S & A expenses (5% of sales)	20,000	30,000	50,000	100,000
Bad debt expenses (5% of sales)	20,000	30,000	50,000	100,000
Total variable expenses............................	$290,000	$435,000	$ 725,000	$1,450,000
Contribution margin	$110,000	$165,000	$ 275,000	$ 550,000
Fixed expenses:				
Fixed mfr. overhead...................................	$ 18,500	$ 18,500	$ 18,500	$ 55,500
Fixed S & A expenses................................	50,000	50,000	50,000	150,000
Total fixed expenses.................................	$ 68,500	$ 68,500	$ 68,500	$ 205,500
Operating income	$ 41,500	$ 96,500	$ 206,500	$ 344,500
Interest income	–0–	1,000[b]	1,417[c]	2,417
Net income before tax....................................	$ 41,500	$ 97,500	$ 207,917	$ 346,917
Income tax expense.......................................	16,600	39,000	83,167	138,767
Net income...	$ 24,900	$ 58,500	$ 124,750	$ 208,150

[a]Consists of the following costs per unit:

Direct materials (20 sq. ft. × $10 per sq. ft.)........................	$200
Direct labour (5 hours per unit × $8 per hour)......................	40
Variable overhead (5 hours per unit × $2 per hour)	10
Total variable production costs per unit...........................	$250

[b]$120,000 invested at the end of January × 10% return × 1/12 = $1,000
[c]$120,000 + $50,000 invested at the end of February × 10% return × 1/12 = $1,417

PROBLEM 7

Cash Budget

	January	February	March	Total
Cash balance, beginning of month................	$105,000	$101,900	$105,700	$ 105,000
Add: Cash collected on accounts receivable.	415,000	500,000	810,000	1,725,000
Cash available...	$520,000	$601,900	$915,700	$1,830,000
Deduct cash payments:				
Accounts payable	$171,600	$298,200	$436,600	$906,400
Direct labour	42,800	64,000	98,000	204,800
Variable mfr. overhead	10,700	16,000	24,500	51,200
Fixed mfr. overhead[a]	8,000	8,000	8,000	24,000
Variable S & A[b]	25,000	20,000	30,000	75,000
Fixed S & A[b]	40,000	40,000	40,000	120,000
Income taxes[c]	–0–	–0–	138,767	138,767
Total cash payments	$298,100	$446,200	$775,867	$1,520,167
Excess cash	$221,900	$155,700	$139,833	$ 309,833
Investing activities:				
Investment in marketable securities	120,000	50,000	30,000	200,000
Ending cash balance.....................................	$101,900	$105,700	$109,833	$ 109,833

[a]Excludes $10,500 of amortization each month (non-cash expense)
[b]5% of previous month's sales
[c]The amount of taxes to be paid in March is determined from the income statement for the quarter prepared in Problem 6.

PROBLEM 8

1. If the expected activity level is 100,000 cases per product, expected activity in direct labour hours is calculated as follows:

   Product X: 100,000 cases × 1.0 DLH = 100,000 DLH
   Product Z: 100,000 cases × 1.2 DLH = 120,000 DLH
   Total direct labour hours   220,000 DLH

2. The overhead budget for the expected activity level of 100,000 cases for each product:

Barth Company
Overhead Budget
For the Year 2004

	Formula	Budgeted Costs at Activity Level of 100,000 Cases Each or 220,000 DLHs	
Variable costs:			
Maintenance	$0.20	$ 44,000	
Utilities	0.10	22,000	
Indirect labour..............................	1.00	220,000	
Total variable costs......................			$286,000
Fixed costs:			
Maintenance		$ 8,000	
Utilities		25,000	
Rent		12,000	
Total fixed costs...........................			45,000
Total overhead costs			$331,000

3. If production increases by 20%, then the number of cases produced would equal 120,000 cases for each product (100,000 × 120%).

If the expected activity level is 120,000 cases per product, expected activity in direct labour hours is calculated as follows:

Product X: 120,000 cases × 1.0 DLH = 120,000 DLH
Product Z: 120,000 cases × 1.2 DLH = 144,000 DLH
Total direct labour hours   264,000 DLH

Barth Company
Overhead Budget
For the Year 2004

	Formula	Budgeted Costs at Activity Level of 120,000 Cases Each or 264,000 DLHs	
Variable costs:			
Maintenance	$0.20	$ 52,800	
Utilities	0.10	26,400	
Indirect labour	1.00	264,000	
Total variable costs			$343,200
Fixed costs:			
Maintenance		$ 8,000	
Utilities		25,000	
Rent		12,000	
Total fixed costs			45,000
Total overhead costs			$388,200

PROBLEM 9

1. Budgeted cost of inspections and setups if the activity level is 50 setups:

	Fixed	Variable	Budgeted Cost (50 Setups)
Inspections	$40,000	$1,050	$92,500[a]
Setups	2,000	900	47,000[b]

[a]$40,000 + ($1,050 × 50 setups) = $92,500
[b]$2,000 + ($900 × 50 setups) = $47,000

2. Budgeted cost of inspection and setups if the activity level is 60 setups:

	Fixed	Variable	Budgeted Cost (60 Setups)
Inspections	$40,000	$1,050	$103,000[a]
Setups	2,000	900	56,000[b]

[a]$40,000 + ($1,050 × 60 setups) = $103,000
[b]$2,000 + ($900 × 60 setups) = $56,000

3. Variable and fixed budget variances for inspection and setup costs would be calculated as follows:

Activity	Actual Cost	Budgeted Cost	Variance	
Inspections:				
Fixed	$ 41,000	$ 40,000	$1,000	U
Variable	60,000	63,000	3,000	F
Total	$101,000	$103,000	$2,000	F
Setups:				
Fixed	$ 1,800	$ 2,000	$ 200	F
Variable	55,500	54,000	1,500	U
Total	$57,300	$56,000	$1,300	

CHAPTER 14
Standard Costing: A Managerial Control Tool

CHAPTER REVIEW

UNIT STANDARDS

❐ A *standard cost* is the expected or budgeted cost of materials, labour, and manufacturing overhead required to produce one unit of product.

❐ A **standard cost sheet** is a formal list of the standard costs for materials, labour, and manufacturing overhead to produce one unit of product. The costs are summed to arrive at the total standard cost for one unit of product.

❐ A **quantity standard** (also referred to as usage or efficiency standard) is the quantity of input allowed per unit of output.

❐ A **price standard** is the price that should be paid per unit of input.

How Standards Are Developed

❐ Standards can be based on:
  ▪ historical experience
  ▪ engineering studies, and
  ▪ input from operating personnel.

Types of Standards

❐ **Ideal standards** are standards that reflect perfect operating efficiency. Ideal standards are virtually unattainable and can result in low employee morale and a decline in performance.

❐ **Currently attainable standards** are demanding but attainable under efficient operating conditions. Such standards allow for normal machine downtime and employee rest periods.

❐ Challenging but attainable standards tend to result in more behavioural benefits than ideal standards. If standards are too tight and never achievable, workers become frustrated and performance levels decline.

Why Standard Cost Systems Are Adopted

❐ Two reasons for adopting a standard cost system are:
  ▪ *To improve planning and control.* A standard cost system compares actual amounts with standard amounts to determine variances from the standard. The variance is broken into its two components; price and quantity (usage or efficiency). The use of a standard cost system for operational control in an advanced manufacturing environment can produce dysfunctional behaviour. However, standards in the advanced manufacturing environment are still useful for planning, such as developing bids.
  ▪ *To facilitate product costing.* Standard costing uses standard costs for direct materials, direct labour, and overhead. Standard cost systems provide readily available unit cost information that can be used for pricing decisions.

❏ Costs under the three product cost assignment approaches are summarized below:

PRODUCT COSTING SYSTEM	MANUFACTURING COSTS		
	Direct Materials	Direct Labour	Overhead
Actual costing system	Actual	Actual	Actual
Normal costing system	Actual	Actual	Budgeted
Standard costing system	Standard	Standard	Standard

STANDARD PRODUCT COSTS

❏ The standard cost sheet for one unit of product might appear as follows:

STANDARD COST SHEET
Production Costs for One Unit of Product

Direct materials
(Standard quantity of materials × Standard price for materials)

Direct labour
(Standard direct labour hours × Standard direct labour rate)

Variable manufacturing overhead
(Standard direct labour hours × Standard variable labour rate)

Fixed manufacturing overhead
(Standard direct labour hours × Standard fixed overhead rate)

Total standard cost per unit of product

❏ The standard cost for direct materials is calculated as follows:

Standard cost for direct materials =
Standard quantity of materials × Standard price for the materials

❏ **Standard quantity of materials allowed** (SQ) is calculated:

SQ = Unit quantity of material standard × Actual output

❏ The standard direct labour cost for a unit of product would be calculated as follows:

Standard direct labour cost =
Standard quantity of direct labour × Standard rate per direct labour hour

❏ **Standard hours allowed** (SH) is calculated:

SH = Unit labour hour standard × Actual output

VARIANCE ANALYSIS: GENERAL DESCRIPTION

Price and Efficiency Variances

❏ The **total budget variance** is the difference between actual cost of inputs and the standard (or planned) cost of inputs based on a flexible budget (i.e., based on actual output).

❑ There are two variances for variable production costs:
  ▪ price or rate variances
  ▪ usage or efficiency variances

❑ **Price (rate) variances** focus on the difference between actual costs of inputs and what the inputs should have cost (standard prices).

❑ **Usage (efficiency) variances** focus on the difference between the actual quantity used and the standard quantity allowed for actual units produced.

❑ The general model for calculating variable cost variances appears below:

Actual quantity of input at actual price $(AP \times AQ)$	Actual quantity of input at standard price $(SP \times AQ)$	Standard quantity of input at standard price $(SP \times SQ)$

$$|\underline{\qquad (AP - SP)AQ \qquad}|\underline{\qquad (AQ - SQ)SP \qquad}|$$

Price or rate variance	Usage or efficiency variance

Total variance = $(AP \times AQ) - (SP \times SQ)$

❑ If the actual price or quantity is less than the standard, the variance is considered **favourable**. Be cautious here: favourable does not imply good performance—it only denotes direction.

❑ If the actual price or quantity exceeds the standard, the variance is considered **unfavourable**. Again, be cautious here: unfavourable does not imply bad performance—it only means actual was more than standard.

The Decision to Investigate

❑ Variances indicate that actual performance is not going according to plan.

❑ Variances do not indicate the cause of the variance or responsibility.

❑ Usually the cause of a variance can be determined only by an investigation. For example, an unfavourable materials quantity variance may not be the fault of the production supervisor. Instead, it may be the result of the purchasing agent buying inferior-quality material.

❑ As a general principle, variances should be investigated if the anticipated benefits of the investigation exceed the expected costs of investigating.

❑ Most firms adopt the general guideline of investigating variances only if they fall outside an acceptable range.

Lower control limit	Upper control limit

|⎿_____⏌|

Acceptable range

❒ The **control limits** of the acceptable range are calculated as follows:

Upper control limit = Standard + Allowable deviation
Lower control limit = Standard – Allowable deviation

❒ The control limits are often expressed as:
- a specified amount, and/or
- a specified percentage of the variance.

❒ For example, management may investigate any variance that exceeds $1,000 or 5% of the standard amount to which the variance relates.

❒ Variance investigation should occur at an appropriate level. A total budget variance may be insignificant but this could be the result of large, significant price and usage variances offsetting each other.

VARIANCE ANALYSIS: MATERIALS AND LABOUR

Direct Materials Variances

Materials Price Variance

❒ The **materials price variance (MPV)** for materials is calculated as follows:

Actual quantity purchased at actual price $(AP \times AQ)$	Actual quantity purchased at standard price $(SP \times AQ)$

$$(AP - SP)AQ$$

Direct materials price variance

❒ The materials price variance can be computed at one of two points:
1. When the raw materials are issued for use in production
2. When the raw materials are purchased

❒ Variances should be calculated at the earliest point possible so management can take any necessary corrective action. Thus, the price variance for materials should be calculated at the time of purchase.

❒ Responsibility for the materials price variance is usually assigned to the purchasing agent.

❒ Using the materials price variance to evaluate performance can produce undesirable behaviour. For example, if the purchasing agent feels pressured to produce favourable price variances:
- materials of lower quality might be purchased (perhaps resulting in unfavourable usage variances), or
- in order to take advantage of quantity discounts, large amounts of inventory might be purchased (eliminating some of the benefits of JIT).

❒ Variance analysis involves the following process:
- Decide whether the variance is significant.
- If insignificant, no further investigation is needed.
- If significant, investigate the cause of the variance and take corrective action if necessary.

Direct Materials Usage Variance

❏ The **materials usage variance (*MUV*)** is calculated as follows:

Actual quantity used at standard price (*SP* × *AQ*)		Standard quantity allowed at standard price (*SP* × *SQ*)
	(*AQ* – *SQ*)*SP*	
	Direct materials usage variance	

❏ The production manager is usually responsible for materials usage because the production manager can minimize scrap, waste, and rework in order to meet the standard.

❏ Using the usage variance to evaluate performance can lead to undesirable behaviour. For example, a production manager who is pressured to produce a favourable materials usage variance might allow defective units to be transferred to finished goods. Although this avoids the problem of wasted materials (which increases actual quantity of material used), it creates customer-relations problems.

❏ The materials usage variance is calculated at the time materials are issued or used in the manufacturing process.

Direct Labour Variances

Labour Rate Variance

❏ The **labour rate variance (*LRV*)** is calculated as follows:

Actual labour hours at actual rate (*AR* × *AH*)		Actual labour hours at standard rate (*SR* × *AH*)
	(*AR* – *SR*)*AH*	
	Direct labour rate variance	

❏ Labour rates are largely determined by external factors, such as labour markets and union contracts.

❏ When labour rate variances occur, it is usually due to:
  - using the *average* wage rate as the standard rate, or
  - using more skilled and higher paid labourers for less skilled tasks.

❏ Responsibility for the labour rate variance is often assigned to the individual, such as the production manager, who decides how labour will be used.

Labour Efficiency Variance

❏ The **labour efficiency variance (*LEV*)** is calculated as follows:

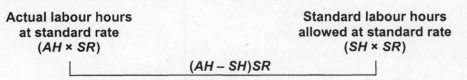

Actual labour hours at standard rate (*AH* × *SR*)		Standard labour hours allowed at standard rate (*SH* × *SR*)
	(*AH* – *SH*)*SR*	
	Direct labour efficiency variance	

❏ Usually production managers are responsible for the direct labour efficiency variance; however, once the cause of the variance is discovered, responsibility may be assigned elsewhere.

❐ The total variance for direct labour would be the sum of the rate variance and the efficiency variance. The total variance can also be calculated as follows:

Total direct labour variance =
(Actual quantity × Actual price) – (Standard quantity × Standard price)

VARIANCE ANALYSIS: OVERHEAD COSTS

❐ One method of analyzing overhead variances is as follows:

1. Divide manufacturing overhead costs into two categories:
   - variable costs
   - fixed costs

2. Determine separate overhead rates for variable and fixed overhead because the two costs react differently to changes in activity.

   The variable overhead rate is determined by analyzing how variable overhead costs react to changes in activity. For example, if a firm determines that $10 of variable manufacturing overhead is incurred for each direct labour hour worked, then the standard variable overhead rate (*SVOR*) would be $10 per direct labour hour.

   The standard fixed overhead rate (*SFOR*) is calculated as follows:

$$\text{Standard fixed overhead rate} = \frac{\textbf{Budgeted fixed overhead costs}}{\textbf{Standard hours allowed for denominator volume}}$$

   Denominator volume is the expected production volume (i.e., the budgeted volume) selected at the beginning of the year when the standard fixed overhead rate is established. The standard fixed overhead rate is determined on an annual basis.

3. Apply manufacturing overhead using the standard variable overhead rate (*SVOR*) and the standard fixed overhead rate (*SFOR*).

   Manufacturing overhead in a standard costing system is applied based on *the standard hours allowed for production achieved* rather than on the actual hours worked.

   The Manufacturing Overhead Control account would include the following items:

Manufacturing Overhead Control

Actual overhead costs	Applied overhead costs (based on standard hours allowed for production)

4. Calculate the two variable overhead variances:
   - variable overhead spending variance
   - variable overhead efficiency variance
5. Calculate the two fixed overhead variances:
   - fixed overhead spending variance
   - fixed overhead volume variance

Variable Overhead Variances
Variable Overhead Spending Variance

❐ The variable overhead spending variance indicates if a firm is paying the budgeted price for the variable manufacturing overhead used.

❏ The **variable overhead spending variance** is calculated as follows:

Actual variable overhead rate × Actual hours   **Standard variable overhead rate × Actual hours**
        (AVOR × AH)   **(SVOR × AH)**

$$(AVOR - SVOR)AH$$

Variable overhead spending variance

❏ Price changes of variable overhead items are essentially beyond the control of supervisors; therefore, the variable overhead spending variance is usually assigned to the production departments.

❏ In order to determine how well costs of individual variable overhead items were controlled, a line-by-line analysis of each variable overhead item is essential.

Variable Overhead Efficiency Variance

❏ The variable overhead efficiency variance results from the efficient or inefficient use of the base used to apply variable manufacturing overhead.

❏ For example, if variable manufacturing overhead is applied using direct labour hours as the base and there is an unfavourable labour efficiency variance, there will also be an unfavourable variable overhead efficiency variance.

❏ The **variable overhead efficiency variance** is calculated as follows:

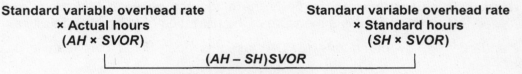

Standard variable overhead rate   **Standard variable overhead rate**
     × Actual hours   **× Standard hours**
      (AH × SVOR)   **(SH × SVOR)**

$$(AH - SH)SVOR$$

Variable overhead efficiency variance

❏ If variable overhead costs change in proportion to changes in the base, such as direct labour hours, then responsibility for the variable overhead efficiency variance should be assigned to the production manager because the production manager has responsibility for the use of direct labour.

Total Variable Overhead Variance

❏ The total variable overhead variance is calculated as follows:

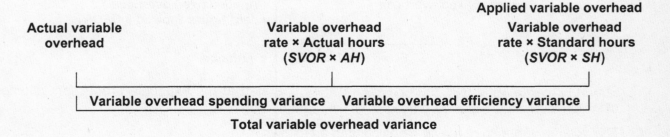

                                                           Applied variable overhead
   Actual variable   **Variable overhead**   **Variable overhead**
      overhead   **rate × Actual hours**   **rate × Standard hours**
                              (SVOR × AH)   **(SVOR × SH)**

   Variable overhead spending variance   **Variable overhead efficiency variance**

Total variable overhead variance

Fixed Overhead Variances

❏ Variance analysis for fixed manufacturing overhead differs from variance analysis for variable manufacturing costs because fixed costs react differently to changes in activity.

❏ Two variances calculated for fixed manufacturing overhead are:
1. the fixed overhead spending or budget variance, and
2. the fixed overhead volume variance.

Fixed Overhead Spending Variance

❏ The **fixed overhead spending variance** compares actual fixed overhead to the fixed overhead budgeted for the production level achieved.

❏ The fixed overhead spending variance is calculated as follows:

Actual fixed overhead   **Budgeted fixed overhead**

Fixed overhead spending variance

❏ Because many fixed overhead items are not subject to change in the short run, fixed overhead costs are often beyond the immediate control of management.

❏ In addition, because fixed overhead consists of a number of items, such as salaries, amortization, property taxes, and insurance, a line-by-line comparison of actual costs and budgeted costs provides more information about the causes of budget variances.

Fixed Overhead Volume Variance

❏ The **fixed overhead volume variance** is the difference between *budgeted* fixed overhead and *applied* fixed overhead. It is a measure of the utilization of production facilities.

❏ The *standard fixed overhead rate (SFOR)* used to apply fixed overhead is calculated as follows:

$$\text{Standard fixed overhead rate} = \frac{\text{Budgeted fixed overhead costs}}{\text{Standard hours allowed for expected capacity}}$$

❏ The expected production volume is selected at the beginning of the year when the standard fixed overhead rate is established.

❏ The output used to calculate the fixed overhead rate can be viewed as the activity capacity acquired. Actual output can be viewed as the activity capacity used.

❏ The fixed overhead volume variance is calculated as follows:

Budgeted fixed overhead   **Applied fixed overhead**
                                     (Standard hours allowed × *SFOR*)

Fixed overhead volume variance

❏ The volume variance tells management if they operated at the expected production volume used to calculate the standard fixed overhead rate.

❏ The volume variance can also be calculated as follows:

Fixed overhead volume variance =
        ***SFOR* × [Expected activity used in *SFOR* – Standard allowed for actual production]**

❏ A volume variance occurs when *actual* production differs from the *expected* production volume used to calculate the standard fixed overhead rate.

❏ There will be no volume variance if actual output equals expected output.

❐ If actual production exceeds expected production, the volume variance is labelled favourable. If actual production is less than expected, the volume variance is labelled unfavourable.

❐ When a volume variance occurs, it might indicate that:

- management did not use the correct expected production level when calculating the standard fixed overhead rate, or

- if the expected output is correct and the volume variance is unfavourable, production facilities were not fully utilized.

Total Fixed Overhead Variance

❐ The total fixed overhead variance is the sum of the fixed overhead spending and volume variances and is calculated as follows:

Actual fixed overhead	Budgeted fixed overhead	Applied fixed overhead ($SH \times SFOR$)
Fixed overhead spending variance	Fixed overhead volume variance	
Total fixed overhead variance		

SUMMARY

❐ The following summarizes the variances:

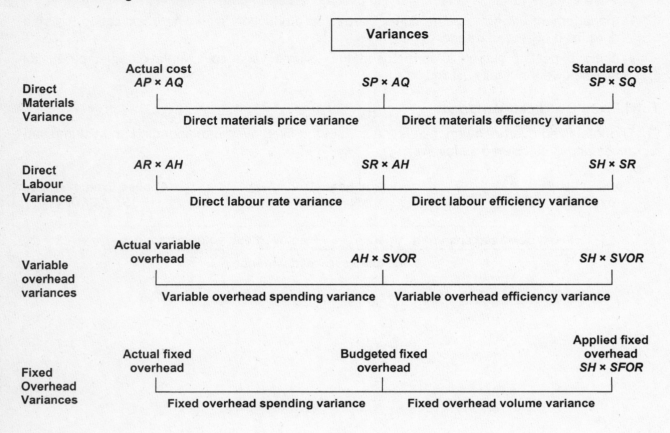

APPENDIX A: PROFITABILITY ANALYSIS

❐ Profitability analysis includes cost variance analysis and revenue variance analysis.

❐ **Total profit variance** is the difference between actual and budgeted profit. Budgeted profit being based on the static budget.

❐ The total profit variance can be broken down into 4 variances:

1. **Sales price variance** measures the direct effect of the change in selling price on profit.
2. **Profit volume variance** measures the effect of sales volume changes on profit.
3. **Variable cost flexible budget variance** measures the effect of variance cost changes on profit.
4. **Fixed cost flexible budget variance** measures the difference between actual and fixed costs on profit.

❐ The profit volume variance can be further broken down as follows:

5. **Profit volume variance (net)** measures the effects on profit of changes in total sales volume, holding sales mix constant.
6. **Sales mix variance** measures the effect of the change in sales mix on profit. It compares budgeted sales mix to actual sales mix.

❐ The profit volume variance (net) can be further broken down as follows:

7. **Industry volume variance** measures the effect on profits of a change in the market volume. It compares budgeted industry volume to actual and how this affects profits.

8. **Market share variance** measures a change in actual market share compared to budget on profits.

APPENDIX B: ACCOUNTING FOR VARIANCES

❑ In a standard costing system, all inventory accounts, raw materials, work-in-process, and finished goods are valued at their standard costs.

❑ If a cost variance is favourable it would be recorded as a credit.

❑ If a cost variance is unfavourable it would be recorded as a debit.

Entries for Direct Materials Variances

❑ The direct material variances are recorded separately because the price variance is based on purchases and the quantity variance is based on usage.

❑ To record the purchase of direct materials:

    Materials .... (SP x AQ)
    Materials price variance (debit if unfavourable, credit if favourable).......... (AP-SP) x AQ
        Accounts Payable .... (AP x AQ)

❑ To record the requisition of materials to work-in-process:

    Work in Process.. (SP x SQ)
    Materials usage variance (debit if unfavourable, credit if favourable)........ (AQ-SQ) x SP
        Materials .... (SP x AQ)

Entries for Direct Labour Variances

❑ Labour variances are recorded in one journal entry, unlike material, because labour cannot be purchased separately from its usage.

    Work in Process.. (SP x SQ)
    Labour rate variance (debit if unfavourable, credit if favourable)..............(AR-SR) x AQ
    Labour efficiency variance (debit if unfavourable, credit if favourable)...... (AH-SH) x SR
        Accrued Payroll .... (AR x AH)

KEY TERMS TEST

Test your recall of the key terms as follows. Try to recall as many key terms as possible without assistance. If you need assistance, refer to the list of key terms at the end of this section.

1. _____ _____ _____ are demanding but achievable under efficient operating conditions. Such standards allow for normal machine downtime and employee rest periods.

2. _____ _____ reflect perfect operating conditions. Such standards are virtually unattainable and can result in low employee morale and a decline in performance.

3. A(n) _____ _____ _____ lists the standard costs and standard quantities of direct materials, direct labour, and overhead for a product.

4. _____ _____ establish the maximum allowable deviation from a standard.

5. _____ _____ _____ are the direct labour hours that should have been used to produce the actual output.

6. _____ _____ ____ _____ _____ is the quantity of materials that should have been used to produce the actual output.

7. A(n) _____ _____ results when the actual amounts are greater than the budgeted or standard allowances.

8. A(n) _____ _____ results whenever the actual amounts are less than the budgeted or standard allowances.

9. The _____ _____ _____ _____ is the difference between the actual direct labour hours used and the standard hours allowed, multiplied by the standard variable overhead rate.

10. The _____ _____ _____ _____ is the difference between the actual variable overhead and the budgeted variable overhead based on actual hours used to produce the actual output.

11. The _____ _____ _____ is the difference between the actual price paid per unit of materials and the standard price allowed per unit, multiplied by the actual quantity of materials purchased.

12. The _____ _____ _____ is the difference between the direct materials actually used and the direct materials allowed for the actual output, multiplied by the standard price.

13. The _____ _____ _____ _____ is the difference between budgeted fixed overhead and applied fixed overhead and is a measure of capacity utilization.

14. The _____ _____ _____ is the difference between the actual hourly rate paid and the standard hourly rate, multiplied by the actual hours worked.

15. The _____ _____ _____ is the difference between the actual direct labour hours used and the standard direct labour hours allowed, multiplied by the standard hourly wage rate.

16. The _____ _____ _____ _____ is the difference between actual fixed overhead and budgeted fixed overhead.

KEY TERMS

control limits

currently attainable standards

favourable variance

fixed overhead spending variance

fixed overhead volume variance

ideal standards

labour efficiency variance

labour rate variance

materials price variance

materials usage variance

standard cost sheet

standard hours allowed

standard quantity of materials allowed

unfavourable variance

variable overhead efficiency variance

variable overhead spending variance

↻ **Compare your answers with those at the end of the chapter. Review any key terms missed.**

CHAPTER QUIZ

Circle the single best answer.

1. All of the following are true of currently attainable standards except: (a) currently attainable standards are based on an efficiently operating workforce; (b) currently attainable standards are based on ideal conditions; (c) currently attainable standards allow for downtime and rest periods; (d) currently attainable standards are based on present production processes and technology.

2. There is a direct relationship between (circle two answers): (a) inputs of direct materials and output of finished product; (b) inputs of direct labour and output of finished product; (c) input of variable manufacturing overhead and output of finished product; (d) input of fixed manufacturing overhead and output of finished product

3. Standards can be based on: (a) historical experience; (b) engineering studies; (c) input from operating personnel; (d) all of the above

4. In order to facilitate control, actual overhead costs for the output level attained should be compared with budgeted costs at the expected activity level: (a) true; (b) false

5. Engineering relationships between inputs and outputs can be established for manufacturing overhead: (a) true; (b) false

6. Separate overhead rates should be calculated for variable and fixed manufacturing overhead because the two costs react differently to changes in activity: (a) true; (b) false

7. The standard fixed overhead rate is calculated as estimated fixed manufacturing overhead costs divided by estimated activity: (a) true; (b) false

8. The standard fixed overhead rate should be determined on a monthly basis: (a) true; (b) false

9. If the selected activity is direct labour hours, manufacturing overhead in a standard costing system would be applied based on the actual direct labour hours worked: (a) true; (b) false

10. The variable manufacturing overhead efficiency variance results from the efficient or inefficient use of the base upon which variable manufacturing overhead is budgeted: (a) true; (b) false

11. The fixed manufacturing overhead budget variance is a measure of the utilization of plant facilities: (a) true; (b) false

12. The fixed manufacturing overhead volume variance indicates to management whether they operated at the expected activity level used to calculate the standard fixed overhead rate. There will be no volume variance if the company operated at the expected activity level: (a) true; (b) false

13. As a general rule, variances should be investigated if the anticipated benefits of the investigation exceed the expected costs of investigating: (a) true; (b) false

Use the following information to answer Questions 14 through 21:

The standard cost sheet for one of the Carver Company's products is presented below:

Direct materials (4 feet @ $6.00).............	$24.00
Direct labour (1 hour @ $12.00)	12.00
Variable overhead (1 hour @ $5.00)........	5.00
Fixed overhead (1 hour @ $3.00ª)...........	3.00
Standard unit cost...................................	$44.00

ªRate based on expected activity of 12,000 hours

The following results for last year were recorded:

Production	10,000 units
Direct materials (39,000 feet purchased and used).........	$241,800
Direct labour (10,500 hours)	$131,250
Variable overhead...	$48,000
Fixed overhead	$40,000

14. The materials price variance is: (a) $7,800 unfavourable; (b) $7,800 favourable; (c) $8,400 unfavourable; (d) $8,400 favourable

15. The materials usage variance is: (a) $4,000 favourable; (b) $4,000 unfavourable; (c) $6,000 favourable; (d) $6,000 unfavourable

16. The labour rate variance is: (a) $5,250 favourable; (b) $5,250 unfavourable; (c) $5,000 favourable; (d) $5,000 unfavourable

17. The labour efficiency variance is: (a) $5,250 favourable; (b) $5,250 unfavourable; (c) $6,000 favourable; (d) $6,000 unfavourable

18. The variable overhead spending variance is: (a) $4,500 favourable; (b) $4,500 unfavourable; (c) $4,800 favourable; (d) $4,800 unfavourable

19. The variable overhead efficiency variance is: (a) $2,500 favourable; (b) $2,500 unfavourable; (c) $2,250 favourable; (d) $2,250 unfavourable

20. The fixed overhead spending variance is: (a) $4,000 unfavourable; (b) $4,000 favourable; (c) $8,000 unfavourable; (d) $8,000 favourable

21. The fixed overhead volume variance is: (a) $4,000 unfavourable; (b) $4,000 favourable; (c) $6,000 unfavourable; (d) $6,000 favourable

↻ Compare your answers with those at the end of the chapter. Review any questions missed.

PRACTICE TEST

PROBLEM 1

The Carver Manufacturing Company has developed the following standards for one of their products, a walnut fern stand:

STANDARD VARIABLE COST SHEET
One Walnut Fern Stand

Materials: 5 square feet × $8 per square foot.........................	$40.00
Direct labour: 2 hours × $10/DLH..	20.00
Variable manufacturing overhead: 2 hours × $5/DLH............	10.00
Total standard variable cost per unit	$70.00

The company records materials price variances at the time of purchase. The following activity occurred during the month of April:

Materials purchased...	5,000 square feet costing $46,000
Materials used..	4,250 square feet
Units produced...	900 units
Direct labour..	2,200 hours costing $19,800
Actual variable manufacturing overhead	$10,500

Instructions:

1. Calculate the direct materials price and usage variances.

PROBLEM 1 (CONTINUED)

2. Prepare the journal entries to record the direct material price and usage variances. (Appendix B)

3. Calculate the direct labour rate variance, the direct labour efficiency variance, and the total direct labour variance.

PROBLEM 1 (*Continued*)

4. Prepare the journal entries to record the direct labour variances. (Appendix B)

5. Compute the variable manufacturing overhead spending and efficiency variances.

PROBLEM 2

The Mills Company manufactures roofing shingles. The production process involves heating and compressing asphalt into sheets and then rolling coarse sand into the hot asphalt. The sheets are then cooled, cut into shingles, and packaged.

The following standard costs were developed:

STANDARD COST SHEET PER SHINGLE

Direct materials:		
Asphalt..	2 lbs. × $0.08/lb.	$0.16
Sand	2 lbs. × $0.02/lb.	0.04
Direct labour	.01 hrs. × $7/hr.	0.07
Variable manufacturing overhead	.01 hrs. × $3/hr.	0.03
Fixed manufacturing overhead......................		?
Total standard cost per shingle		?

The following information is available regarding the company's operations for the period:

Shingles produced	500,000
Materials purchased:	
Asphalt..	800,000 pounds @ $0.07 per pound
Sand	900,000 pounds @ $0.03 per pound
Materials used:	
Asphalt..	775,000 pounds
Sand	850,000 pounds
Direct labour	5,100 hours costing $36,000
Manufacturing overhead incurred:	
Variable...	$16,500
Fixed	$48,000

Budgeted fixed manufacturing overhead for the period is $60,000, and the standard fixed overhead rate is based on expected capacity of 6,000 direct labour hours.

Instructions:

1. Calculate the standard fixed manufacturing overhead rate.

PROBLEM 2 *(Continued)*

2. Complete the standard cost card for roofing shingles.

3. Calculate the following variances:

    a. Materials price and usage variances for asphalt and sand

PROBLEM 2 *(Continued)*

Use this space to continue your answer.

b. Direct labour rate and efficiency variances

PROBLEM 2 *(Continued)*

c. Variable manufacturing overhead spending and efficiency variances

d. Fixed manufacturing overhead spending and volume variances

PROBLEM 3

The Commodore Company uses standard costing for direct materials and direct labour. Management would like to use standard costing for variable and fixed overhead also.

The following monthly cost functions were developed for manufacturing overhead items:

Overhead Item	Cost Function
Indirect materials	$0.10 per DLH
Indirect labour....................................	$0.40 per DLH
Repairs and maintenance................	$0.20 per DLH
Utilities	$0.25 per DLH
Insurance..	$2,000
Rent...	$4,000
Amortization......................................	$20,000

The cost functions are considered reliable within a relevant range of 30,000 to 55,000 direct labour hours.

Commodore expects to operate at 40,000 direct labour hours per month.

Information for the month of September is as follows:

Actual overhead costs incurred:	
Indirect materials	$ 4,500
Indirect labour..	17,000
Repairs and maintenance	8,000
Utilities	10,000
Insurance..	2,100
Rent...	4,000
Amortization..	20,000
Total..	$65,600
Actual direct labour hours worked....................	42,000
Standard direct labour hours allowed for production achieved.....................................	44,000

Instructions:

1. Calculate the standard manufacturing overhead rate based upon expected capacity, showing the breakdown between the fixed overhead rate and the variable overhead rate.

PROBLEM 3 *(Continued)*

Use this space to continue your answer.

2. Calculate the variable manufacturing overhead spending variance.

3. Calculate the variable manufacturing overhead efficiency variance.

PROBLEM 3 *(Continued)*

4. Calculate the fixed manufacturing overhead spending variance.

5. Calculate the fixed manufacturing overhead volume variance.

ANSWERS

KEY TERMS TEST

1. Currently attainable standards
2. Ideal standards
3. standard cost sheet
4. Control limits
5. Standard hours allowed
6. Standard quantity of materials allowed
7. unfavourable variance
8. favourable variance
9. variable overhead efficiency variance
10. variable overhead spending variance
11. materials price variance
12. materials usage variance
13. fixed overhead volume variance
14. labour rate variance
15. labour efficiency variance
16. fixed overhead spending variance

CHAPTER QUIZ

1. b
2. a and b
3. d
4. b False. To facilitate control, actual overhead costs should be compared with budgeted costs for the same level of output.
5. b False
6. a True
7. a True
8. b False. The fixed manufacturing overhead rate should be determined on a yearly basis.
9. b False. Manufacturing overhead would be applied based on the standard hours allowed for production achieved.
10. a True

11. b False. The fixed manufacturing overhead volume variance is a measure of the utilization of plant facilities.
12. a True
13. a True
14. a 39,000($6.20 – $6.00) = $7,800 unfavourable
15. c $6.00(39,000 – (4 feet × 10,000)) = $6,000 favourable
16. b 10,500 hours($12.50 – $12.00) = $5,250 unfavourable
17. d $12(10,500 – 10,000) = $6,000 unfavourable
18. a $48,000 – (10,500 × $5) = $4,500 favourable
19. b $5(10,500 – 10,000) = $2,500 unfavourable
20. a $40,000 – ($3 × 12,000) = $4,000 unfavourable
21. c $36,000 budgeted – ($3 × 10,000) applied = $6,000 unfavourable

PRACTICE TEST

PROBLEM 1

1. **Direct materials price variance:**

Actual quantity purchased at actual price		Actual quantity purchased at standard price
5,000 sq. ft. × $9.20/sq. ft. $46,000		5,000 sq. ft. × $8/sq. ft. $40,000

$6,000 Unfavourable

Direct materials price variance
5,000($9.20 – $8.00) = $6,000 Unfavourable

Direct materials usage variance:

Actual quantity used at Standard price		Standard quantity allowed at Standard price
4,250 sq. ft. × $8/sq. ft. $34,000		900 units × 5 sq. ft. × $8/sq. ft. $36,000

$2,000 Favourable

Direct materials usage variance
$8(4,250 – 4,500) = $2,000 Favourable

4. Journal entries to record direct materials price and usage variances:

Materials	40,000	
Direct materials price variance	6,000	
Accounts payable		46,000
Work in process	36,000	
Direct materials usage variance		2,000
Materials		34,000

3. Direct labour rate variance:

Actual labour hours at actual rate	Actual labour hours at standard rate
2,200 hours × $9/hour	2,200 hours × $10/hour
$19,800	$22,000

$2,200 Favourable

Direct labour rate variance
2,200($9 − $10) = $2,200 Favourable

Direct labour efficiency variance:

Actual labour hours at standard rate	Standard labour hours allowed at standard rate
2,200 hours × $10/hour	(900 units × 2 hours) × $10/hour
$22,000	$18,000

$4,000 Unfavourable

Direct labour efficiency variance
$10(2,200 − 1,800) = $4,000 Unfavourable

Total direct labour variance:

Actual hours at actual price	$19,800	
Standard hours allowed for production ((900 × 2) × $10)	18,000	
Total direct labour variance	$ 1,800	U

The total direct labour variance can be broken down as follows:

Direct labour rate variance	$2,200	F
Direct labour efficiency variance	4,000	U
Total direct labour variance	$1,800	U

4. Journal entry to record direct labour variances:

Work in process	18,000	
Direct labour efficiency variance	4,000	
Direct labour rate variance		2,200
Accrued payroll		19,800

5. Variable manufacturing overhead spending variance:

Actual variable overhead	Standard variable overhead rate × Actual hours (AQ × SVOR)
	2,200 hours × $5/hour
$10,500	$11,000

$500 Favourable

Variable overhead spending variance

Variable manufacturing overhead efficiency variance:

Standard variable overhead rate × Actual hours ($AQ \times SVOR$) 2,200 hours × \$5/hour \$11,000	Standard variable overhead rate × Standard hours ($SQ \times SVOR$) (900 units × 2 hours) × \$5/hour \$9,000

$$\text{\$2,000 Unfavourable}$$
Variable overhead efficiency variance

PROBLEM 2

1. Standard fixed manufacturing overhead rate $= \dfrac{\text{Estimated fixed overhead}}{\text{Estimated direct labour hours}}$

$$= \dfrac{\$60,000}{6,000 \text{ direct labour hours}}$$

$$= \$10 \text{ per direct labour hour}$$

2.   **STANDARD COST SHEET PER SHINGLE**

Direct materials:
Asphalt..	\$0.16
Sand	0.04
Direct labour	0.07
Variable manufacturing overhead	0.03
Fixed manufacturing overhead (.01 hrs. × \$10/hr.)	<u>0.10</u>
Total standard cost per shingle	<u>**\$0.40**</u>

3. a. **Materials price variance—Asphalt:**

Actual quantity purchased × Actual price 800,000 lbs. × \$0.07/lb. \$56,000	Actual quantity purchased × Standard price 800,000 lbs. × \$0.08/lb. \$64,000

$$\text{\$8,000 Favourable}$$
Materials price variance—Asphalt

Materials price variance—Sand:

Actual quantity purchased × Actual price 900,000 lbs. × \$0.03/lb. \$27,000	Actual quantity purchased × Standard price 900,000 lbs. × \$0.02/lb. \$18,000

$$\text{\$9,000 Unfavourable}$$
Materials price variance—Sand

Materials usage variance—Asphalt:

Actual quantity used × Standard price 775,000 lbs. × \$0.08/lb. \$62,000	Standard quantity × Standard price 500,000 × 2 lbs. × \$0.08/lb. \$80,000

$$\text{\$18,000 Favourable}$$
Materials usage variance—Asphalt

Materials usage variance—Sand:

Actual quantity used × Standard price		Standard quantity × Standard price
850,000 lbs. × $0.02/lb. $17,000		500,000 × 2 lbs. × $0.02/lb. $20,000

$3,000 Favourable

Materials usage variance—Sand

b. Direct labour rate variance:

Actual labour hours × Actual rate		Actual labour hours × Standard rate
5,100 DLH × $7.06*/hr. $36,000		5,100 DLH × $7/hr. $35,700

$300 Unfavourable

Direct labour rate variance

*rounded

Direct labour efficiency variance:

Actual labour hours × Standard rate		Standard labour hours × Standard rate
5,100 DLH × $7/hr. $35,700		500,000 units × .01 DLH × $7/hr. $35,000

$700 Unfavourable

Direct labour efficiency variance

c. Variable manufacturing overhead spending variance:

Actual variable overhead		Standard variable overhead rate × Actual hours (SVOR × AH)
		5,100 DLH × $3/hr. $15,300
$16,500		

$1,200 Unfavourable

Variable overhead spending variance

Variable manufacturing overhead efficiency variance:

Standard variable overhead rate × Actual hours (SVOR × AH)		Standard variable overhead rate × Standard hours (SVOR × SH)
5,100 DLH × $3/hr. $15,300		500,000 units × .01 DLH × $3/hr. $15,000

$300 Unfavourable

Variable overhead efficiency variance

d. Fixed manufacturing overhead spending variance:

Actual fixed overhead		Budgeted fixed overhead
$48,000		$60,000

$12,000 Favourable

Fixed overhead spending variance

Fixed manufacturing overhead volume variance:

Budgeted fixed overhead

Applied fixed overhead
(Standard activity × *SFOR*)

500,000 units × .01 DLH × $10/hr.

$60,000

$50,000

$10,000 Unfavourable

Fixed overhead volume variance

The volume variance could also be calculated as follows:

FMO volume variance = *SFOR* × [Expected capacity – Standard hours allowed for production level achieved]

= ($10)(6,000 DLH – 5,000 DLH allowed)

= ($10)(1,000 DLH)

= $10,000

The Mills Company produced 500,000 shingles, a level for which 5,000 direct labour hours are allowed.

The Mills Company budgeted 6,000 direct labour hours. The volume variance resulted from the company operating at a level other than the budgeted level of 6,000 direct labour hours.

PROBLEM 3

1. Standard manufacturing overhead rate:

Manufacturing overhead items:

Indirect materials		$0.10 per DLH
Indirect labour		0.40 per DLH
Repairs and maintenance		0.20 per DLH
Utilities		0.25 per DLH
Insurance	$ 2,000	
Rent	4,000	
Amortization	20,000	
Variable manufacturing overhead		$0.95 per DLH
Fixed manufacturing overhead	$26,000	

SVOR = $0.95 per direct labour hour

$$SFOR = \frac{\text{Estimated fixed manufacturing overhead}}{\text{Estimated direct labour hours}}$$

$$= \frac{\$26,000}{40,000 \text{ direct labour hours}}$$

= $0.65 per direct labour hour

Total manufacturing overhead rate = *SFOR* + *SVOR*

= $0.65 + $0.95

= $1.60 per direct labour hour

2. Variable manufacturing overhead spending variance:

Actual variable overhead

Standard variable overhead
rate × Actual hours
(*SVOR* × *AH*)

($4,500 + $17,000 + $8,000 +
$10,000)
$39,500

42,000 DLH × $0.95/hr.
$39,900

$400 Favourable

Variable overhead spending variance

3. **Variable manufacturing overhead efficiency variance:**

Standard variable overhead
rate × Actual hours
(*SVOR* × *AH*)

42,000 DLH × $0.95/hr.
$39,900

Standard variable overhead
rate × Standard hours
(*SVOR* × *SH*)

44,000 DLH × $0.95/hr.
$41,800

$1,900 Favourable
Variable overhead efficiency variance

4. **Fixed manufacturing overhead spending variance:**

Actual fixed overhead
$26,100

Budgeted fixed overhead
$26,000

$100 Unfavourable
Fixed overhead spending variance

5. **Fixed manufacturing overhead volume variance:**

Budgeted fixed overhead

$26,000

Applied fixed overhead
(Standard activity × *SFOR*)

44,000 DLH × $0.65/hr.
$28,600

$2,600 Favourable
Fixed overhead volume variance

The volume variance could also be calculated as follows:

FMO volume variance = *SFOR* × [Expected capacity – Standard hours allowed for production level achieved]

= ($0.65)(40,000 DLH – 44,000 DLH allowed)

= ($0.65)(4,000 DLH)

= $2,600 Favourable

CHAPTER 15
Quality Costs and Productivity: Measurement, Reporting, and Control

CHAPTER REVIEW

MEASURING THE COSTS OF QUALITY

❒ Quality improvement can increase profitability in two ways:
1. By increasing customer demand
2. By decreasing costs

❒ Studies indicate that costs of quality for American companies are typically 20 to 30 percent of sales. Quality experts maintain that the optimal quality level should be about 2 to 4 percent of sales.

Quality Defined

❒ A **quality product** is a product that meets or exceeds customer expectations. Quality is customer satisfaction.

❒ A quality product or service meets or exceeds customer expectations on the following eight dimensions:

- **Performance**—how consistent and well a product performs
- **Aesthetics**—the appearance of the product as well as the appearance of the facilities, equipment, personnel, and communication materials associated with services
- **Serviceability**—ease of maintaining and/or repairing a product
- **Features (quality of design)**—characteristics of a product that serve the same function but have different design specifications, such as the type and quality of materials used in the product (for example, 14-karat gold jewellery and gold-plated jewellery)
- **Reliability**—the probability that the product or service will perform its intended function for a specified length of time
- **Durability**—the length of time a product functions
- **Quality of conformance**—how a product meets its design specifications. Is the product manufactured as the design specifies?
- **Fitness for use**—suitability of the product for carrying out its advertised functions

❒ Conformance is viewed by experts to be the essence of quality. Conformance is the basis for defining what is meant by a nonconforming or defective product.

❒ A **defective product** does not conform to specifications.

❒ **Zero defects** requires that all products and services conform to specifications. The *traditional view* of conformance assumes an acceptable range on either side of a target value for each specification or quality characteristic. The *robust quality view* redefines defective units as those that do not meet the target value.

Costs of Quality Defined

❏ **Costs of quality** are costs incurred because poor quality may exist or poor quality does exist.

❏ Quality costs are associated with two subcategories of quality-related activities:

- **Control activities**—activities performed by an organization to prevent or detect poor quality (because poor quality may exist). Control activities consist of prevention and appraisal activities. **Control costs** are the costs of performing control activities.
- **Failure activities**—activities performed by an organization or its customers in response to poor quality (poor quality does exist). **Failure costs** are the costs incurred by an organization because failure activities are performed.

❏ Four categories of quality costs include the following:

1. **Prevention costs** are incurred to prevent poor quality. Examples of prevention costs include:
    - quality engineering
    - quality training programs
    - quality planning
    - quality reporting
    - supplier evaluation and selection
    - quality audits
    - quality circles
    - field trials
    - design reviews

2. **Appraisal costs** are incurred to determine whether products and services are conforming to requirements or customer needs. The main objective is to prevent nonconforming goods from being shipped to customers. Examples of appraisal costs include:
    - inspecting and testing of raw materials
    - packaging inspection
    - supervising appraisal activities
    - *process acceptance* (sampling goods in process to see if the process is in control and producing nondefective goods)
    - *product acceptance* (sampling finished goods to determine if the finished goods meet an acceptable quality level)
    - measurement (inspection and test) equipment
    - outside endorsements

3. **Internal failure costs** are incurred because products or services do not meet requirements and the defect is discovered before the external sale. Examples of internal failure costs include:
    - scrap
    - rework
    - downtime (due to defects)
    - reinspection
    - retesting
    - design changes

    If there are no defects, there are no internal failure costs.

4. **External failure costs** are incurred because products fail to meet requirements after delivery to customers. Examples include:
    - the cost of recalling defective products

- lost sales because of poor product performance
- returns and allowances because of poor quality
- warranty costs
- repair costs
- product liability
- customer dissatisfaction
- lost market share
- complaint adjustment

Measuring Quality Costs

❑ Quality costs can be classified as:

- **observable quality costs**—quality costs available from an organization's accounting records.
- **hidden quality costs**—opportunity costs resulting from poor quality. Hidden quality costs are usually not recorded in the accounting records. Three methods of estimating hidden quality costs are:
  - the multiplier method
  - the market research method, and
  - the Taguchi quality loss function.

❑ The multiplier method assumes that total failure costs are a multiple of measured failure costs.

❑ Market research methods, such as customer surveys, are used to assess the effect of poor quality on sales and market share.

❑ The **Taguchi loss function** assumes any variation from the target value of a quality characteristic causes hidden quality costs. The Taguchi loss function is:

$$L(y) = k(y - T)^2$$

where k = a proportionally constant dependent upon the organization's external failure cost structure

y = actual value of quality characteristic

T = target value of quality characteristic

L = quality loss

REPORTING QUALITY COST INFORMATION

❑ The first step in a quality cost reporting system is to prepare a detailed listing of actual quality costs by category.

❑ This serves two purposes:

1. It permits managers to assess the financial impact of quality costs.
2. It reveals the relative emphasis currently placed on each category.

Quality Cost Reports

❑ In the quality cost report, quality costs are grouped into one of four categories:

- prevention costs
- appraisal costs
- internal failure costs

- external failure costs
☐ In addition, each category of quality costs is expressed as a percentage of sales.
☐ An example of a quality cost report appears in Exhibit 15-3 in the text.
☐ There are two views concerning optimal quality costs:
  - the acceptable quality (traditional) view that uses an acceptable quality level
  - the contemporary view that uses total quality control

Quality Cost Function: Acceptable Quality View

☐ The acceptable quality view uses an **acceptable quality level (AQL)** that permits a predetermined level of defective units to be produced and sold. AQL is the level where the number of defects allowed minimizes total quality costs.

☐ The reasoning of this traditional approach is that there is a trade-off between failure costs and prevention and appraisal costs (control costs). As prevention and appraisal costs increase, internal and external failure costs are expected to decrease. As long as the decrease in failure costs is greater than the corresponding increase in prevention and failure costs, a company should continue increasing its efforts to prevent or detect defective units.

Quality Cost Function: Zero-Defects View

☐ The zero-defects model views the optimal level of quality costs as the level where zero defects are produced.

☐ The robust quality model redefines a defective unit. The robust model focuses on hitting the *target value* for product specifications rather than an acceptable range.

Activity-Based Management and Optimal Quality Costs

☐ Activity-based management classifies activities as:
  - value-added activities, and
  - nonvalue-added activities.

☐ Internal and external failure activities and their associated costs are nonvalue-added and should be eliminated.

☐ Prevention activities performed efficiently are value-added. (Costs caused by inefficiency in prevention activities are nonvalue-added costs.)

☐ Appraisal activities may be value-added or nonvalue-added, depending upon the activity. For example, quality audits may serve a value-added objective.

Trend Analysis

☐ A **multiperiod quality trend report** is used to identify if quality costs have decreased as planned over time.

USING QUALITY COST INFORMATION

☐ The principal objective of reporting quality costs is to improve and facilitate managerial planning, control, and decision making.

☐ Potential uses of quality cost information include:
  - quality program implementation decisions

- evaluation of the effectiveness of quality programs
- strategic pricing decisions (For example, improved reporting of quality costs might be used by managers to target specific quality costs for reductions. A reduction in quality costs might enable a firm to reduce its selling price, improve its competitive position, and increase market share.)
- inclusion of quality costs in cost–volume–profit analysis (For example, overlooking quality cost savings results in a higher breakeven and possible rejection of a profitable project.)

PRODUCTIVITY: MEASUREMENT AND CONTROL

❏ **Productivity** is concerned with producing output efficiently.

❏ **Total productive efficiency** is the point at which the following two conditions are met:
- **technical efficiency**—the point at which, for any mix of inputs that will produce a given output, no more of any one input is used than is absolutely necessary.
- **input trade-off efficiency**—the least-cost, technically efficient mix of inputs.

❏ Productivity can be improved as follows:
1. Improve technical efficiency by:
   - using less input to produce the same output, or
   - using the same input to produce more output.
2. Improve input trade-off efficiency by using a less costly mix of inputs.

Partial Productivity Measurement

❏ **Productivity measurement** involves measuring productivity changes so that efforts to improve productivity can be evaluated.

❏ Productivity can be measured using:
- a **partial productivity measure** that assesses productivity for each input separately, or
- a **total productivity measure** that assesses productivity for all inputs combined.

❏ A partial productivity measure assesses productivity efficiency for one input by comparing output to input:

Productivity ratio = Output/Input

❏ An **operational productivity measure** uses *physical quantities* to measure input and output.

❏ A **financial productivity measure** uses dollars to measure input and output.

❏ To assess changes in productivity, the actual productivity measure for the current period is compared with the **base period** (a prior period that serves as a benchmark for measuring changes).

❏ Advantages of partial productivity measures include the following:
- They permit managers to focus on the use of a particular input.
- They provide feedback that operating personnel can relate to and understand—measures that deal with the specific inputs they control.

❏ A disadvantage of partial productivity measures is that because partial productivity measures focus on a particular input, they do not consider trade-offs between the productivity of different inputs. For example, less direct labour might be used (direct labour productivity increased), but more scrap and waste might result (material productivity decreased).

Total Productivity Measurement

☐ A **total productivity measurement** is an assessment of productivity efficiency for all inputs combined in order to value a change in productivity.

☐ One way to value productivity changes is to calculate the effects of productivity changes on profits.

Profile Productivity Measurement

☐ **Profile measurement** is a series or vector of separate and distinct partial operational measures. Productivity ratio profiles are shown for a series of years.

Profit-Linked Productivity Measurement

☐ **Profit-linked productivity measurement** is an assessment of the amount of profit change from the base period to the current period attributable to productivity changes.

☐ The *profit-linkage rule* determines the profit effect by computing the difference between the cost of the inputs that would have been used without any productivity changes and the cost of the actual inputs used.

$$\text{Profit-linked effect} = \frac{\text{Cost of inputs that would have been}}{\text{used without any productivity changes}} - \frac{\text{Cost of actual}}{\text{inputs used}}$$

$$\text{Profit-linked effect} = (PQ \times P) - (AQ \times P)$$

where PQ = the inputs that would have been used for the current period without any productivity changes). PQ is calculated as follows:

$$PQ = \text{Current output/Base-period productivity ratio}$$

P = current input price

AQ = actual quantity

Price-Recovery Component

☐ The **price-recovery component** indicates the change in profit that would have occurred without the productivity improvement.

☐ The price-recovery component is calculated as follows:

$$\text{Price recovery} = \text{Profit change} - \text{Profit-linked productivity change}$$

Quality and Productivity

☐ Improving quality is one way to improve productivity. For example, by improving quality and reducing the number of defective units, rework time and materials are reduced. Thus, fewer inputs are used to produce the same output and productivity increases.

KEY TERMS TEST

Test your recall of the key terms as follows. Try to recall as many key terms as possible without assistance. If you need assistance, refer to the list of key terms at the end of this section.

1. _____ _____ is a quality performance standard that requires all products and services to be produced and delivered according to specifications.

2. _____ _____ _____ are incurred because products fail to conform to requirements after being sold to outside parties.

3. _____ _____ _____ are incurred because products and services fail to conform to requirements where lack of conformity is discovered prior to external sale.

4. _____ _____ are incurred to determine whether products and services are conforming to requirements.

5. _____ _____ are incurred to prevent defects in products or services being produced.

6. _____ _____ _____ are costs incurred because poor quality may exist or because poor quality does exist.

7. _____ _____ _____ are expressed in physical terms.

8. A(n) _____ _____ _____ is a productivity measure that expresses inputs and outputs in dollars.

9. _____ concerns producing output efficiency, using the least quantity of inputs possible.

10. _____ _____ _____ is the point at which technical efficiency and price efficiency are achieved.

11. _____ _____ _____ is an assessment of productive efficiency for all inputs combined.

12. A(n) _____ _____ _____ is a ratio that measures productive efficiency for one input.

13. _____ _____ is the point at which for any mix of inputs that will produce a given output, no more of any one input is used than is absolutely necessary.

14. _____ _____-_____ _____ is the least-cost, technically efficient mix of inputs.

15. _____-_____ _____ _____ is an assessment of the amount of profit change—from the base period to the current period attributable to productivity changes.

16. _____ _____ is an assessment of productivity changes.

17. A(n) _____ _____ _____ or _____ is a predetermined level of defective products that a company permits to be sold.

18. The difference between the total profit change and the profit-linked productivity change is the _____-_____ _____.

19. _____ _____ _____ is a measure of how well a product meets its design specifications.

20. _____ _____ are activities performed by an organization to prevent or detect poor quality because poor quality may exist.

21. _____ _____ are activities performed by an organization or its customers in response to poor quality (poor quality does exist).

22. _____ _____ _____ are opportunity costs resulting from poor quality.

23. _____ _____ _____ are quality costs available from an organization's accounting records.

KEY TERMS

acceptable quality level (AQL)
appraisal costs
control activities
costs of quality
external failure costs
failure activities
financial productivity measure
hidden quality costs
input trade-off efficiency
internal failure costs
observable quality costs
operational productivity measures

partial productivity measurement
prevention costs
price-recovery component
productivity
productivity measurement
profit-linked productivity measurement
quality of conformance
technical efficiency
total productive efficiency
total productivity measurement
zero defects

↻ **Compare your answers with those at the end of the chapter. Review any key terms missed.**

CHAPTER QUIZ

Write your answers in the spaces provided.

1. List the four categories of quality costs:

    1. _____

    2. _____

    3. _____

    4. _____

2. In a quality cost report, quality costs are grouped into categories and then each category of quality costs is expressed as a percentage of _____.

3. There are two views concerning optimal quality costs:

    1. the traditional view that uses a(n) _____ quality level

    2. the contemporary view that uses _____ quality control

4. Productivity is concerned with producing output _____.

5. Productivity is measured as _____ divided by _____.

Use the following information to answer Questions 6 through 15:

Classify the following costs as one of the following:

- prevention cost
- appraisal cost
- internal failure cost
- external failure cost

_____   **6.** Warranty work

_____   **7.** Quality training programs

_____   **8.** In-process inspection

_____   **9.** Reinspection of reworked products

_____   **10.** Product recalls

_____   **11.** Inspection labour costs

_____   **12.** Downtime attributed to quality problems

_____   **13.** Product inspection

_____   **14.** Consumer complaint department

_____   **15.** Labour and overhead incurred for rework of defective products

Circle the single best answer.

16. A quality product is a product that meets or exceeds customer expectations: (a) true; (b) false

17. As prevention and appraisal costs increase, internal and external failure costs are expected to increase: (a) true; (b) false

18. The robust quality model focuses on hitting the target value for product specifications rather than an acceptable range: (a) true; (b) false

Use the following information to answer Questions 19 through 27:

The following information pertains to the Sunshine Company.

	2004	2005
Output	8,000	10,000
Output prices	$12	$12
Materials (pounds)	5,000	5,500
Material unit price	$4	$5
Labour (hours)	3,000	2,500
Labour rate per hour	3,000	2,500
Power (kilowatt hours)	1,200	1,800
Price per kilowatt hour	$2.50	$3

19. The partial operational productivity measure for materials for 2004 is: (a) 0.625; (b) 1.60; (c) 1.67; (d) 1.10

20. The partial operational productivity measure for materials for 2005 is: (a) 1.82; (b) 1.87; (c) 2.0; (d) 1.55

21. From 2004 to 2005, productivity for materials: (a) increased; (b) decreased

22. The partial operational productivity measure for labour for 2004 is: (a) 2.67; (b) 4.00; (c) 0.375; (d) 1.20

23. The partial operational productivity measure for direct labour for 2005 is: (a) 2.5; (b) 2.8; (c) 4; (d) 4.2

24. From 2004 to 2005, productivity for labour: (a) increased; (b) decreased

25. The partial operational productivity measure for power for 2004 is: (a) 0.15; (b) 1.5; (c) 8.33; (d) 6.67

26. The partial operational productivity measure for power for 2005 is: (a) 5.52; (b) 5.56; (c) 7.24; (d) 16.67

27. From 2004 to 2005, power usage productivity: (a) increased; (b) decreased

↻ **Compare your answers with those at the end of the chapter. Review any questions missed.**

PRACTICE TEST

PROBLEM 1

The following information pertains to Magic, Inc., for 2004:

Sales	$30,000,000
External failure costs	900,000
Internal failure costs	1,800,000
Prevention costs	400,000
Appraisal costs	600,000

Instructions:

1. Calculate each category of quality costs as a percentage of sales.

   External failure costs: _____

   Internal failure costs: _____

   Prevention costs: _____

   Appraisal costs: _____

2. Calculate total quality costs as a percentage of sales.

3. If quality costs were reduced to 2.5% of sales, determine the increase in profit that would result.

PROBLEM 2

At the beginning of the year, Westfall Company initiated a quality improvement program. The program was successful in reducing scrap and rework costs.

To help assess the impact of the quality improvement program, the following data were collected for the current and preceding years:

	Preceding Year	Current Year
Sales	$4,000,000	$4,000,000
Quality training.....................................	10,000	15,000
Materials inspection	25,000	35,000
Scrap	200,000	180,000
Rework	250,000	200,000
Product inspection	40,000	60,000
Product warranty.................................	300,000	250,000

Instructions:

1. Classify each of the costs as one of the following:
    - prevention cost
    - appraisal cost
    - internal failure cost
    - external failure cost

    Quality training: _____

    Materials inspection: _____

    Scrap: _____

    Rework: _____

    Product inspection: _____

    Product warranty: _____

2. Compute each category of quality costs as a percentage of sales.

	Preceding Year	Current Year
Prevention costs	_____	_____
Appraisal costs	_____	_____
Internal failure costs	_____	_____
External failure costs	_____	_____

PROBLEM 2 *(Continued)*

3. **a.** How much has profit increased as a result of quality improvement?

    b. If quality costs can be reduced to 2.5% of sales, how much additional profit would result?

PROBLEM 3

The following pertains to the last two years of operation of the Lowell Company:

	2004	2005
Output..	15,000	18,000
Selling price per unit...........................	$20	$20
Input quantities:		
Materials (pounds).........................	5,000	5,000
Labour (hours).................................	4,000	4,500
Input prices:		
Materials (per pound)	$4	$4.50
Labour (per hour)	$8	$8.10

Instructions:

1. **a.** Calculate the partial operational productivity ratios for materials and labour for each year.

	2004	2005
Material	_____	_____
Labour	_____	_____

    b. Did material and labour productivity improve from 2004 to 2005?

PROBLEM 3 *(Continued)*

2. a. Compute the profit-linked productivity measure.

b. By how much did profits increase due to changes in productivity?

PROBLEM 4

The following information pertains to the Starr Company:

	2004	2005
Output...	4,000	4,500
Output prices	$8	$8
Materials (pounds).............................	2,500	3,000
Material unit price	$2	$3
Labour (hours)....................................	2,000	1,800
Labour rate per hour..........................	$7	$7
Power (kilowatt hours)	800	900
Price per kilowatt hour	$1.50	$2

Instructions:

1. Compute the partial operational measures for each input for 2004 and 2005. Discuss productivity improvement.

	2004	2005
Material	_____	_____
Labour	_____	_____
Power	_____	_____

PROBLEM 4 *(Continued)*

2. Prepare an income statement for each year and calculate the total change in profits.

	2004	2005

3. Calculate the profit-linked productivity measure for 2005. Discuss the results.

4. Calculate the price-recovery component. Explain the results.

ANSWERS

KEY TERMS TEST

1. Zero defects
2. External failure costs
3. Internal failure costs
4. Appraisal costs
5. Prevention costs
6. Costs of quality
7. Operational productivity measures
8. financial productivity measure
9. Productivity
10. Total productive efficiency
11. Total productivity measurement
12. partial productivity measurement
13. Technical efficiency
14. Input trade-off efficiency
15. Profit-linked productivity measurement
16. Productivity measurement
17. acceptable quality level, AQL
18. price-recovery component
19. Quality of conformance
20. Control activities
21. Failure activities
22. Hidden quality costs
23. Observable quality costs

CHAPTER QUIZ

1. 1. prevention costs
    2. appraisal costs
    3. internal failure costs
    4. external failure costs
2. sales
3. 1. acceptable
    2. total
4. efficiently
5. output, input
6. external failure cost
7. prevention cost
8. appraisal cost
9. internal failure cost
10. external failure cost
11. appraisal cost
12. internal failure cost
13. appraisal cost
14. external failure cost
15. internal failure cost
16. a   True
17. b   False. As prevention and appraisal costs increase, internal and external failure costs are expected to decrease.
18. True
19. b   8,000/5,000 = 1.60
20. a   10,000/5,500 = 1.82
21. a
22. a   8,000/3,000 = 2.67
23. c   10,000/2,500 = 4
24. a
25. d   8,000/1,200 = 6.67
26. b   10,000/1,800 = 5.56
27. b

PRACTICE TEST

PROBLEM 1

1. External failure costs: $900,000/$30,000,000 = 3.0%
   Internal failure costs: $1,800,000/$30,000,000 = 6.0%
   Prevention costs: $400,000/$30,000,000 = 1.3%
   Appraisal costs: $600,000/$30,000,000 = 2.0%

2. Total quality costs: $3,700,000/$30,000,000 = 12.3%

3. Current quality costs $3,700,000
   Goal (2.5% × $30,000,000)   750,000
   Increase in profit $2,950,000

PROBLEM 2

1. Quality training: prevention cost
   Materials inspection: appraisal cost
   Scrap: internal failure cost
   Rework: internal failure cost
   Product inspection: appraisal cost
   Product warranty: external failure cost

2.

	Preceding Year		Current Year	
Prevention costs:				
Quality training	$ 10,000	.25%	$ 15,000	.38%
Appraisal costs:				
Materials inspection	$ 25,000		$ 35,000	
Product inspection	40,000		60,000	
Total appraisal costs	$ 65,000	1.63%	$ 95,000	2.38%
Internal failure costs:				
Scrap	$200,000		$180,000	
Rework	250,000		200,000	
Total internal failure costs	$450,000	11.25%	$380,000	9.50%
External failure costs:				
Product warranty	$300,000	7.50%	$250,000	6.25%

3. a.

Total quality costs—preceding year	$825,000
Total quality costs—current year	740,000
Increase in profit	$ 85,000

b.

Total quality costs—current year	$740,000
Goal (2.5% × $4,000,000)	100,000
Increase in profit	$640,000

PROBLEM 3

1. a. Partial operational productivity ratios:

	2004	2005
Material	15,000/5,000 = 3.00	18,000/5,000 = 3.60
Labour	15,000/4,000 = 3.75	18,000/4,500 = 4.00

b. Yes. Both materials and labour productivity improved from 2004 to 2005.

2. a. Profit-linked productivity measure:

	(1) PQ[a]	(2) PQ × P	(3) AQ	(4) AQ × P	(2) – (4) (PQ × P) – (AQ × P)
Materials	6,000	$27,000	5,000	$22,500	$4,500
Labour	4,800	38,880	4,500	36,450	2,430
		$65,880		$58,950	$6,930

[a]Materials: 18,000/3.00 = 6,000
Labour: 18,000/3.75 = 4,800

b. Profits increased by $6,930 due to improvements in productivity.

PROBLEM 4

1. Partial operational measures:

	2004	2005
Material	4,000/2,500 = 1.60	4,500/3,000 = 1.50
Labour	4,000/2,000 = 2.00	4,500/1,800 = 2.50
Power	4,000/800 = 5.00	4,500/900 = 5.00

Productive efficiency has decreased for materials, increased for labour, and remained the same for power. Overall productivity improvement can be evaluated by valuing the trade-off.

2.

	2004	2005
Sales		
(4,000 × $8)	$32,000	
(4,500 × $8)		$36,000
Cost of Inputs:		
Materials		
(2,500 × $2)	(5,000)	
(3,000 × $3)		(9,000)
Labour		
(2,000 × $7)	(14,000)	
(1,800 × $7)		(12,600)
Power		
(800 × $1.50)	(1,200)	
(900 × $2.00)		(1,800)
Income	$11,800	$12,600

Total change in profit = $12,600 − $11,800 = $800 increase

3. Profit-linked productivity measure:

	(1) PQ^a	(2) $PQ \times P$	(3) AQ	(4) $AQ \times P$	(2) − (4) $(PQ \times P) − (AQ \times P)$
Materials	2,813	$ 8,439	3,000	$ 9,000	$ (561)
Labour	2,250	15,750	1,800	12,600	3,150
Power	900	1,800	900	1,800	–0–
		$25,989		$23,400	$2,589

^{a}Materials: 4,500/1.60 = 2,813
Labour: 4,500/2 = 2,250
Power: 4,500/5 = 900

The value of the increase in efficiency for labour more than offsets the decrease in efficiency for materials. There was no change in value of the productivity efficiency of power usage.

4. Price-recovery component:

Price-recovery component = Profit change − Profit-linked productivity change
Price-recovery component = $800 − $2,589 = $(1,789)

Without the productivity improvement, profits would have declined by $1,789. The $4,000 increase in revenues would not have offset the increase in the cost of inputs. It is only because of the productivity increase that the firm showed an increase in profitability.

CHAPTER 16
Financial Performance Evaluation and Transfer Pricing in Decentralized Companies

CHAPTER REVIEW

RESPONSIBILITY ACCOUNTING

❐ Responsibility accounting is a system that measures the results of responsibility centres according to the information managers need to operate their centre.

❐ A **responsibility centre** is a segment of a business whose manager is accountable for specified sets of activities. Four types of responsibility centres are:

- **cost centre**—the manager is financially responsible only for costs
- **revenue centre**—the manager is financially responsible only for sales (revenues)
- **profit centre**—the manager is financially responsible for both revenues and costs
- **investment centre**—the manager is financially responsible for revenues, costs, and investments

DECENTRALIZATION

❐ To manage diverse and complex activities, organizations usually choose one of two approaches:

- **centralized decision making**—a system in which decisions are made at the top level of an organization and lower-level managers implement the decisions
- **decentralized decision making**—a system in which decisions are made and implemented by lower-level managers pertaining to their responsibility centre.

❐ **Decentralization** is the practice of delegating or decentralizing decision-making authority to lower levels.

❐ The majority of firms tend to be decentralized.

Reasons for Decentralization

❐ Reasons for using a decentralized organizational structure include:

- *Utilization of local information.* The quality of decisions is affected by the quality of information. Because lower-level managers have access to information about operating conditions, customers, and competition, they are often in a position to make better decisions.
- *Strategic focus of central management.* Decentralization allows top management to concentrate on company-wide problems, strategic planning, and decision making.
- *Training and motivational opportunities for managers.* Divisional management is a source of personnel for promotion to top management positions. A decentralized organization provides better training for top management positions than a more centralized organization where managers simply carry out top management's orders. Also, greater responsibility can produce more job satisfaction and motivate the local manager to exert greater effort.

- *Enhanced competition among divisions.* In a highly centralized company, large overall profit margins can mask inefficiencies within the various subdivisions. More fully exposing a division to market forces can help reveal noncompetitive divisions and improve divisional performance.

The Units of Decentralization

❏ Decentralization is usually achieved by creating decentralized units called *divisions*.

❏ Divisions might be differentiated by:
  - types of products or services produced
  - geographic regions
  - type of responsibility given to the divisional manager (cost centre, revenue centre, profit centre, or investment centre)

MEASURING THE PERFORMANCE OF INVESTMENT CENTRES

❏ Since it is possible for a division to perform well or poorly irrespective of the efforts of its manager, companies try to separate the evaluation of the segment from the evaluation of the segment manager.

❏ Two methods used to evaluate division performance of investment centres are:
  - return on investment (ROI)
  - residual income (RI)
  - economic value added (EVA)

Return on Investment

❏ **Return on investment (ROI)**, the most common measure of performance for an investment centre, is calculated as follows:

$$\text{ROI} = \text{Operating income/Average operating assets}$$

❏ **Operating income** is earnings before interest and taxes.

❏ **Operating assets** are those assets used to generate operating income, usually including cash, receivables, inventories, property, plant, and equipment.

$$\text{Average operating assets} = \frac{(\text{Beginning net book value} + \text{Ending net book value})}{2}$$

Most firms use net book value when calculating average operating assets.

Margin and Turnover

❏ ROI can be broken into two components:

$$\text{ROI} = \text{Margin} \times \text{Turnover}$$

$$= \frac{\text{Operating income}}{\text{Sales}} \times \frac{\text{Sales}}{\text{Average operating assets}}$$

❏ **Margin** shows the amount of each dollar of net sales that is available for interest expense, income tax expense, and profit.

❏ **Turnover** compares a division's investment in operating assets with the ability of those assets to generate revenues.

❏ Firms with a low profit margin, such as discount stores, may rely upon a high turnover to generate profits. Conversely, a firm with a low turnover, such as a fine jeweller, may rely upon high profit margins.

Advantages of ROI

❏ Three positive results from using ROI are:

- It encourages managers to focus on the relationship among sales, expenses, and investment.
- It encourages managers to focus on cost efficiency.
- It encourages managers to focus on operating asset efficiency.

Disadvantages of the ROI Measure

❏ Two disadvantages associated with ROI are:

- It encourages managers to focus on the short run at the expense of the long run (myopic behaviour). For example, a manager might cut research and development expenses in the short run to improve ROI, but the cuts may not be in the best long-term interests of the division.
- It discourages managers from investing in projects that would decrease the division's ROI but would increase the profitability of the company as a whole. Generally, projects with an ROI less than a division's current ROI would be rejected by the division manager.

❏ Example: Assume a division is expected to have income of $100,000 with an investment base of $500,000.

Expected ROI for the division excluding the proposed project is 20%, calculated as follows:

$$\text{Current ROI} = \text{Income/Investment}$$
$$= \$100,000/\$500,000$$
$$= 20\%$$

A proposed project has been evaluated and found to be acceptable using discounted cash flow analysis. The project would increase divisional income by $24,000 and divisional investment by $160,000.

ROI of the proposed project is 15%, calculated as follows:

$$\text{ROI of proposed project} = \text{Incremental income/Incremental investment}$$
$$= \$24,000/\$160,000$$
$$= 15\%$$

Since the proposed project has a lower ROI than the expected ROI for the division, acceptance of the project will lower the division's ROI.

ROI for the division including the proposed project is 18.8%, calculated as follows:

$$\text{ROI including proposed project} = \frac{\$100,000 + \$24,000}{\$500,000 + \$160,000}$$
$$= 18.8\%$$

If the division manager accepts the proposed project, it will lower his division's ROI from 20% to 18.8%. Thus, it is not in the manager's best interests to accept the project even if it might be in the best interests of the firm.

In fact, the manager would not want to accept any project with a return of less than 20% since it would lower the division's ROI.

Residual Income

❏ **Residual income** is the difference between operating income and the minimum dollar return required on a company's operating assets. It is calculated as follows:

Residual income = Operating income – (Minimum rate of return x Operating assets)

Advantages of Residual Income

❏ Residual income overcomes the problem ROI had of discouraging investing in projects that would decrease the division's ROI but would increase the profitability of the company as a whole.

❏ Using the above example, if the minimum required rate of return was set at 12% the project would be accepted because it earns a return of 15%, and would thus increase residual income by:

Residual income of project = 24,000 – (12% x 160,000)

= 4,800

Disadvantages of Residual Income

❏ There are two disadvantages associated with residual income:
- It encourages managers to focus on the short run at the expense of the long run.
- Since the residual income result is an absolute number, it is not comparable between divisions of different size.

Economic Value Added

❏ **Economic value added (EVA)** is a performance measure calculated as after-tax operating profit minus the total annual cost of capital.

❏ EVA is calculated as follows:

EVA = After-tax operating income – (Weighted average cost of capital × Total capital employed)

❏ To calculate weighted average cost of capital (WACC) the company must identify all sources of invested funds, like debt (loans) and equity (issued shares). The interest on debt funding is adjusted for its tax deductibility to form the cost of debt. The cost of equity is the opportunity cost to investors, usually expressed as the average return on equity. Next a weighting is applied to the cost of debt and cost of equity to determine the WACC. For example, a project may be 60% financed by debt and 40% financed by equity. These percentages would be used as the weighting.

❏ Total capital employed includes:
- amounts paid for buildings, land, and machinery
- other expenditures meant to have a long-term payoff, such as research and development and employee training. These costs are included in total capital employed even if they are expensed as required by GAAP for financial accounting purposes.

❏ A positive EVA indicates that the company earned operating profit greater than the cost of the capital used. The company is creating wealth. If EVA is negative, then the company is destroying capital.

❒ Like RI, EVA is a dollar figure. EVA emphasizes *after-tax* operating profit and the *actual* cost of capital.

❒ Stock prices follow EVA better than earnings per share or return on equity.

Using EVA for Individual Projects

❒ EVA can be calculated for individual projects as follows:

EVA = Project income – Cost of capital

= Project income – (Cost of capital % × Assets employed)

Behavioural Aspects of EVA

❒ Using EVA encourages managers to accept any project that earns above the minimum rate.

❒ EVA encourages managers to consider the cost of financial investment (the cost of capital) when making decisions. Thus, EVA helps encourage desirable behaviour from division managers; an emphasis on operating income alone cannot do this.

Multiple Measures of Performance

❒ ROI, RI, and EVA are only measures of financial performance and all are focused on the short-term; thus, many companies may use nonfinancial operating measures to balance the performance measurement.

TRANSFER PRICING IN DECENTRALIZED COMPANIES

❒ If divisions of a company are operated independently but engage in transactions amongst themselves frequently a **transfer price** of the goods and services must be established.

❒ **Transfer prices** are prices charged for goods transferred between two divisions of the same company. The output of the selling division is used as input of the buying division.

Impact on Performance Measures

❒ Transfer pricing affects the transferring divisions and the overall firm through its impact on:
  - divisional performance measures
  - firmwide profits, and
  - divisional autonomy.

Impact on Divisional Performance Measures

❒ The price charged for transferred goods is revenue to the selling division and cost of goods sold to the buying division.

❒ Thus, profits and profit-based performance measures (ROI, RI, and EVA) of both divisions are affected by the transfer price.

Impact on Company-wide Profits

❒ The actual transfer price nets out for the company as a whole. It is revenue to one division and an expense in the other, so when you add the divisions together to get company-wide profits the effect is cancelled out.

❏ Transfer pricing can affect company-wide profits earned by the company as a whole if it affects divisional behaviour. For example, divisions, acting independently, may set transfer prices that maximize divisional profits but adversely affect company-wide profits.

Impact on Autonomy

❏ Because transfer pricing decisions can affect company-wide profitability, top management is often tempted to intervene and dictate desirable transfer prices.

❏ If such intervention becomes a frequent practice, however, the organization has effectively abandoned decentralization and all of its advantages.

The Transfer Pricing Problem

❏ The **transfer pricing problem** concerns finding a transfer pricing system that simultaneously satisfies the following three objectives:

1. *Accurate performance evaluation.* No one divisional manager should benefit at the expense of another.
2. *Goal congruence.* Divisional managers are motivated to select actions that maximize firm-wide profits.
3. *Divisional autonomy.* Central management should not interfere with the decision-making freedom of divisional managers.

❏ Although direct intervention by central management to set specific transfer prices may not be advisable, general transfer pricing guidelines or policies may be useful.

The Opportunity Cost Approach as a Guide for Transfer Pricing

❏ The **opportunity cost approach** identifies:

■ the **minimum transfer price**, which is the transfer price that would leave the selling division indifferent between selling the goods to an outside party or transferring the goods to an internal division

■ the **maximum transfer price**, which is the transfer price that would leave the buying division indifferent between buying the goods from an outside party or purchasing from an internal division

❏ The transferred goods should be transferred internally whenever the opportunity cost (minimum price) of the selling division is less than the opportunity cost (maximum price) of the buying division.

Market Price

❏ If there is a perfectly competitive outside market for the transferred goods, the optimal transfer price is the market price. (In a perfectly competitive market, the selling division can sell all it wishes at the prevailing market price.)

❏ The opportunity cost approach also identifies the market price as the optimal transfer price.

❏ If the selling division could sell the product externally for the market price, it would not accept anything less than market price.

❏ The minimum transfer price for the selling division is the market price, because the selling division would receive the market price whether it sells the product externally or internally.

❐ The maximum transfer price for the buying division is the market price, because the buying division would pay the market price whether it purchases the product internally or from an outside supplier.

Negotiated Transfer Prices

❐ If a perfectly competitive market for the transferred goods exists, the optimal transfer price is the market price.

❐ If a perfectly competitive market for the transferred goods does *not* exist, a negotiated transfer price may be a practical alternative.

❐ Opportunity costs for the buying division and selling division form the upper and lower boundaries for the transfer price.

Minimum Transfer Price	Maximum Transfer Price
Opportunity Cost for Selling Division	Opportunity Cost for Buying Division

❐ The selling division wants a high transfer price that will increase *its* income. The buying division wants a low transfer price that will increase *its* income.

Avoidable Distribution Costs

❐ If the selling division avoids costs such as distribution costs by selling internally, the opportunity cost to the selling division is the market price minus the avoidable cost.

❐ The opportunity cost to the buying division is the market price.

❐ The lower limit of the bargaining range is the market price minus avoidable costs, and the upper limit is the market price.

Minimum Transfer Price	Maximum Transfer Price
Market Price Less Selling Division's Avoidable Costs	Market Price

Excess Capacity

❐ When the selling division has excess capacity, a bargaining range exists.

❐ The lower limit of the bargaining range is the selling division's incremental costs. This is the minimum the selling division would be willing to accept.

❐ The upper limit of the range is the lower of:
  ▪ the buying division's outside purchase price, or
  ▪ the transfer price that results in a zero contribution margin on the goods for the buying division.

  This is the maximum amount the buying division would be willing to pay.

❐ At the lower limit of the range, the entire profit goes to the buying division.

❐ At the upper limit of the range, the entire profit goes to the selling division.

Disadvantages of Negotiated Transfer Prices

❒ Three disadvantages of negotiated transfer prices are as follows:
   1. One divisional manager who has private information may take advantage of another divisional manager.
   2. Performance measures may be distorted by the negotiating skills of managers.
   3. Negotiation can consume considerable time and resources.

Advantages of Negotiated Transfer Prices

❒ Negotiated transfer prices can help achieve the three objectives of:
   ▪ goal congruence
   ▪ autonomy, and
   ▪ accurate performance evaluation.

❒ If negotiation helps ensure goal congruence, top management is not as likely to intervene and divisional autonomy is not diminished.

❒ If the negotiating skills of managers are comparable or if the firm views negotiating skills as an important part of being a manager, concerns about accurate performance evaluation are avoided.

Cost-Based Transfer Prices

❒ Three types of cost-based transfer prices are:
   ▪ full cost
   ▪ full cost plus markup, and
   ▪ variable cost plus fixed fee.

❒ If cost-based transfer prices are used, *standard costs* should be used in order to avoid passing on the inefficiencies of one division to another.

Full-Cost Transfer Pricing

❒ Transfer prices should be determined based upon the opportunity costs of the buying and selling divisions.

❒ Full cost rarely provides accurate information about opportunity costs; therefore, using full-cost transfer prices can result in dysfunctional manager behaviour.

❒ If the selling division transfers products at the standard full cost, the selling division will not recognize any profit on the transfer.

Full Cost Plus Markup

❒ Using standard full cost plus a markup for profit for transfer prices can lead to decisions that are not in the best interests of the entire company.

❒ In addition, if the profit markup is determined by formula (such as 20 percent of cost), the transfer price is of limited usefulness in evaluating the division's performance.

❒ If the markup is negotiated, then it is negotiated transfer pricing.

Variable Cost Plus Fixed Fee

❒ If the fixed fee is negotiable, the variable-cost-plus-fixed-fee approach is equivalent to negotiated transfer pricing.

Appropriateness of Use

❑ Reasons for using cost-based transfer prices include:

- Cost-based transfer prices are objective and simple to apply.
- If the transfers between divisions have a small impact on the profit of either division, it may be cost-beneficial to use a cost-based formula rather than spending valuable resources on negotiations.
- The use of the full-cost plus markup formula may be the agreed-upon result of negotiations.

Special Issues in Multinational Companies

❑ Multinational companies have operations in several countries.

❑ Cultural, geographic, economic, and other differences often result in the divisions of multinational companies operating as investment centres. These differences also result in unique problems for performance evaluation and transfer pricing.

Performance Evaluation

❑ Interdivisional comparisons of ROI, RI, and EVA are misleading in multinational companies due to the differences in environmental and other factors.

❑ One way to discourage myopic behaviour is to use additional measures of performance that relate more closely to the long-run health of the division.

Transfer Pricing

❑ Multinational companies with subsidiaries in both high-tax and low-tax countries may use transfer pricing to shift costs to the high-tax countries (where their deductibility will lower tax payments) and to shift revenues to low-tax countries.

❑ Canadian-based multinationals are governed by the Canada Customs and Revenue Agency, which requires that sales between divisions be made at "arm's length."

KEY TERMS TEST

Test your recall of the key terms as follows. Try to recall as many key terms as possible without assistance. If you need assistance, refer to the list of key terms at the end of this section.

1. _____ . _____ _____ is a system in which decisions are made at the top level of an organization and local managers are given the charge to implement these decisions.

2. _____ is the granting of decision-making freedom to lower operating levels.

3. _____ _____ _____ is a system in which decisions are made and implemented by lower-level managers.

4. _____ _____ _____ is a performance measure calculated by taking the after-tax operating profit minus the total annual cost of capital.

5. _____ _____ _____ or _____ is the ratio of operating net income to operating assets.

6. _____ is the ratio of net operating income to sales.

7. _____ is the ratio of sales to average operating assets.

8. _____ _____ are assets used to generate operating income, consisting of cash, inventories, receivables, property, plant, and equipment.

9. _____ _____ is earnings before interest and taxes.

10. _____ _____ is the amount of operating income remaining after a minimum charge has been deducted.

11. The price charged for goods transferred from one division to another is called the _____ _____.

12. The _____ _____ _____ is the problem of finding a transfer pricing system that simultaneously satisfies the three objectives of accurate performance evaluation, goal congruence, and autonomy.

13. The _____ _____ _____ is the transfer price that will make the buying division no worse off if an input is acquired internally.

14. The _____ _____ _____ is the transfer price that will make the selling division no worse off if the intermediate product is sold internally.

15. _____ _____ _____ is a transfer pricing system that identifies the minimum price a selling division is willing to accept and the maximum price a buying division is willing to pay.

16. A(n) _____ _____ is a segment of the business whose manager is accountable for specified sets of activities.

17. A(n) _____ _____ is a division of a company that is evaluated on the basis of cost.

18. A(n) _____ _____ is a segment of the business that is evaluated on the basis of sales.

19. A(n) _____ _____ is a division of a company that is evaluated on the basis of operating income or profit.

20. A(n) _____ _____ is a division of a company that is evaluated on the basis of return on investment.

KEY TERMS

centralized decision making
cost centre
decentralization
decentralized decision making
economic value added
investment centre
margin
maximum transfer price
minimum transfer price
operating assets

operating income
opportunity cost approach
profit centre
residual income
responsibility centre
return on investment (ROI)
revenue centre
transfer price
transfer pricing problem
turnover

↻ **Compare your answers with those at the end of the chapter. Review any key terms missed.**

CHAPTER QUIZ

Write your answers in the spaces provided.

1. Four types of responsibility centres are:

   1. _____

   2. _____

   3. _____

   4. _____

2. Three methods used to evaluate investment centre performance are:

   1. _____

   2. _____

   3. _____

3. In order for decentralization to be effective, performance must be evaluated for control purposes. The measures used to evaluate performance can affect a manager's behaviour; therefore, the performance measures used should encourage _____ _____.

4. Return on investment is calculated as follows:

   ROI = _____ / _____

5. A disadvantage of ROI as a performance measure is that it may encourage _____ _____.

6. Residual income is calculated as follows:

   RI = _____ - (_____ x _____)

7. Economic value added is calculated as follows:

   EVA = _____ – (_____ × _____)

8. Nonfinancial operating measures of performance include:

   1. _____

   2. _____

   3. _____

   4. _____

9. Three objectives of a transfer pricing system should be:

   1. _____

   2. _____

   3. _____

10. Under conditions of perfect competition, when the selling division has no excess capacity, the optimal transfer price is the _____ _____.

11. The opportunity cost approach to transfer pricing identifies a minimum transfer price and a maximum transfer price. If a perfectly competitive market for the transferred goods does *not* exist, a negotiated transfer price can be used. The lower boundary for the transfer price is _____. The upper boundary for the transfer price is _____.

12. With regard to transfer prices, if the selling division has excess capacity, a bargaining range exists. The floor of the bargaining range is the selling division's _____ . The ceiling of the bargaining range is the maximum amount the buying division is willing to pay, which is the lower of _____ or_____.

13. Transfer prices based on _____ _____ do not encourage the selling division to be efficient.

Circle the single best answer.

Use the following information to answer Questions 14 and 15:

The following results for the year pertain to the Russell Division of TADD Corporation:

Revenues	$500,000
Variable expenses	250,000
Fixed expenses	100,000
After-tax operating profit	130,000

Total capital employed is $800,000. The firm's weighted average cost of capital is 10%.

14. EVA for the Russell Division is: (a) $50,000; (b) $70,000; (c) $150,000; (d) $170,000

15. Return on investment for the Russell Division is: (a) 5.34%; (b) 10%; (c) 12.5%; (d) 18.75%

☺ Compare your answers with those at the end of the chapter. Review any questions missed.

PRACTICE TEST

PROBLEM 1

The Kendall Division of Stephens Enterprises expects the following results for 2000:

Revenues	$500,000
Variable expenses	200,000
Contribution margin	$300,000
Fixed expenses	180,000
Operating income	$120,000

Total divisional assets are $1,000,000.

Instructions:

Calculate profit margin, asset turnover, and ROI for the division.

PROBLEM 2

The following information pertains to Roger Corporation:

After-tax operating profit..................................	$ 100,000
Financing:	
Bonds (10% interest)....................................	600,000
Common shares (average risk)...................	400,000
Total capital employed	1,200,000
Marginal tax rate	40%

Instructions:

1. Calculate the weighted average cost of capital for the company.

PROBLEM 2 *(Continued)*

2. Calculate economic value added for the company.

3. Discuss the significance of Roger's EVA.

PROBLEM 3

Colby, Incorporated, has just formed a new division, and the following four investment opportunities are available to the division:

Investment Opportunity	Income	Investment
1	$ 80,000	$200,000
2	120,000	600,000
3	80,000	500,000
4	50,000	200,000

The firm requires a minimum return of 20%.

Instructions:

1. If you were the division manager and your evaluation was based on ROI, which investment opportunities would you accept?

PROBLEM 3 *(Continued)*

2. If you were the division manager and your evaluation was based on RI, which investment opportunities would you accept?

3. If you were president of Colby, Incorporated, which projects would you want the division to accept?

PROBLEM 4

Goldwasser Industries has two divisions, the Lauren Division and the Lindsey Division. Information about a component that the Lauren Division produces is as follows:

Revenue..	$100 per unit
Variable manufacturing costs...................	$25 per unit
Fixed manufacturing overhead.................	$15 per unit
Expected sales in units............................	7,000 units

The Lauren Division can produce up to 8,000 components per year. The Lindsey Division needs 500 units of the component for a product it manufactures.

Instructions:

1. Determine the minimum transfer price that the Lauren Division would accept.

PROBLEM 4 *(Continued)*

2. Determine the maximum transfer price that the manager of the Lindsey Division would pay.

3. How would your answers to Requirements 1 and 2 change if the Lauren Division did not have excess capacity?

PROBLEM 5

Alexander Industries is a decentralized company that evaluates its divisions based on ROI.

Division K has the capacity to make 10,000 units of a product. Division K's variable costs are $60 per unit.

Division N can use the product as a component in one of its products. Division N would incur $40 of variable costs to convert the component into its own product, which sells for $200.

Instructions:

The following requirements are independent of each other.

1. Division K can sell all that it produces for $120 each. Division N needs 1,000 units. What is the correct transfer price?

PROBLEM 5 *(Continued)*

2. Division K can sell 8,000 units at $150 each. Any excess capacity will be unused unless the units are purchased by the N division, which could use up to 1,000 units. Determine the floor and ceiling of the bargaining range.

ANSWERS

KEY TERMS TEST

1. Centralized decision making
2. Decentralization
3. Decentralized decision making
4. Economic value added
5. Return on investment, ROI
6. Margin
7. Turnover
8. Operating assets
9. Operating income
10. Residual income
11. transfer price
12. transfer pricing problem
13. maximum transfer price
14. minimum transfer price
15. Opportunity cost approach
16. responsibility centre
17. cost centre
18. revenue centre
19. profit centre
20. investment centre

CHAPTER QUIZ

1. 1. cost centres
    2. revenue centres
    3. profit centres
    4. investment centres
2. 1. return on investment
    2. residual income
    3. economic value added
3. goal congruence
4. Operating income/Average operating assets
5. dysfunctional behaviour (or myopic behaviour)
6. Operating income – (Minimum required rate × Operating assets)
7. After-tax operating income – (Weighted average cost of capital × Total capital employed)
8. 1. market share
    2. customer complaints

    3. personnel turnover ratios
    4. personnel development
9. 1. accurate performance evaluation
    2. goal congruence
    3. divisional autonomy
10. market price
11. the opportunity cost for the selling division, the opportunity cost for the buying division
12. incremental costs, the buying division's outside purchase price, the transfer price that results in a zero contribution margin on the goods for the buying division
13. actual costs
14. a $\$130,000 - (10\% \times \$800,000) = \$50,000$
15. d $\$500,000 - \$250,000 - \$100,000 = \$150,000$; $\$150,000/\$800,000 = 18.75\%$

PRACTICE TEST

PROBLEM 1

ROI = Operating income/Average operating assets
    = $\$120,000/\$1,000,000$
    = 12%

ROI = Margin × Turnover
    = (Operating income/Sales) × (Sales/Average operating assets)
    = ($\$120,000/\$500,000$) × ($\$500,000/\$1,000,000$)
    = .24 × .50 = .12 or 12%

PROBLEM 2

1. After-tax cost of bonds = (.10 × .60) = .06 or 6%

   Cost of common shares= Return on long-term treasury bonds + Average premium
                        = 6% + 6% = 12%

   Weighted average cost of capital:

	Amount	Percent	x	After-Tax Cost	=	Weighted Cost
Bonds.........................	$600,000	.60	x	.06	=	.036
Common shares	400,000	.40	x	.12	=	.048
Weighted average cost of capital						.084

2. Cost of capital = $1,200,000 × .084 = $100,800

Economic value added:

After-tax profit...	$100,000
Less: Weighted average cost of capital...........	100,800
EVA	$ (800)

3. Roger's EVA was a negative $800, indicating that capital was destroyed. If the EVA had been positive, this would indicate that wealth had been created.

PROBLEM 3

1.

Investment Opportunity	Income	Investment	ROI
1	$ 80,000	$200,000	40%
2	120,000	600,000	20%
3	80,000	500,000	16%
4	50,000	200,000	25%

If the division manager accepts only Project 1, his ROI will be 40%. Accepting any of the other projects would lower his ROI. For example, if the divisional manager accepts Project 1 and Project 4, his ROI would drop from 40% to 32.5%.

ROI = ($80,000 + $50,000)/($200,000 + $200,000) = 32.5%

2.

Investment Opportunity	Income	- (Investment	x 20%)	RI
1	$ 80,000	$200,000	20%	$40,000
2	120,000	600,000	20%	$0
3	80,000	500,000	20%	$(20,000)
4	50,000	200,000	20%	$10,000

The division manager would accept Projects 1 and 4, reject Project 3 and be indifferent as to Project 2.

3. The president of the firm would want the division to accept any project with a return in excess of the firm's required return of 20%, that being Projects 1 and 4, with 2 being indifferent.

PROBLEM 4

1. The lower boundary of the bargaining range would be the selling division's variable cost of $25. This would be the minimum amount the selling division would accept.

2. The upper boundary of the range would be $100 (the amount the buying division would pay an outside supplier).

3. If the Lauren Division could sell 8,000 units to outside customers for $100 each, the Lauren Division would have to receive $100 per unit from the Lindsey Division.

If the Lauren Division sells to the Lindsey Division, it forgoes $100 per unit from outside customers. Therefore to be as well off, the Lauren Division must receive $100 per unit from the Lindsey Division.

PROBLEM 5

1. The transfer price would be the market price of $120 each.

If Division K sells to Division N, it would forgo $120 per unit; therefore to be as well off, Division K must receive $120 per unit from Division N. Division N would pay the market price of $120 whether it purchased the component from Division K or from an outside supplier.

2. The floor of the bargaining range is $60 per unit (Division K's variable cost to produce the component).

The ceiling of the range would be the lower of:
a. the buying division's outside purchase price ($150), or
b. the transfer price that results in a zero contribution margin on the goods for the buying division ($200 − $40 variable cost = $160).

The ceiling would be $150 (the amount Division N would pay to acquire the component from an outside supplier).

CHAPTER 17
Strategic Performance Evaluation and Management

CHAPTER REVIEW

STRATEGIC PERFORMANCE MANAGEMENT ENVIRONMENT

❏ The type of environment a company operates in can have a significant effect on the type of control and communication systems for the company.

❏ Organizations operating in a dynamic, rapidly changing environment find that adaptation, change, and continuous improvement are necessary. **Continuous improvement** is the process of constantly searching for ways to eliminate waste. Waste reduction tools attempt to eliminate waste in the form of inventories, unnecessary activities, defective products, rework, setup time, and underutilization of employee talents and skills. Waste reduction tools include:

- JIT purchasing and manufacturing
- reengineering
- total quality management
- employee empowerment
- computer-aided manufacturing

Organizational Control Environment

❏ **Organizational environment** includes factors that are largely controllable by the organization in the long term but may be fixed in the short term, such as production capacity.

❏ **External environment** consists of factors that are largely uncontrollable by the organization, such as weather conditions.

❏ **Contingency theory** advises that there is no one best or universal management control system.

❏ An organization's control system should be compatible with its own unique organizational and external environment.

❏ The following table summarizes the organizational factors and external factors that affect a company's management control system.

Organizational Factors	Environmental Factors
Size	Technology
Strategy	Competition
Structure	Economy
Systems	Culture
Resources	Social Values
Staff Skills	Regulation and Legislation
Management Philosophy	Politics
Organizational Norms	

Performance Management and Control Systems

❐ Responsibility accounting uses the accounting system to measure actions and outcomes.

❐ The objective of responsibility accounting is to influence behaviour such that the individual's and organization's goals are aligned.

❐ The responsibility control model has four elements:
  - assigning responsibility
  - establishing performance measure or benchmarks
  - evaluating performance
  - rewarding performance

❐ **Management control** is the process by which managers ensure that resources are obtained and used effectively and efficiently to achieve the organization's objectives.

❐ **Performance management** is broader that management control. It entails the effective use of information provided by the management control system for strategic planning, decision-making, and management.

Management Control Systems

❐ Three types of management control systems are:
  1. *functional-based*
  2. *activity-based*, and
  3. *strategic-based*

❐ The system selected is *contingent* on the environment in which the firm operates. Firms that operate in a stable environment with standardized products and low competitive pressures may use the functional-based responsibility accounting system. As the competitive environment becomes more dynamic, activity-based and strategic-based systems may be more suitable.

COMPARISON OF FUNCTIONAL-BASED, ACTIVITY-BASED, AND STRATEGIC-BASED CONTROL SYSTEMS

❐ A **functional-based control system**:
  - focuses on organizational units such as departments and plants
  - uses financial outcome measures and static standards and benchmarks to evaluate performance
  - emphasizes status quo and organizational stability

❏ An **activity-based control system**:
  ▪ focuses on processes
  ▪ uses both operational and financial measures and dynamic standards
  ▪ emphasizes continuous improvement

❏ A **strategic-based control system** (or **Balanced Scorecard**) translates the mission and strategy of an organization into operational objectives and measures from the following four perspectives:
  1. Financial perspective
  2. Customer perspective
  3. Process perspective
  4. Infrastructure (learning and growth) perspective

Strategic-based responsibility accounting uses directed continuous improvement, whereby continuous improvement is related to the overall mission and strategy of the organization.

❏ The four responsibility elements for functional-based, activity-based, and strategic-based control systems are summarized below:

Responsibility Element	Functional-Based Control Systems	Activity-Based Control Systems	Strategic-Based Control Systems
Assign responsibility	▪ Responsibility assigned to individual in charge of an organizational unit such as a department, division, or production facility ▪ Responsibility defined in financial terms (costs)	▪ Responsibility assigned to teams or processes such as product development	▪ Responsibility system maintains perspectives that serve as a potential source for a competitive advantage ▪ Focuses on financial, customer, process, and infrastructure (learning and growth) perspectives

Establish performance measures or benchmarks	▪ Budgets
	▪ Standard costing using currently attainable standards
		▪ Performance measures are dynamic and process-oriented.
		▪ Focuses on continual improvement and increasing customer value
			▪ Performance measures are perspective oriented.
			▪ Performance measures are integrated and linked to the organization's goals and initiatives.
			▪ Measures balanced between:[a]
			  ▪ lag and lead measures
			  ▪ objective and subjective measures
			  ▪ financial and nonfinancial measures
			  ▪ external and internal measures

Responsibility Element	Functional-Based Control Systems	Activity-Based Control Systems	Strategic-Based Control Systems
Evaluate performance	<ul><li>Compare actual costs with budgeted (or standard) costs</li><li>Individuals held accountable only for items they can control</li></ul>	<ul><li>Financial measures</li><li>Nonfinancial measures such as quality, efficiency, on-time delivery, cycle time, productivity</li></ul>	<ul><li>Performance measures relate to:<ul><li>process efficiency</li><li>customer satisfaction</li><li>infrastructure factors that enable an organization to learn, change, and use new and improved process (employee satisfaction and skills)</li><li>economic or financial consequences of processes (cost trends)</li></ul></li></ul>
Assign rewards	<ul><li>Rewards individuals based on financial performance</li><li>Rewards include promotions, salary increases, bonuses, and profit sharing.</li></ul>	<ul><li>Rewards based on multidimensional performance</li><li>Group-based or team rewards</li><li>Rewards include gain sharing—sharing in gains related to specific improvement projects.</li></ul>	<ul><li>Rewards based on multidimensional performance</li><li>Incentive compensation may be distributed among the four perspectives: financial, customer, process, and infrastructure (learning and growth) perspectives.</li></ul>

[a]**Lag measures** are outcome measures of results from past efforts, such as customer profitability.

Lead measures or **performance drivers** are factors that drive future performance, such as hours of employee training.

Objective measures are readily quantified and verified, such as market share.

Subjective measures are less quantifiable and more judgmental, such as employee capabilities.

Financial measures are expressed in monetary terms.

Nonfinancial measures are expressed in nonmonetary terms, such as effects of dissatisfied customers.

External measures relate to customers and shareholders, such as customer satisfaction.

Internal measures relate to processes and capabilities that create value for customers and shareholders, such as process efficiency and employee satisfaction.

PROCESS VALUE ANALYSIS

❏ Process value analysis is essential to strategic-based control systems.

❏ Process value analysis is concerned with:
  - activity value analysis
  - value chain analysis
  - supply chain management

Activity Value Analysis

❏ **Activity value analysis** is the process of identifying, describing, and evaluating the activities an organization performs.

❏ Activity value analysis requires an understanding of what causes activity costs.

❏ **Activity inputs** are resources consumed by the activity in producing its outputs.

❏ **Activity outputs** are the results of performing an activity.

❑ **Activity output measure** is the number of times the activity is performed. It is a measure of the demands placed on an activity.

❑ **Driver analysis** is the effort expended to identify those factors that are the root causes of activity costs. Once the root cause of activity costs is known, then action can be taken to improve the activity.

❑ Activity value analysis should produce four outcomes:
1. Identify the activities to be performed
2. Identify the individuals performing the activities
3. Identify the time and resources required to perform the activities
4. Identify the value of the activities to the organization, including a recommendation to select and keep only value-added activities

❑ **Value-added activities** are activities that are necessary to achieve corporate objectives and remain in business.

❑ An activity is valued added if it satisfies three conditions:
1. the activity produces a change of state
2. change of state was not achievable by preceding activities
3. activities enable other activities to be performed.

❑ **Value-added costs** are costs caused by value-added activities.

❑ **Nonvalue-added activities** are unnecessary activities and are all activities other than those that are absolutely essential to remain in business.

❑ **Nonvalue-added costs** are costs caused by either:
- nonvalue-added activities, or
- the inefficient performance of value-added activities.

❑ Activity analysis attempts to:
- identify and eliminate all unnecessary activities, and
- increase the efficiency of necessary activities.

❑ An unnecessary activity is wasteful and should be eliminated. Managing costs may increase the efficiency of an activity—but if the activity is unnecessary, what does it matter if it is performed efficiently?

❑ Five major categories of nonvalue-added activities are:
- *Scheduling*—an activity that uses time and resources to determine when different products have access to processes (or when and how many setups must be done) and how much will be produced.
- *Moving*—an activity that uses time and resources to move raw materials, work in process, and finished goods from one department to another.
- *Waiting*—an activity in which raw materials or work in process use time and resources by waiting on the next process.
- *Inspecting*—an activity where time and resources are spent on ensuring that the product meets specifications.
- *Storing*—an activity that uses time and resources while a good or raw material is held in inventory.

❑ None of the above activities adds any value for the customer.

❑ Activity analysis can reduce costs in four ways:

1. **Activity elimination**—eliminating nonvalue-added activities.

2. **Activity selection**—choosing among different sets of activities caused by competing strategies.

3. **Activity reduction**—decreasing the time and resources required by an activity. This approach to cost reduction should be primarily aimed at:

   ▪ improving the efficiency of necessary activities, or

   ▪ improving the nonvalue-added activities until they can be eliminated.

   Reducing setup time is an example of improving the efficiency of a necessary activity.

4. **Activity sharing**—increasing the efficiency of activities by using economies of scale. An example is designing a product to use components already used in other products. By using existing components, activities associated with these components, such as design and machine tooling, are not duplicated.

Value Chain Analysis

❑ **Value chain analysis** is a strategic tool that can be used to understand a company's competitive advantage and its relationships with suppliers, customers, and competitors.

❑ Value chain analysis is concerned not only with value activity analysis, but also with higher-level evaluation of strategic alternatives and their long-term consequences.

❑ The value chain consists of 6 interrelated sets of activities:

32. Research and development

33. Design

34. Production

35. Marketing

36. Distribution

37. Customer service

❑ Administrative functions are not included in the value chain, as they consist mostly of non-valued activities.

❑ Not all the value chain activities are important to all companies. A company needs to consciously decide which value chain activities it wants to pursue. For example, if a company's competitive advantage rests in the production area, it may want to outsource its marketing or research and development activities and concentrate on production efficiencies only.

Supply Chain Management

❑ A **supply chain** is all the activities involved in the efficient and effective movement and transformation of raw materials, through the manufacturing process, to final products to end users.

❑ **Supply chain management** refers to the integrated and process-orientated approach to design, manage, and control the supply chain.

❑ Good supply chain management can lead to increased customer satisfaction, loyalty, and increased market share.

❏ Before the implementation of supply chain management, a cost benefit analysis should be performed.

STRATEGIC PERFORMANCE MEASUREMENT

❏ Strategic performance measurement is a process concerned with the assessment of the performance of organizations, organizational units, and programs.

❏ Strategic performance measurement's primary function is to monitor processes toward an organization's strategic objectives. It serves as an important planning, control, and accountability device.

❏ A direct measure of the well-being of all stakeholders does not exist so we must use proxies.

Nonfinancial Performance Measures

❏ Nonfinancial measures are often more easily understood by low-level managers than financial measures because lower-level managers can see the effect they have directly on the nonfinancial measure.

❏ Nonfinancial measures can be collected and analyzed on a timelier basis than financial measures.

❏ Poor financial results can often be predicted by early nonfinancial measures related to productivity, quality, etc., as can good financial results.

❏ Performance measures can be developed and used at different organizational levels. As the responsibility broadens (going up the hierarchy), the focus becomes more on effectiveness and less on efficiency and the number of measures decrease.

❏ Each organizational level warrants its own set of performance measures based on its own unique characteristics. There is no one set of performance measures suitable for every organization.

❏ Effective performance measures will have the following measurement criteria: relevance, reliability, accessibility, and simplicity.

❏ The main difficulty with performance measurement systems lies in the use of performance measures. A performance measure should be controllable by the employee held accountable for the measure, communicated clearly to the employee, and used in evaluating and rewarding employees. Also, employees should have a voice in designing the performance measure they will be held accountable for.

❏ Exhibit 17-8 of the text lists 18 factors that significantly contribute to the success of performance measurement systems.

❏ There are three performance measurement frameworks:

  ▪ The **balanced scorecard**, which consists of a balanced mix of financial and nonfinancial measures in 4 different areas; learning and growth, processes, customer satisfaction, and financial.

  ▪ The **business excellence model**, which consists of nine criteria; leadership, people management, policy and strategy, resources, people satisfaction, customer satisfaction, impact on society, and business results. It emphasizes total quality management.

  ▪ The **performance prism**, which focuses on stakeholders rather than strategies. There are five elements to this approach: strategies, processes, capabilities, stakeholder satisfaction, and stakeholder contribution.

❏ All three approaches allow for benchmarking. **Benchmarking** is an approach to standard setting that uses best practices as the standard for evaluating activity performance.

The Balanced Scorecard

❏ The **Balanced Scorecard** is a strategic control system that translates an organization's mission and strategy into operational objectives and performance measures from four different perspectives:

1. **Financial perspective**, which describes the economic consequences of actions taken in the other three perspectives

2. **Customer perspective**, which defines the customer and market segments in which the business operates

3. **Internal business process perspective**, which describes the internal processes needed to provide value for customers and owners

4. **Learning and growth (infrastructure) perspective**, which defines the capabilities that an organization needs to create long-term growth and improvement: employee capabilities, information systems capabilities, and employee attitudes of motivation, empowerment, and alignment

❏ A business's **strategy** specifies the desired relationships among the above four perspectives.

❏ *Strategy translation* specifies objectives, measures, targets, and initiatives for each perspective.

❏ **Single-loop feedback** provides information about the effectiveness of the strategy implementation.

❏ **Double-loop feedback** provides information about both the *effectiveness* of the strategy implementation and the *validity* of the assumptions underlying the strategy.

The Financial Perspective

❏ The financial perspective has three strategic themes:

1. *Revenue growth.* Objectives may include increasing the number of new products, developing new markets, changing the pricing strategy.

2. *Cost reduction.* Objectives may include reducing the cost per unit. Accuracy of cost assignment is important when evaluating cost reduction performance objectives.

3. *Asset utilization.* Financial measures include return on investment and economic value added.

Customer Perspective

❏ The customer perspective defines and selects the customer and market segments in which the company chooses to compete.

❏ **Core objectives and measures** are common across all organizations.

Core Objectives	Measures
Increase market share	Market share (percentage of market)
Increase customer retention	Percentage growth from existing customers Percentage of repeating customers
Increase customer acquisition	Number of new customers
Increase customer satisfaction	Ratings from customer surveys
Increase customer profitability	Customer profitability

❏ **Customer value** is the difference between what the customer receives (realization) and what the customer gives up (sacrifices).

❏ Realization objectives and measures are summarized below:

Realization Objectives	Measures
Decrease price	Reduce price
Decrease postpurchase costs	Reduce postpurchase costs
Improve production functionality	Satisfaction ratings of product features
Improve product quality	Percentage of returns
Increase delivery reliability	On-time delivery percentage Aging schedule
Improve product image and reputation	Ratings from customer surveys

Process Perspective

❏ The process perspective identifies the processes needed to achieve the customer and financial perspectives.

❏ The **process value chain** consists of three processes:
1. The **innovation process** creates new products and services to satisfy the emerging and potential needs of customers.
2. The **operations process** produces and delivers existing products and services to customers. Cycle time and velocity are two operational measures of responsiveness to customer orders. **Cycle time** is the time it takes to produce a unit of output (cycle time = time/units produced). **Velocity** is the number of units of output that can be produced in a given period of time (velocity = units produced/time).
3. The **postsales service process** provides critical and responsive services to customers after the product or service has been delivered.

❐ Objectives and measures for the three processes of the process perspective are summarized below:

Objectives	Measures
Innovation process:	
Increase the number of new products	Number of new products versus planned products
Increase proprietary products	Percentage of revenue from proprietary products
Decrease new product development time	Time to market (from start to finish)
Operations process:	
Increase process quality	Quality costs Output yields Percentage of defective units
Increase process efficiency	Unit cost trends Output/input(s)
Decrease process time	Cycle time and velocity MCE (Manufacturing Cycle Efficiency)
Postsales service process:	
Increase service quality	First-pass yields
Increase service efficiency	Cost trends Output/Input
Decrease service time	Cycle time

Learning and Growth Perspective

❐ The learning and growth perspective provides the capabilities that enable the accomplishment of the other three perspectives' objectives.

❐ The objectives and measures of the learning and growth perspective are summarized below:

Objectives	Measures
Increase employee capabilities	Employee satisfaction ratings Employee turnover percentages Employee productivity (revenue/employee) Hours of training
Increase motivation, empowerment, and alignment	Suggestions per employee Suggestions implemented per employee
Increase information systems capabilities	Percentage of processes with real-time feedback capabilities Percentage of customer-facing employees with on-line access to customer and product information

MEASURING AND REWARDING MANAGERIAL PERFORMANCE

❐ The performance of the division should be separated from the performance of managers because certain items under the division responsibility are not controllable by the managers.

❐ **Uncontrollable** factors cannot be influenced by a manager, where as **controllable** factors can.

Goal Congruence and Managerial Motivation

❑ **Goal congruence** exists when individuals and groups in an organization work toward the achievement of organizational goals.

❑ **Managerial motivation** is an exertion of effort toward achieving organizational goals.

❑ Organizations may encourage goal congruence by using management compensation programs that reward managers for taking actions that benefit the organization.

❑ **Organizational goals** set specific short and medium term performance targets. The target should be well defined (specific), and challenging but attainable.

❑ **Participation** in goal setting by employees is important for three reasons:

- It can increase employee ownership of the goals, which fosters employee commitment to attaining the goals.
- It utilizes employee skills and knowledge and can motivate employees to further develop their skills.
- It can promote the customer perspective since when employees are in closer contact with customers they have a better understanding of the customers' needs.

❑ For effective participation three conditions must be met:

- Employees must possess the necessary information and skills.
- Employee contributions must be taken seriously by upper-level managers.
- Performance measures and rewards must fairly reflect the employee's contribution to the organization.

Managerial Incentive Compensation

❑ In a corporation, the shareholders (owners) are represented by the board of directors, who hire a CEO to manage the corporation. The CEO hires division managers to operate the divisions on behalf of the owners.

❑ There are three reasons why managers might not provide good service:

1. They may have low ability.
2. They may prefer to not work as hard as needed.
3. They may prefer to spend company resources on perquisites.

❏ The first reason requires owners to discover information about the manager before hiring him or her. The second and third reasons require the owner to monitor the manager or to arrange an incentive scheme that will closely align the manager's goals with those of the owners.

Monetary Compensation

❏ Monetary compensation includes salaries and bonuses.

❏ Bonuses give a company more flexibility than salary increases.

❏ Many companies use a combination of salary and bonus to reward performance, keeping salaries fairly stable and basing bonuses on divisional income or targeted increases in net income.

❏ Income-based compensation can encourage dysfunctional behaviour, such as postponing research and development or maintenance.

Nonmonetary Compensation

❏ Nonmonetary compensation might consist of titles, office location, expense accounts, and other perquisites.

❏ **Perquisites** are a type of fringe benefit received by managers over and above salary. Examples include use of a company car and expense accounts.

Gainsharing

❏ **Gainsharing** provides cash incentives for a company's entire workforce, with the incentives keyed to quality and productivity gains. For example, instead of using profit-driven bonuses, a company might use performance-based measures such as product quality or customer loyalty.

Performance Measures and Behavioural Effects

❏ Performance measures promote positive behaviours and goal congruence if used properly.

Activity Drivers and Behaviour

❏ If an individual's or team's performance is judged by the ability to reduce nonvalue-added costs, then the selection and use of activity drivers as output performance measures can affect behaviour.

❏ A **value-added standard** is the optimal output level for an activity. This can then be used to define a specific objective and create desirable behaviours.

❏ Value-added standards focus on continual improvement and movement toward the ideal.

Incentive Compensation and Behaviour

❏ The behavioural effects of performance measurement are intensified if these measures are used as a basis for incentive compensation plans.

❏ Managers may "boost" short-term performance at the expense of long-term performance. For example, if compensation is based on a percentage of net income, managers may choose to defer research and development activities, because such activities decrease short-term income, although they improve the organization's long-term prospects. These types of behaviours are referred to as gaming behaviours.

Multiple Measures and Behaviour

❑ To mitigate gaming behaviours, **multiple measures** that balance financial and nonfinancial criteria in the compensation formula are required. The aim should be to balance the measure so that when one measure is manipulated, the other criteria moves in the opposite direction, thereby deterring manipulation of the measures.

❑ The balance of the measure will be contingent upon each individual organization's strategy.

APPENDIX A: SPECIAL ISSUES IN PERFORMANCE MANAGEMENT AND REPORTING

Value- and Nonvalue-Added Cost Reporting

❑ An activity-based cost report should include:
- value-added costs
- nonvalue-added costs

❑ This enables management to focus on reducing and eventually eliminating nonvalue-added costs.

❑ The steps involved in reporting value-added and nonvalue-added costs are as follows:
- Identify output measures for each activity.
- Determine value-added standard quantities for each activity.
- Calculate value-added costs as the value-added standard quantities multiplied by the price standard.

$$\text{Value-added costs} = \text{Standard quantity} \times \text{Standard price}$$
$$= SQ \times SP$$

- Nonvalue-added costs are the difference between the actual quantity of the activity's output and the value-added level, multiplied by the unit standard cost.

$$\text{Nonvalue-added costs} = (\text{Actual quantity} - \text{Standard quantity}) \times \text{Standard price}$$
$$= (AQ - SQ) \times SP$$

- For flexible resources (resources acquired as needed), AQ is the actual quantity of activity used.
- For committed resources (resources acquired in advance of usage), AQ is the actual quantity of activity capacity acquired (the activity's practical capacity).
- For nonvalue-added activities that are unnecessary, the value-added standard quantity is zero.

Trend Report

❑ Trend reporting involves comparing costs for each activity over time. If activities are reduced, eliminated, selected, and shared, cost reductions should follow and there should be a decline in nonvalue-added costs from one period to the next.

The Role of Kaizen Standards

❑ **Kaizen costing** focuses on reducing the costs of existing products and processes using two major subcycles:
1. The kaizen or continuous improvement cycle
2. The maintenance cycle

❐ The kaizen or continuous improvement cycle consists of a Plan-Do-Check-Act sequence:

1. *Plan.* Plan the amount of improvement (such as reduction in nonvalue-added costs). A **kaizen standard**, a type of currently attainable standard, reflects planned improvement for the upcoming period.

2. *Do.* Implement the planned improvements.

3. *Check.* Check the actual improvement attained with the kaizen standard.

4. *Act.* Set a new minimum standard for future performance, initiate a maintenance cycle, and search for additional improvement opportunities.

❐ The maintenance cycle also uses a Plan-Do-Check-Act sequence; however, the standard is based on prior improvements to lock in realized improvements. For example, if actual improvement achieved resulted in setup costs of $125, then setup costs of $125 should be maintained until further improvements are made.

Activity Capacity Management

❐ **Activity capacity** is the number of times an activity can be performed. Activity drivers measure activity capacity.

❐ There are two capacity variances:

1. **Activity volume variance** is the difference between the actual activity level acquired (practical capacity or AQ) and the capacity that should be used (value-added standard quantity or SQ). The volume variance is the nonvalue-added cost of the activity. For a nonvalue-added activity, the standard quantity (SQ) equals zero.

2. **Unused capacity variance** is the difference between activity availability (AQ) and activity usage (AU).

❐ The capacity variances are calculated as follows:

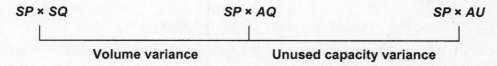

$$SP \times SQ \qquad SP \times AQ \qquad SP \times AU$$

|_____|_____|
Volume variance   **Unused capacity variance**

where AQ = activity capacity acquired (practical capacity)
$\quad\quad\quad SQ$ = activity capacity used
$\quad\quad\quad AU$ = actual usage of the activity
$\quad\quad\quad SP$ = fixed activity rate

❐ Activity improvement can create unused capacity, but managers must be willing to reduce resource spending to increase profits.

Life-Cycle Cost Budgeting

❐ **Product life cycle** is the time a product exists from conception to abandonment.

❐ **Life-cycle costs** are all costs associated with the product for its entire life cycle.

❐ Life-cycle costs include:

- development (planning, design, and testing)
- production (conversion activities)
- logistics support (advertising, distribution, and warranty)

❏ **Whole-life cost** is the life-cycle cost of a product plus postpurchase costs that consumers incur, including operation, support, maintenance, and disposal.

❏ **Life-cycle cost management** focuses on managing value-chain activities so that a long-term competitive advantage is created.

❏ The *value chain* is the set of activities required to design, develop, produce, market, and service a product (or service).

Cost Reduction

❏ Because 90 percent or more of a product's costs are *committed* (but not incurred) during the development stage, it is logical to focus on managing activities during this stage.

❏ Studies have shown that every dollar spent on premanufacturing activities saves $8–$10 on manufacturing and postmanufacturing activities.

❏ More opportunities for cost reduction exist during product planning than in production.

❏ The traditional emphasis has been on controlling costs during the production stage. In addition, development and logistics costs have been virtually ignored when computing product profitability for managerial purposes.

Whole-Life Product Cost

❏ A whole-life product cost consists of four elements:
  ▪ nonrecurring costs (planning, designing, and testing)
  ▪ manufacturing costs
  ▪ logistic costs
  ▪ the customer's postpurchase costs

Role of Target Costing

❏ Target costing is a useful tool for establishing cost reduction goals.

❏ A **target cost** is the difference between the sales price needed to capture a predetermined market share and the desired profit per unit.

$$\text{Target cost per unit} = \text{Sales price needed to capture a predetermined market share} - \text{Desired profit unit}$$

❏ If the target cost is less than what is currently achievable, cost reductions are budgeted to achieve the target cost. Progress is measured by comparing actual costs with target costs.

KEY TERMS TEST

Test your recall of the key terms as follows. Try to recall as many key terms as possible without assistance. If you need assistance, refer to the list of key terms at the end of this section.

1. _____-_____ _____ are all activities other than those that are absolutely essential to remain in business.

2. _____-_____ _____ are activities necessary to achieve corporate objectives and remain in business.

3. A(n) _____-_____ _____ is the optimal output level for an activity.

4. Costs caused by value-added activities are _____-_____ _____.

5. Costs caused by nonvalue-added activities or the inefficient performance of value-added activities are _____-_____ _____.

6. _____ _____ is the process of identifying, describing, and evaluating the activities an organization performs.

7. _____ _____ is the process of eliminating nonvalue-added activities.

8. _____ _____ decreases the time and resources required by an activity.

9. _____ _____ is the process of choosing among sets of activities caused by competing strategies.

10. _____ _____ increases the efficiency of necessary activities by using economies of scale.

11. _____ _____ advises that there is no one best management control system.

12. _____ _____ is the process by which managers ensure that resources are obtained and used effectively and efficiently to achieve organizational objectives.

13. When individuals and groups in an organization work toward achieving organizational goals this is _____ _____.

14. _____ _____ are outcomes of results of past efforts, whereas _____ _____ are indicators or factors that predict or drive future performance.

15. All the activities involved in the efficient and effective movement and transformation of raw materials into an end product are known as the _____ _____. _____ _____ is a process-orientated approach to design, manage, and control these activities.

16. The performance measurement framework which consists of these criteria—leadership, people management, policy and strategy, resources, people satisfaction, customer satisfaction, impact on society, and business results—is the _____ _____ _____.

17. _____ provides cash incentives for quality and productivity gains.

18. _____ is an approach that uses best practices as the standard for evaluating activity performance.

19. A(n) _____-_____ _____ _____ is a control system that centres responsibility on organizational units and individuals with budgets and standard costing used to evaluate and monitor performance.

20. _____-_____ _____ _____ is a control system that centres responsibility on processes and teams where activity performance is measured in terms of time, quality, and efficiency.

21. In order to mitigate gaming behaviour, _____ _____ that are balanced between non-financial and financial criteria should be used in the compensation formula.

22. _____ is the number of units that can be produced in a given period of time (e.g., output per hour).

23. _____ _____ is the length of time required to produce one unit of a product.

24. A(n) _____-_____ _____ _____ or _____ _____ is a control system that translates an organization's mission and strategy into operational objectives and measures for four different perspectives: the financial perspective, the customer perspective, the process perspective, and the learning and growth (infrastructure) perspective.

25. _____ _____ are resources consumed by the activity in producing its output.

26. _____ _____ is the result or product of an activity.

27. _____ _____ _____ is the number of times the activity is performed.

28. _____ _____ is a Balanced Scorecard viewpoint that defines the customer and market segments in which the business will compete.

29. _____ _____ is a Balanced Scorecard viewpoint that describes the financial consequences of actions taken in the other three perspectives.

30. _____ _____ _____ _____ is a Balanced Scorecard viewpoint that describes the internal processes needed to provide value for customers and owners.

31. _____ _____ _____ _____ is a Balanced Scorecard viewpoint that defines the capabilities that an organization needs to create long-term growth and improvement.

The following questions relate to the appendix material:

32. _____ _____ _____ is the time a product exists from conception to abandonment.

33. _____-_____ _____ is managing value-chain activities so that a long-term competitive advantage is created.

34. Costs associated with the product for its entire life cycle are called _____-_____ _____.

35. _____ _____ is an effort to reduce the costs of existing products and processes.

36. _____ _____ is the difference between the sales price needed to achieve a projected market share and the desired per unit profit.

KEY TERMS

activity-based control systems
activity elimination
activity inputs
activity output
activity output measure
activity reduction
activity selection
activity sharing
activity value analysis
Balanced Scorecard
Benchmarking
Business excellence model
Contingency theory
customer perspective
cycle time
financial perspective
functional-based control system
gainsharing
goal congruence
internal business process perspective
kaizen costing
lag measures
lead measures
learning and growth (infrastructure) perspective
life-cycle cost management
life-cycle costs
management control
multiple measures
nonvalue-added activities
nonvalue-added costs
product life cycle
strategic-based control system
supply chain
supply chain management
target cost
value-added activities
value-added costs
value-added standard
velocity
whole-life cost

Compare your answers with those at the end of the chapter. Review any key terms missed.

CHAPTER QUIZ

Write your answers in the spaces provided.

1. The emphasis of a functional-based control system is on managing ____________.
2. The key to successful control in an activity-based system is to manage ______________.
3. Cycle time = ______________________________ / ________________________________
4. Delivery performance can be improved by decreasing _________ _______ or increasing __________.
5. The traditional emphasis has been on controlling costs during the _________________ stage; however, because 90 percent or more of a product's costs are committed during the _________________ stage, it is logical to focus on managing activities during this stage.
6. The eight organizational factors that affect a company's management control system are:

   1. ____
   2. ____
   3. ____
   4. ____

5. _____

6. _____

7. _____

8. _____

7. Five major categories of nonvalue-added activities are:

1. _____

2. _____

3. _____

4. _____

5. _____

8. Activity elimination, activity selection, activity reduction, and activity sharing are all ways to reduce nonvalue-added costs: (a) true; (b) false

9. Which of the following performance measurement frameworks focuses on stakeholders rather than strategy? (a) balanced scorecard; (b) business excellence model; (c) performance prism.

10. Financial measures are more easily understood by lower-level managers because they can see the effect they have on the measure: (a) true; (b) false

11. The four perspectives of the balance scorecard are:

1. _____

2. _____

3. _____

4. _____

12. Which of the following would likely be a lag measure: (a) number of employee suggestions; (b) return on investment; (c) cycle time improvements.

13. Which of the following is required for effective performance measures: (a) relevance; (b) reliability; (c) accessibility; (d) simplicity; (e) all of the before-mentioned.

14. When designing a compensation system one has to be aware of the potential behavioural implications of each measure: (a) true; (b) false

15. Process value analysis is not concerned with: (a) market analysis; (b) activity value analysis; (c) supply chain analysis; (d) value chain analysis.

The following questions relate to the appendix material:

16. Value-added costs = _____ × _____

17. Nonvalue-added costs =

(_____ – _____) × _____

18. For nonvalue-added activities that are unnecessary, the standard quantity is _____.

19. Target cost = _____

   – _____

20. Life-cycle costs include:

   1. _____

   2. _____

   3. _____

Circle the single best answer.

Use the following information to answer Questions 21 through 27:

King Manufacturing has developed optimal standards for labour usage, receiving, and packing. The optimal levels of the inputs for each of the activities, their actual levels achieved, and the standard prices are as follows:

	Cost Driver	SQ	AQ	SP
Labour usage	Labour hours	15,000	20,000	$ 10
Receiving	Purchase orders	600	750	120
Packing	Sales orders	700	1,000	90

The actual prices paid for the inputs equal the standard price.

21. Value-added costs for labour are: (a) $145,500; (b) $150,000; (c) $160,000; (d) $200,000

22. Nonvalue-added costs for labour are: (a) $50,000; (b) $60,200; (c) $68,400; (d) $105,000

23. Value-added costs for receiving are: (a) $68,000; (b) $72,000; (c) $84,600; (d) $90,000

24. Nonvalue-added costs for receiving are: (a) $15,600; (b) $16,200; (c) $16,800; (d) $18,000

25. Value-added costs for packing are: (a) $63,000; (b) $70,000; (c) $72,000; (d) $90,000

26. Nonvalue-added costs for packing are: (a) $18,900; (b) $25,200; (c) $27,000; (d) $28,400

27. If the company wants to reduce nonvalue-added costs for labour by 20 percent next year, the currently attainable standard for labour hours would be: (a) 17,000; (b) 18,600; (c) 19,000; (d) 20,000

☼ **Compare your answers with those at the end of the chapter. Review any questions missed.**

PRACTICE TEST

PROBLEM 1

Instructions:

For each activity listed below, determine the amount of value-added and nonvalue-added costs.

1. A company has 10 days of finished goods inventory on hand to avoid stockouts. The carrying costs of the inventory average $20,000 per day.

    Value-added costs: $_____

    Nonvalue-added costs: $_____

2. Setup time for a product is 5 hours. A firm that produces the same product and uses JIT has reduced setup time to 15 minutes. Setup labour is $10 per hour.

    Value-added costs: $_____

    Nonvalue-added costs: $_____

3. Warranty work costs the firm $1,000,000 per year. A competitor's warranty costs are $200,000 per year.

    Value-added costs: $_____

    Nonvalue-added costs: $_____

4. Downtime for bottleneck machinery averages 200 hours per year resulting in $600,000 in lost sales.

    Value-added costs: $_____

    Nonvalue-added costs: $_____

5. A time and motion study revealed it should take 12 minutes to produce a product that currently takes 30 minutes to produce. Labour is $15 per hour.

    Value-added costs: $_____

    Nonvalue-added costs: $_____

6. The company keeps 5 days of raw materials on hand to avoid shutdowns due to raw materials shortages. Carrying costs average $10,000 per day.

    Value-added costs: $_____

    Nonvalue-added costs: $_____

7. By redesigning the manufacturing layout, the time required to move materials can be reduced from 2 hours to 30 minutes. The labour cost is $12 per hour.

    Value-added costs: $_____

    Nonvalue-added costs: $_____

8. Each unit of product requires 10 pounds of raw material. Due to scrap and rework, each unit has been averaging 10.8 pounds of raw material. The raw material costs $5 per pound.

Value-added costs: $ _____

Nonvalue-added costs: $ _____

PROBLEM 2 (APPENDIX)

Bass Company has developed ideal standards for four activities: labour, materials, inspection, and receiving. Information about each activity is provided below:

Activity	Cost Driver	Standard Quantity	Actual Quantity	Standard Price
Labour	Hours	5,000	6,000	$ 6
Materials	Pounds	20,000	24,000	8
Inspection	Inspection hours	–0–	30,000	7
Receiving	Orders	200	225	500

The actual prices paid per unit of each cost driver were equal to the standard prices.

Instructions:

1. Prepare a cost report that lists the value-added costs, nonvalue-added costs, and actual costs for each activity using the following format.

Activity	Value-Added Costs	Nonvalue-Added Costs	Actual Costs
Labour	$ _____	$ _____	$ _____
Materials	_____	_____	_____
Inspection	_____	_____	_____
Receiving	_____	_____	_____
Totals	_____	_____	_____

2. Assume that continuous improvement efforts reduce the demand for inspection by 20% during the year (i.e., actual activity usage drops by 20%). Calculate the activity volume variance and the unused capacity variance below:

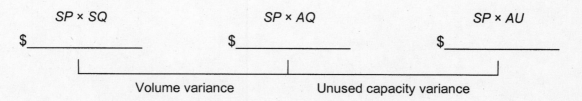

SP × SQ	*SP × AQ*	*SP × AU*
$_____	$_____	$_____

             Volume variance   Unused capacity variance

PROBLEM 3

At the beginning of 2000, Mollett Company installed a JIT purchasing and manufacturing system. The following information has been gathered about one of the company's products:

	2000	2001
Theoretical annual capacity in units	20,000	20,000
Actual production in units	15,000	16,000
Production hours available	4,000	4,000
On-time deliveries	1,000	1,500
Total deliveries	2,000	2,200
Scrap (pounds)	6,000	5,500
Materials used (pounds)	60,000	62,000
Actual cost per unit	$25	$24
Days of inventory	4	2
Number of defective units	1,000	1,200

Instructions:

1. Compute the following measures for 2000 and 2001 as compared to the company's goal:

Activity	2000	2001	Goal
a. Actual velocity	_____	_____	_____
b. Actual cycle time	_____	_____	_____
c. On-time delivery percentage	_____	_____	_____
d. Scrap as a percentage of total materials used	_____	_____	_____
e. Days of inventory	_____	_____	_____
f. Defective units as a percentage of total units produced	_____	_____	_____

2. Indicate any areas that need further improvement.

PROBLEM 4 (APPENDIX)

Ashley, Inc., sells one of its products for $120 each. Sales volume averages 1,000 units per year. Recently, its main competitor reduced the price of its product to $100. Ashley expects its own sales to plummet unless it matches the competitor's price. In addition, the current profit per unit must be maintained. Information about the product (for production of 1,000 units) is as follows:

	Standard Quantity	Actual Quantity	Actual Cost
Materials (pounds)	7,800	8,000	$40,000
Labour (hours)...................................	1,800	2,000	20,000
Setups (hours)..................................	–0–	1,000	10,000
Material handling (moves)................	–0–	500	5,000
Warranties (number repaired)	–0–	300	15,000

Instructions:

1. Calculate the target cost for maintaining current market share and profitability.

2. Calculate the nonvalue-added cost per unit. If nonvalue-added costs can be reduced to zero, can the target cost be achieved?

PROBLEM 5 (APPENDIX)

Michaels, Inc., developed the following budgeted life-cycle income statement for two proposed products. Each product's life cycle is expected to be two years.

	Product A	Product B	Total
Sales	$1,000,000	$1,400,000	$2,400,000
Cost of goods sold	800,000	1,000,000	1,800,000
Gross margin	$ 200,000	$ 400,000	$ 600,000
Period expenses:			
Research and development			(220,000)
Marketing			(180,000)
Life-cycle income			$ 200,000

An 11% return on sales is required for new products; therefore, because the proposed products did not have an 11% return on sales, the products were going to be dropped. Relative to Product B, Product A requires more research and development costs but requires fewer resources to market the product. Seventy percent of the research and development costs are traceable to Product A, and 20% of the marketing costs are traceable to Product A.

PROBLEM 5 *(Continued)*

Instructions:

1. Prepare a revised life-cycle income statement for each product.

	Product A	Product B

2. If an 11% return on sales is required, should Product A be produced?

3. If an 11% return on sales is required, should Product B be produced?

PROBLEM 6

Complete the following chart:

Responsibility Element	Functional-Based Control Systems	Activity-Based Control Systems	Strategic-Based Control Systems
Assign responsibility			
Establish performance measures or benchmarks			
Evaluate performance			
Assign rewards			

PROBLEM 7

Complete the following chart, indicating which balanced scorecard perspective the measure relates to and whether each performance measure is a lead or lag measure

Performance measure	Perspective	Lead or lag measure
1.On time delivery percentage		
2.Cycle time		
3.Economic Value Added		
4.Number of employee training hours		
5.Number of defects		
6.Number of customer complaints		

ANSWERS

KEY TERMS TEST

1. Nonvalue-added activities
2. Value-added activities
3. value-added standard
4. value-added costs
5. nonvalue-added costs
6. Activity value analysis
7. Activity elimination
8. Activity reduction
9. Activity selection
10. Activity sharing
11. Contingency theory
12. Management control
13. goal congruence
14. Lag measures; lead measures
15. supply chain; supply chain management
16. business excellence model
17. gainsharing
18. Benchmarking
19. functional-based control system
20. Activity-based control system
21. multiple measures
22. Velocity
23. Cycle time
24. strategic-based control system, Balanced Scorecard
25. Activity input
26. Activity output
27. Activity output measure
28. Customer perspective
29. Financial perspective
30. Internal business process perspective
31. Learning and growth perspective (or Infrastructure perspective)
32. Product life cycle
33. Life-cycle management
34. life-cycle costs
35. Target cost
36. Kaizen costing

CHAPTER QUIZ

1. costs
2. activities
3. Total production time/Number of units produced
4. cycle time, velocity
5. production, development
6. 1. Size, 2. Strategy, 3. Structure, 4. Systems, 5. Resources, 6. Staff Skills, 7. Management Philosophy, 8. Organizational norms
7. 1. Scheduling, 2. Moving, 3. Waiting, 4. Inspecting, 5. Storing
8. true
9. c
10. False
11. 1. Learning and growth, 2. Internal business processes, 3. Customer, 4. Financial
12. b
13. e
14. true
15. a
16. Standard quantity × Standard price
17. (Actual quantity – Standard quantity) × Standard price
18. zero
19. Sales price needed to capture a predetermined market share – Desired profit per unit
20. 1. development
    2. production
    3. logistics support
21. b 15,000 × $10 = $150,000
22. a (20,000 – 15,000) × $10 = $50,000
23. b 600 × $120 = $72,000
24. d (750 – 600) × $120 = $18,000
25. a 700 × $90 = $63,000
26. c (1,000 – 700) × $90 = $27,000
27. c 5,000 hours × 20% = 1,000 hours; 20,000 – 1,000 = 19,000 hours

PRACTICE TEST
PROBLEM 1

1. Value-added costs: $–0–
   Nonvalue-added costs: $200,000

2. Value-added costs: $10 × (15/60) = $2.50
   Nonvalue-added costs: $10 × 4.75 = $47.50

3. Value-added costs: $–0–
   Nonvalue-added costs: $1,000,000
   Note that with zero defects there should be no warranty costs.

4. Value-added costs: $–0–
   Nonvalue-added costs: $600,000

5. Value-added costs: $15 × (12/60) = $3.00 per product
   Nonvalue-added costs: $15 × [(30 – 12)/60] = $4.50 per product

6. Value-added costs: $–0–
   Nonvalue-added costs: $50,000

7. Value-added costs: $12 × (30/60) = $6
   Nonvalue-added costs: $12 × 1.5 = $18

8. Value-added costs: $5 × 10 = $50
   Nonvalue-added costs: $5 × .8 = $4

PROBLEM 2

1.

Activity	Value-Added Costs	Nonvalue-Added Costs	Actual Costs
Labour	$ 30,000	$ 6,000	$ 36,000
Materials	160,000	32,000	192,000
Inspection	–0–	210,000	210,000
Receiving	100,000	12,500	112,500
Totals	$290,000	$260,500	$550,500

The previous amounts would be calculated as follows:

Activity	Value-Added Costs $(SQ \times SP)$	Nonvalue-Added Costs $(AQ - SQ)(SP)$	Actual Costs $(AQ \times AP)$
Labour	5,000 × $6	(6,000 – 5,000)($6)	6,000 × $6
Materials	20,000 × $8	(24,000 – 20,000)($8)	24,000 × $8
Inspection	0 × $7	(30,000 – 0)($7)	30,000 × $7
Receiving	200 × $500	(225 – 200)($500)	225 × $500

2.

$SP \times SQ$	$SP \times AQ$	$SP \times AU$
$7 × 0	$7 × 30,000	$7 × 24,000
$0	$210,000	$168,000

|———————— $210,000 U ————————|———————— $42,000 F ————————|
                Volume variance   Unused capacity variance

PROBLEM 3

1. **a.**

	2000	2001	Goal
Actual velocity			
15,000/4,000	3.75 units/hr.		
16,000/4,000		4 units/hr.	
20,000/4,000			5 units/hr.

   b.

	2000	2001	Goal
Actual cycle time			
4,000/15,000	.27 hrs./unit		
4,000/16,000		.25 hrs./unit	
4,000/20,000			.20 hrs./unit

   c.

	2000	2001	Goal
On-time delivery percentage			
1,000/2,000	50%		
1,500/2,200		68%	
			100%

   d.

	2000	2001	Goal
Scrap as a percentage of total materials used			
6,000 lbs./60,000 lbs.	10%		
5,500 lbs./62,000 lbs.		8.87%	
			0%

   e.

	2000	2001	Goal
Days of inventory	4	2	0

f.	2000	2001	Goal
Defective units as a percentage of total units produced			
1,000/15,000	6.67%		
1,200/16,000		7.5%	
			0%

2. All areas need further improvement in order to meet the goals.

PROBLEM 4

1.

Current selling price	$120
Current cost ($90,000/1,000)	90
Current profit per unit	$ 30
Selling price to maintain market share	$100
Desired profit per unit	30
Target cost	$ 70

2. **Nonvalue-Added Costs**

Materials:
$40,000/8,000 = $5/pound

(8,000 – 7,800) × $5	$ 1,000

Labour:
$20,000/2,000 = $10/hour

(2,000 – 1,800) × $10	2,000
Setups	10,000
Materials handling	5,000
Warranties	15,000
Nonvalue-added costs..............................	$33,000

Nonvalue-added costs per unit

($33,000/1,000 units)	$33/unit

If nonvalue-added costs can be reduced to zero, the cost per unit would be $57 ($90 – $33), which is below the target cost of $70.

PROBLEM 5

1.

	Product A	Product B
Sales	$1,000,000	$1,400,000
Cost of goods sold..................................	800,000	1,000,000
Gross margin..	$ 200,000	$ 400,000
Traceable expenses:		
Research and development		
(70% × $220,000).............................	(154,000)	
(30% × $220,000).............................		(66,000)
Marketing expenses		
(20% × $180,000).............................	(36,000)	
(80% × $180,000).............................		(144,000)
Life-cycle income...................................	$ 10,000	$ 190,000

2. Return on sales (Product A) = $10,000/$1,000,000 = 1%
If an 11% return on sales is required, Product A should not be produced.

3. Return on sales (Product B) = $190,000/$1,400,000 = 13.6% If an 11% return on sales is required, Product B should be produced

PROBLEM 6

See page 321-322 of study guide

PROBLEM 7

Performance measure	Perspective	lead or lag measure
1.On time delivery percentage	customer	lag for processes, lead for customer satisfaction
2.Cycle time	internal business processes	lag or lead—depends how you are using the measure, it is a lag measure of the current process efficiencies, but it is lead indicator for future efficiency improvements
3.Economic Value Added	financial	lag
4.Number of employee training hours	learning and growth	lead
5.Number of defects	internal business processes	lag for processes, lead for customer satisfaction
6.Number of customer complaints	customer	lag or lead—depends how you are using the measure, it is a lag measure of the current customer satisfaction, but it is lead indicator for future customer satisfaction